BACKPACKING: One Step at a Time

BACKPACKING
One Step at a Time

Revised 1980s Edition

BY HARVEY MANNING

Foreword by Jim Whittaker
Cartoons by Bob Cram
Photos by Keith Gunnar

VINTAGE BOOKS

A Division of Random House • New York

VINTAGE BOOKS EDITION, MAY 1980

Copyright © 1972, 1975, 1980 by Recreational Equipment, Inc.,
1525 11th Avenue, Seattle, Washington 98122

Library of Congress Cataloging in Publication Data

Manning, Harvey.
  Backpacking, one step at a time.

  Bibliography: p.
  1. Backpacking.   2. Backpacking—Equipment and
supplies.   I. Title.
GV199.6.M36   1980   796.5′1   79–3580
ISBN 0–394–74290–7

BACKPACKING, camping, and mountaineering have grown tremendously in popularity since I came to Recreational Equipment Inc. (REI Co-op) in 1955. As one measure, REI's 1979 *increase* in sales over the previous year was more than its *total* sales in 1972, which could be interpreted to mean that more *new* people got out on the trails and into the mountains in 1979 than *all* the people who were there in 1972.

My brother and I operated the guide service on Mount Rainier from 1949 to 1952. In 1951, 291 persons attained the summit. In 1978, 6,436 registered for summit climbs, and over 3,000 reached the top! In our era the garbage at 10,000-foot Camp Muir amounted to so little that it was jettisoned without qualms in the nearest crevasse, and the single privy precariously overhanging Cowlitz Glacier handled every visitor. Now the guides backpack 60-pound loads of garbage down from Muir twice a week and helicopters are dispatched to haul away the remainder, plus the 50-gallon containers that support the four latrines.

The population explosion on Rainier's high rock and ice has been more than matched in meadows and valleys which are nowhere near as tough, in fact are very fragile and in danger of being crushed by masses of backpackers and campers. The delicate ecosystems of alpine parklands, desert oases, ocean dunes, lakeshores, marshes, riverbanks, and the like are everywhere threatened.

We must lessen the impact of the human animal on the trail country, the wilderness. One way is by education. We must teach people to be as unobtrusive as possible by adopting practices such as using small backpacking stoves instead of wood fires, dipping water out of lakes and streams to wash dishes and bodies rather than using soap in the lakes and streams, stopping in established campsites, staying on man-made or game trails, packing out all garbage, taking only pictures, and leaving only footprints. The alternative is to limit the number of people who walk the trails and climb the mountains, and thus deprive others of the opportunity to satisfy the basic human need to experience a wilderness environment.

I think the need exists even where it is not recognized or expressed. Throughout our nation are children of the cities who never have known any "valleys" but avenues with paved floors and concrete walls, any "mountains" but skyscrapers of glass and aluminum. If we can lead them into natural valleys and mountains and teach them how to be comfortable there, so they can grow and expand in an environment which, even when hostile, is fair, so they can feel the freedom of wild places, high places, then I think they will learn to enjoy, perhaps love, and surely respect nature, and realize all things natural —including themselves—are beautiful. With John Muir I say: "Climb the mountains and get their good tidings; Nature's peace will flow into you as sunshine into flowers; the winds will blow their freshness into you and the storms their energy, and cares will drop off like autumn leaves."

My climbs on Mount Everest and K-2 have left me with vivid impressions of the world's beauty. One moment I never will forget came on Everest in 1963. On May 22 we began our long descent from the basecamp established on March 21, having been more than 60 days above 17,500 feet, entirely in the realm of snow, ice, and rock. Coming down the Khumbu Glacier, we left the ice at last, walked onto moraine, then down to Gorak Shep. Seventeen years later, one of my sharpest recollections of Everest is that startling vision of small green plants, and that incredible odor of warm, musty earth. Several days on Rainier or any other peak rising far above timberline give a similar sensation. I wish everyone could know that feeling.

In the 1980s even greater pressures will be placed on the environment. Climbers, backpackers, skiers—the type of people who join REI —are an elite corps, you might say, in preserving natural values. No one knows better that we need the wilderness to bring people closer to their better selves, that we need places to be alone, where the wilds can bring us their good tidings. But we know full well that we also need, for survival, the raw materials of the earth. Our backpacks are aluminum, our pitons steel, our fabrics and insulation are synthetics made from petroleum. Even as we stand alone on some rock outcrop looking at a landscape few have ever seen, we know we are part of the world of men and women, of industry and energy, of expanding demands on a fragile planet.

I long have urged REI members and others to take the lead in finding appropriate ways to use and enjoy and preserve our most precious resource—nature. I now urge you again. We are all, like it or not, on a dangerous voyage into the future. The exigencies of energy and economics will be constant companions—and not very pleasant ones. And in some quarters, sight may be lost of traditional environmental values. Not, I hope, among us who cherish the experiences of wilderness.

We realize the need humans have for experiencing our environment. I feel we have a responsibility to protect it, and to set an example for new climbers, campers, and backpackers to travel carefully and considerately, to fit unobtrusively into the landscape, and to remember they are part of nature and any damage they do is—in the end—to themselves.

JIM WHITTAKER

INTRODUCTION TO THE THIRD EDITION

IT is said of hiking, as of shooting pool, that being expert in it is the sign of a misspent youth. However, as all children know, the blame for just about anything can be shifted to parents. For example, my father grew up in Lowell, Massachusetts, roaming Shedd Park, a vast wildland of oaks and hickories, woods violets and sweetferns. He fished for trout in Marshall's Brook, flowing from Tewksbury to the Concord River, and for kibbies and pickerel in the Concord. His headquarters was the Secret Camp, a giant glacial erratic. Banquets there featured potatoes baked in coals, apples roasted on sticks, ears of corn roasted in the husk, and whatever else farmers donated when they weren't looking. Meanwhile, across the continent, my mother was hiking the beaches of Puget Sound, exploring the inland sea by ferry and mosquito-fleet steamer and naphtha launch and rowboat and canoe, and digging clams and trolling for king salmon. All this was in my blood, or perhaps my genes, when I was introduced as a child barely walking to the World-Outside-the-City on fishing trips to streams of the Cascades and Olympics.

We were among the first Americans to exploit the new freedom—the freedom of proliferating roads and fast wheels—to pioneer a new way to the wilderness. The automobile brought within easy, inexpensive weekend reach places previously accessible to city folk only on lengthy vacations (which not many had) at considerable expense (which not many could afford). We were not long alone in the woods. The good tidings were heard. Car-campers thronged.

Decades later, when universities came to have professors of wild-land sociology, their research confirmed the expectation of common sense: the recreation of the youth and adult is determined by the recreation of the child. The *form* is not necessarily the same. The crux is the *feeling.* When forests of the car campground are lonesome and dark and quiet, the child is thrillingly scared. But when the camp-ground becomes people-stomping and lantern-glaring and radio-blar-ing, the youth and adult must go deeper in the woods to be satisfactorily frightened. Thus it was that in 1937 I joined the Boy Scouts.

I was a second-generation Scout, among the earliest, because only in 1910 had Scouting arrived in America. In 1915 Dad joined the local troop. On overnight hikes to remote Baptist Pond he learned to roll equipment and food in a blanket, tie the ends, and drape the "horse collar" across his body from one shoulder to the opposite hip, in the manner of the U.S. Army in the Spanish-American War.

My troop, north of Seattle, had plenty of room to find adventure in second-growth forests and along Puget Sound beaches. The climax of the year, though, was the summer week or two at Camp Parsons, on the shores of Hood Canal, at the foot of the Olympic Mountains. There I was trained in a unique hiking style, a synthesis of official-handbook Scouting, the local lore of wilderness mountaineering, and some special Parsons techniques, such as near-nudity and semistarva-tion, that permitted little boys to carry exceedingly light packs, en-abling us to walk remarkably far and high. My first trip to camp, in 1938, I stood at 6,000-foot Marmot Pass in a July sunset and gazed into wilderness and for the first time *knew it was wilderness.* That night at Camp Mystery, a mile above sea level, I lay me down to try to sleep and for the first time was utterly exposed to the infinite iciness and eternal blackness of a totally wild mountain night. Never got over it.

Still on the trails these decades later, I find them much changed. There aren't as many of them, what with encroachments by subdivi-sions and highways and logging roads and ORVs and ATVs. And there are more of us. Indeed, in the 1960s, seemingly overnight, the trails became mobbed. To explain the abrupt transformation of the wildland scene, dismayed hikers propounded Devil Theories, charging various scapegoats with responsibility for destroying the old solitude. However, more widely accepted now is a less impassioned General Theory of Trail Demography that goes something like this:

In the 1920s and 1930s the automobile carried city folk to the wilderness edge. There we car-camping children heard the owls and felt shivers up and down our spines. But as car campgrounds grew tame we became the hiking youths and adults of the 1930s and 1940s. In the 1950s and 1960s we took along our children, who as youths and adults in the 1960s and 1970s, finding crowds in camps of childhood, moved to more pristine wilderness, on and off the trails.

Meanwhile, following our example and aided by faster cars, more and better roads, more money, and more leisure, another generation took over the car campgrounds in the 1940s and 1950s. Their children, following our example and aided by better equipment and more information, and more money and more leisure, moved to the trails in the 1960s and 1970s.

Two population waves rolled from cities to car campgrounds to trails to wilder trails. Both waves were enormously swollen by the baby boom of the 1940s and 1950s. And in the 1960s and 1970s they merged to become a single tsunami.

Though other factors have played a role, very clearly the popularity of backpacking today is largely the fault of Columbus, John Muir, Henry Ford, the Boy Scouts, the New Deal, World War II, my parents, and my wife and me and our kids. But in my confession I must also implicate DuPont, Dick Kelty, Kraft Dinner, and geese. If hikers today had to endure 1938 equipage and diet, few would last more than a night at Camp Mystery. Few did then.

Rainproof shelter, comfortable packs, edible foods, and warm sleeping bags have removed much torture from wilderness travel. At a price. If wilderness could speak, it would protest bulldozers and chain saws and motorcycles—but also boots boots boots. And many hikers do speak up to declare themselves miserable in the equipment shops, tortured by a bewilderment of riches.

Commiserating with wilderness and hikers, in 1971 Jim Whittaker asked me to do a book that would (1) teach the "new ethic" of light-foot walking and no-trace camping and the Luddite responsibility to dismantle the Great American Energy Machine; and (2) guide hikers through the thickets of equipment, helping them assemble outfits good for them—and good for the fragile land.

Almost a decade later, here we are at the third edition of *Backpacking*. The book remains the same in substance and spirit, but all the equipment information has been updated, new photos have been added where appropriate, and a few more cartoons have been thrown in for clarity and fun.

A little should be said about the book's credentials. My career as a mountain bum, as noted earlier, began in the Olympics and Cascades. I spent a year of childhood in Massachusetts as well, hiking with Dad to the Secret Camp in Shedd Park, where we baked potatoes and roasted apples, once again donated by farmers when they weren't looking. Over the years I've also visited Canada's Cascades, Coast Range, Selkirks, and Rockies; Montana's Madison Range and other Rockies; Wyoming's Tetons; Oregon's Cascades and Wallowas; and California's Cascades, Whites, and High, Middle, and Low Sierra, from Desolation to Mineral King. Meanwhile, my bookmaking began as chairman of the editorial committee which in 1960 produced the first edition of *Mountaineering: The Freedom of the Hills.*

However, the unique credentials of this book derive not from my misspent youth, nor from any time misspent since then, but from the experience of the men and women of REI who since the founding of "The Co-op" in 1938 have hiked and climbed from Seattle to Greenland, Denali to Aconcagua, Alps to Himalaya, and in serving thousands of hikers and climbers have absorbed their experience as well.

Many contributions of my mentors to the first and second editions live on herein, though their names are now regretfully consigned to the archives. For this third edition Jim Whittaker placed me in the capable hands of REI's Ken Blaker, who in addition to other invaluable assistance and support provided the splendid services of Jim

Cross as manuscript coordinator and dean of faculty. He assembled the professors and organized the seminars at which I was lectured by Phil Bender, Jim Cross, Mike Dwyer, Jeff Fong, Kim Frank, Anna Marie Herfindahl, Arleen Hiuga-Musgrove, Miller Myers, Mary Michel, Carol Momoda, Gary Rose, Suzanne Silletto, Katie Venables-Waldrop, Jerry Watt, Barbara Weldon, and Jenny Zimmerman. Many of these subsequently reviewed chapter drafts, as did Laura Blachman, Becky and Stan Fishburn, Eric Lundblad, Scott McCleery, Gary Ranz, Dji Seaborn, Joel Stromwell, Jim Wall, and Jim Whittaker.

Other backpacking shops around Puget Sound were helpful, whether the clerks knew it or not, and all were friendly, despite some doubts about the anonymous customer. ("Who *was* that masked man?") David Beaton of Eddie Bauer supplied text materials from the course he teaches. Catalogs of outfitters located from Seattle to Maine were intensively mined, as were the magazines noted in Chapter 7. Jim Poth of *Sunset* was a rich lode of borrowable research.

For information on the early years of Scouting I'm indebted to Harvey Simpson Manning, and on military history to Harvey Paul Manning, and on how to lead children in the wilderness, to Penelope Lou, Rebecca Jo, and Claudia Anne Manning. Betty Manning served as rear guard and omelette cook and mushroom tester, permitting the rest of us to enjoy new species in perfect safety, forty-eight hours later. Other companions of peaks and bushes have requested they not be named here.

Indispensable to this edition were letters from readers of the prior two editions. A girl poignantly described her first venture on wildland trails, at the same age I was at Marmot Pass. (Many things change, but many remain the same, all is not lost.) A fellow troglodyte recalled certain memorably disgusting meals of the 1930s. (For some changes, thank golly.) Hikers from just about everywhere corrected errors, criticized opinions and prejudices, offered their own, compensated for my provincialism by describing how it is in their home provinces. Obviously a great many American childhoods, youths, and adulthoods are being very profitably misspent.

HARVEY HAWTHORNE MANNING

CONTENTS

Part One

OFF AND AWAY ON THE TRAIL

1: HOW TO WALK

PEOPLE not so very old can remember when nearly every American was an expert walker, traveling by foot to work and school, taking morning constitutionals and evening strolls, idling away Sunday afternoons on park paths or country lanes.

Nowadays, though, in an age and nation where the definition of Homo sapiens has been amended to "featherless *wheeled* biped," few urban folk know more than the rudiments. Everyone legs it around town a little, but awkwardly. City walking is too disjointed—from stoplight to stoplight, from parking lot to supermarket—to develop rhythm. Hard sidewalks heat the feet and gelatinize cartilage and rattle the vertebrae. Walkers sweat—considered impolite in mixed company. And in three-cars-per-home suburbs the mere fact of being unwheeled—unless huffing and jiggling in jogger's skivvies—is prima facie evidence of criminal intent.

Nevertheless, any nondisabled person readily can master the refinements, even if his longest habitual journey afoot is from subway to elevator. Mark Twain pronounced Russia a nation of geniuses, observing that tiny children there were fluent in a language so formidable that despite listening intently he couldn't understand a word. Americans similarly marvel at how adeptly their offspring skip about. Yet in every creaky adult is the nimble child—once off wheels onto feet, the body recovers old skills. No coaching is necessary, no manual solemnly instructing how to point the toes and bend the knees and what to do with arms and teeth. Such manuals have been written; the U.S. Army prepared a definitive volume but abandoned it when the troops concentrating on doing everything right, all fell down. To learn (to remember) to walk well, one simply goes walking.

The major obstacles are mental. The beginner (relearner) may be alarmed by a new awareness of heart, lungs, and muscles and imagine he is at the point of death. Also, after years of swift motion on wheels, the slow passage of the landscape may lead to a sense of futility.

The following discussion, therefore, pretty much ignores mechanics and concentrates on attitude; the intent is to help the reader overcome superstitions and enjoy an easy and pleasant transition from enslavement by machines to the freedom of the feet.

PACE

How fast a pace is too fast? Too slow? Just right?

Manuals often declare 2 miles an hour is the proper rate for such-and-such circumstances and 3 mph or 4 for others, and that 1,000 feet of elevation gain per hour is socially respectable if not quite admirable. All such pronouncements should be ignored; there are too many variations among individuals, and trails, for any rules to be meaning-

ful. A small child may do well to toddle half a mile an hour while a troop of competitive boys are running 5 miles. Gaining 500 feet of elevation an hour may destroy an accountant wheezing after a long winter at a desk; a logger may climb 3,000 feet an hour while chewing a jawful of snoose.

Travel times given by guidebooks must be viewed with suspicion. One guide has been published by an egomaniac plainly aiming to humiliate all who follow in his path. Another was written by two hill-hardened geologists whose legs separate just below the neck. At best a guide inevitably is hung up on the elusive "average." Average *what*? A hiker must test each book individually, comparing his own times on sample trips with those stipulated, and in this manner find a personal conversion factor.

How fast a hiker *can* go is one thing; how fast he *wants* to go is another. Some find joy whizzing through wildlands, jotting in their journals: "Made it from Bug Bog to Blister Pass in 3 hours 7 minutes flat—18½ minutes better than my previous best and possibly a new record." To each his own. Racers don't hurt anyone except competitors gnashing teeth because their best time from Bug to Blister is 3½ hours.

Most hikers, though, aren't out to set records but to enjoy the full walk, the trees and flowers and birds and waterfalls, the clouds and breezes and horizons. The most pleasurable pace gives each of these

its due and thus is somewhat or considerably slower than the maximum. (Of course, when darkness is near and the goal distant, or clouds of flies gather for the kill, the rule is to say the heck with fun and *run.* Or at least stagger as rapidly as possible.)

SETTING THE PACE

The beginner must understand that despite superficial similarities, walking is not akin to jogging or running. Its goal is not to expiate sins by self-flagellation, nor to batter the consciousness into a mystical experience. The walker sets his pace to make the body feel good, not bad.

Legs and lungs and heart are the monitors. When legs feel leaden —slow down. When lungs seem about to burst into flame—slow down. When the heart is battering the ribs—slow down. When a chipmunk by the path dispels all awareness of legs and lungs and heart, the pace is just right.

Comfort is important not merely for its own sake but because only a tolerable pace can be sustained. The dash-and-drop tactics of novices —going at top speed until completely breathless, gasping to a halt, then resuming all-out attack—are a constant misery and over the long haul slower than a steady plod.

The first stretch of trail should be taken at a deliberate loiter; the body, slothful from sleeping bag or car, complains less if introduced gradually to the task. Speed automatically increases as muscles loosen and juices flow free and easy; often there is a sensation of "second wind," indicating the system has gotten it all together.

HOW LONG A WALK?

The beginner, while experimenting to see how fast he can walk comfortably, must also find how far he can walk, taking into account not only mileage but elevation gain—5 miles with a rise of 5,000 feet demand more energy than 15 miles on the flat.

Each hiker must learn his own potential and adjust ambitions to match. One may cover 20 miles a day, or gain 6,000 feet, with ease; another may struggle to make 5 miles or 1,500 feet, or 2 miles or 500 feet. When personal abilities are defined, future trips can be planned accordingly, keeping in mind the beauty part—that the more one walks, the farther and faster one can walk.

Some hikers love traversing great distances in a grand rush, rambling a dozen or two miles in a day to feel a wildland unity—"the One that remains while the Many change and pass." Others are content with several miles a day, lingering over rocks and springs and mosses.

A related matter is how many *hours* a hiker can travel in a day, regardless of pace. Fresh from a city desk a person may not be able to stand erect, much less move, more than 4 or 5 hours; a trail-toughened veteran may pick 'em up and lay 'em down 10 or 12 consecutive hours with no pain, or 16 or 20 when seized by the mood.

WATER, FOOD, AND SALTS

Water is as essential to life as air; at rest the normal adult may require 2 quarts a day, more when working hard. In desert travel 4 quarts a day is a commonly recommended ration. Except in deserts, death by dehydration is a rare threat, but not debilitation—the average body is reduced in efficiency 25 percent by losing 1½ quarts of water, and during strenuous activity in hot weather this much can be perspired in an hour.

The old Puritan formula was to suck prune pits or pebbles, on the theory that excessive drinking endangers the soul. With booze maybe, but not water. Except in areas where pollution is a problem, the hiker should sample every tempting spring and creek and even in wet country carry a loaded canteen in case the dry spells are long. To be sure, moderation is the rule: gulping too much cold water can shock the stomach; also, dumping pounds of liquid into the body may require an extended rest while the bloated tank empties into the bloodstream.

Similarly, nibbling a snowball while walking a high, hot ridge—slowly, of course, to avoid "ice cream headache"—can prevent a blazing sun from shriveling the brain.

During hard hiking, lunch should be an all-day meal, consumed in

small, frequent installments to provide a steady flow of fuel without overloading the stomach. Weariness tends to kill the appetite, leading to a vicious circle of deeper weariness, less appetite. Though the thought of food may be loathsome, the tired hiker should take a bit of candy, a sip of fruit juice; the shot of quick calories often miraculously revitalizes a depleted system by almost instantly raising the level of blood sugar. (However, a sudden *excess* of sweets can in some people trigger a complex physiological reaction in which the blood-sugar level is actually lowered.)

A person's precious bodily fluids are more than a simple sugar solution. As water is lost through perspiration, both in the *sensible* form (visible, palpable sweat) and the *insensible* (vapor exhaled unseen and unfelt from pores), so too are sodium chloride and other salts essential to the inner chemistry. A hiker may nibble constantly and chug-a-lug at every stream and still grow weaker than the work alone can explain. Worse, he may develop headache, nausea, or muscle cramps. Or he may topple to the ground with heat prostration and awake, if lucky, in a hospital. The traditional remedy, sufficient in most circumstances, is to swallow a salt tablet or two every several hours, washed down with water, and preferably accompanied by food. However, nowadays hot-country travelers and heavy exercisers anywhere drink synthetic sweat, packaged as Gatorade or Gookinade or the like, and thus restore not only sodium chloride but the other vital salts. These preparations are said to win football games in Florida.

They surely help one climb steep trails naked to the sun. In deserts they have saved lives. Never mind that to some they taste like what they are.

UPHILL

Rambling happily along the flat is easy enough—when the trail turns upward, that's the time of testing.

Physically speaking, the secret of success is meeting steepness with slowness, constantly adjusting the pace to maintain uniform—comfortable—energy output, heeding signals from legs and lungs and heart. For very steep grades and weary hours the *rest step* combines mental discipline with robot regularity: (1) one foot advances; (2) motion halts momentarily while the forward leg rests, unweighted, knee bent, the body entirely supported by the rear leg with knee locked; (3) the rear foot advances to rest.

Occasionally as low as 7,000 feet and commonly above 9,000, oxygen shortage may cause *mountain sickness,* the symptoms including lack of appetite, nausea, and debilitation. The immediate remedy is getting more air into the lungs, using the rest step and at each pause taking a deep breath or two. The long-term cure is to *acclimatize,* devoting several days to a reduced level of ambition, accepting that for a time every High Sierra mile, for example, will be twice as long as an ocean beach mile. *Warning:* If bad headache or cough develops and persists, descend to richer air; if symptoms continue, hasten to a doctor.

Deterioration of the spirit often is the major uphill hazard. Hope dwindles as the ridge crest seems as far above in afternoon as in morning. Panic may trigger a mad assault, but as each crazed dash ends in collapse, the certainty of final defeat erodes the will. Despair is deepened by boredom; one may grow terribly sick of a tree that cannot be left behind, that stands there eternally mocking the sluggish pace. The answer is to forget the impossible ridge, ignore the wicked tree, and retreat into a revery about baking brownies over a campfire, what tactics might have won for Darius at Arbela, the plot line of a Marx Brothers movie.

At last the best energies are spent and still the path climbs and the sun falls. What now? Cry a little perhaps, but better shift gears farther down, grind out a step at a time, and sink deeper into thoughts of other times, other places.

In the extremity, think no farther ahead than some easy objective. Decide, for example, "I will walk exactly 20 minutes and sit down," and be sustained by anticipation of a chunk of candy and a swallow of water. Or, "I will take exactly 200 steps and stop for a breather." Or, "I will go to that boulder, then decide if I can continue or must lay my bones down, nevermore to rise again."

DOWNHILL

Downhill travel is simpler than uphill, as witness a falling rock. However, though some muscles and organs can pretty much relax, on a steep and rough trail other parts of the body take their lumps.

One alternative, typical of the young, is a semi-run, letting gravity have its way; but the jolt of each hard landing may reverberate up the spine and hit the head like a club.

The other method, favored by older folk, is patient restraint; but the knees, in holding back body weight, may become as loose as a rag doll.

And it is on the downhill that blisters blossom. Before beginning a sustained drop, boots should be laced tight, perhaps a pair of socks added, tender places taped. The first sensation of hot spots on soles or toes demand an instant halt for repairs (see Chapter 8).

REST STOPS

Walking is two separate and equally important actions—moving and not moving. Rest stops do not in themselves advance a party toward its destination but are an integral part of the long day's journey —and at least half the fun.

Manuals are full of rules. One expert dictates a mandatory stop every 40 minutes, lasting precisely 2 minutes. The hiker is forbidden to sit down, presumably lest he forget his sinful nature or even succeed in sucking juice from the prune pits. Rules are excellent for games, and for wars, too—resting by the clock and marching in column by the bugle are appropriate en route to battle. Civilian pedestrians, though, generally lean more toward a comfortable anarchy.

Particularly with a party of any size, a halt usually is necessary in the first half-hour for relacing boots, shedding sweaters, adjusting packs, and stepping privately into the bushes.

Beyond that there is no formula for frequency. Many hikers like to charge from trailhead or camp an hour or two without pause to get a few quick miles under the boots for the sake of a lazy afternoon. An interval of 30–40 minutes is more typical; near the end of a tough day, 15–20 minutes. A person who must stop every 5–10 minutes should try a slower pace. But when time is plentiful, each waterfall, vista, and marmot-on-a-boulder demands attention—after all, this is what the hike is about.

Neither is there any formula for duration. A party on a tight schedule must be content with efficiency stops of several minutes and resume walking before muscles cool and blood slows. Another party, on so loose a leash that wherever they are is exactly where they're supposed to be, may pause a half-hour to hear out a bird song all the way to the coda or watch a bumblebee creep inside every bluebell in the meadow.

In early hours, with the entire day's task yet to be done, hikers tend to rest briefly. In late hours of a slog they commonly go down like falling trees and lie inert like logs until moss grows on their boots. At any hour a standing breather lets legs and lungs and heart catch up with past overexertion—as in commencing a long uphill grind too fast —in preparation for resuming at a more respectful pace.

Morning, noon, or evening, after a very long rest hikers should go gently a bit, just as at the start of the trip, while muscles re-loosen and the heart works back up to speed.

Stops are so important that they should, whenever possible, be selected carefully. That is, if a rest will be wanted sometime soon, it is well not to collapse in a swamp but to glance at the map to see what lies ahead and then totter on a few more minutes to a bubbling creek, a splendid view, a field of flowers, a patch of cool shade.

SOCIAL PROBLEMS

The complexity of walking increases geometrically with party size, as Napoleon found on the retreat from Moscow. Many problems can be eliminated by abandoning the Grand Army and traveling in small groups.

The lone hiker has no social difficulties at all, except the possibility of discovering, while talking to himself, that he's a bore. He must walk more carefully, suspecting every pebble and twig of plotting to kill him—in lonesome country they may be able to do so merely by twisting his ankle.

The etiquette of social hiking reduces to simply thinking about the other fellow. For example, a swift walker who crowds the heels ahead may lose a friend—or on a brushy trail suffer the retaliating dis-courtesy of willow whips released in his face without warning. By the same token, a slow walker should not frustrate friends by hogging the centerline but step graciously aside and wave them on with a smile. The dozens more rules that could be stated are adequately covered by the Golden Rule.

Strangers met on the trail deserve the same consideration—unless they are riding motorbikes, in which case the proper response is every manner of hostility short of lynching.

Marching in a crowd is far more exhausting and nerve-racking than tramping alone or with several companions. The pace of a bunch in close formation is always too slow for some, too fast for others, a pain for all. The garrulous walker also is disruptive, constantly forcing conversation; the big mouth has plenty of spare breath but the gasper may be prevented by politeness (which develops into hatred) from settling into an efficient breathing rhythm. Thus, unless individual paces are nearly identical, an experienced party generally strings out on the trail, regathering for sociability at rest stops.

However, if the route is obscure or the party green, safety takes precedence and the rule is: *stay together.* The inconvenience is nothing compared to that of a search.

A WORD TO WOMEN (AND THEIR MALE COMPANIONS)

All but hopelessly brainwashed sexists, of whichever sex, now realize that when it comes to hiking, a woman is just like a man—just as fast (or slow), just as strong (or weak), just as tough (or delicate), just as brave (or cowardly), just as smart (or dumb). If short-legged or small, perhaps she can't hold the same pace as a long-legged man or haul the same load as a broad-shouldered man, but these are consequences of size, not sex.

However, one sexual characteristic has occasional significance, and novice hikers (both women and their male companions) should be aware of the possibility. In a few women the exertions of hiking or the effects of high altitude sometimes upset the menstrual cycle; the period may come earlier than usual and/or with an exceptionally heavy flow. Therefore, until a woman learns by experience how backpacking affects her, she must on every trip be prepared for the unexpected with a sufficient supply of tampons or napkins—plus plastic bags to carry them out of the wilderness if they cannot be *completely* burned in a wood fire.

Moreover, such common accompaniments of the period as cramps, nausea, weakness, dizziness, irritability, and headache may be intensified. Modifications of the planned schedule may be necessary, per-

13

haps not hiking as far as intended or laying over in camp a day.

Finally, the odor of a woman's period attracts bears, aggravating danger to the party's foodstuffs, and may anger them—especially to be kept in mind when visiting grizzly country.

It should be noted that pregnancy need not deter hiking. Many a woman continues backpacking virtually until ready for the delivery room and is off on the trails again in a matter of weeks, baby on back.

GETTING IN CONDITION

Most hikers earn their bread in sedentary occupations that tend to make them soft and sloppy and miserable. Partly this is why they go walking—to toughen the flesh and gain the smug self-satisfaction of

healthy animals. However, to go directly from city to trail can be humiliating, depressing. Legs wobble, heart pounds, lungs heave—is it worth it? Why not buy a motorcycle and exploit the only part of the body in top condition after years of freeway and desk and television?

Despicable thought. Pride forces the alternative—to restore function to other parts of the body that have been allowed to atrophy or bloat. The best conditioning for the trail is the trail, and the ideal schedule is trails every week the whole year, but if a person can enjoy trails only for a limited season, he should commence with short trips on easy paths, the length and difficulty gradually increased. If trail country is far from home, strictly for vacations, city prisoners can get into shape—or better, stay in shape—through any exercises (swim-

14

ming, bicycling, canoeing, handball, tennis, calisthenics, pushing away from the table) that expand lungs and toughen muscles and slim guts.

Once thoroughly out of condition a hiker must be prudent. Unless the exercise—walking or any other—forces the heart to speed up and the lungs to labor, they are not being improved. Indeed, a healthy person should go at his conditioning with verve, to the point of racing heart and gasping lungs, because when pushed near limits, the body most rapidly extends its limits. However, at those limits lie (having fallen) the tennis-court cardiacs. Medical advice is the essential preliminary to any rigorous conditioning program; the prescription may well be to forget the verve, to go slow and easy on a longer but safe program.

Jogging and running, whatever their intrinsic merits, are not as good preparations for walking as walking. They use and thus condition different muscles. They require special equipment and care to avoid tendonitis, shin splints, runner's knee, crushed vertebrae, and dogbite. In fact, the booming business reported by podiatrists, plus a growing opinion that running is boring, seem to be engendering a new fad. Walking. Looming on the horizon is a tidal wave of manuals telling us how to point the toes and bend the knees. A parade of authors promoting books on TV talk shows. A new uniform to distinguish respectable middle-class walkers from hoboes. A nationwide epidemic of falling down.

If there is indeed a new fad, the prophets can render important service by reminding us that walking is every doctor's universal remedy for what ails civilized man. Without the medical risks of jogging and running it does as much to strengthen the cardiovascular system, relieve hypertension, tone muscles, improve posture, and burn calories that otherwise would turn to fat. Granted, the medicine is not as strong—an hour's brisk walk may be the equivalent of a half-hour jog or a quarter-hour run.

Granted, too, walking lacks expiation and mystic vision. But it's more fun. The runner looks inward to his soul, not always a pretty sight. The walker looks outward to flowers and clouds, dependably nice. And though the dogs bark, they seldom bite.

THE LIGHT FOOT

When the country was young and empty the lonesome pioneer, fearing for his survival, built paths and roads for safety and convenience without concern for how they affected the health of the wilds. Now the country is getting older and very full, freeway promoters are not cheered but hissed, and the reflective walker fears for survival of the wilds.

Most of the world is so traumatized by plow and wheel and house, chain saw and bulldozer and motorcycle, that a regiment of King Kongs wearing army boots couldn't walk heavy enough to make a perceptible dent. But in some of the world—the best part, hikers would say—machines are banned and a major punisher of the landscape is the human foot. One easily can slip over the line into silliness about this. After all, avalanches and floods and elk radically remodel the scene and nobody denounces *them* from a pulpit. But that's because avalanches and floods and elk *live* in the wilds; the human walker, a visitor, must be respectful and polite, must walk with a light foot.

Just as cities and highways can be very good things in their proper places, so too can trails, despite being strips of devastation, if they stay where they belong. To help maintenance crews keep them under control, hikers should not kick dirt for the sheer heck—such as by running wantonly downhill, whooping and hollering and jumping and skidding and churning. They should not cut switchbacks—shortcuts become erosion gullies. They should walk on the trail, not beside it to stay out of the rut—the parallel tracks in turn become ruts.

Off the trail the rules are more complex, require more judgment. The aim is twofold: (1) to avoid building new trails with the boots; (2) to avoid damaging plants and soils. For the sake of the first goal, in suitable terrain a party should fan out rather than travel single file, should shun incipient paths, choose rock or snow in preference to flowers and dirt. Often easier said than done. And often for the sake of the second goal it's better to follow an obvious game trail, already for, lo, these many centuries a brown track beaten through the green.

Common sense tells us where feet hurt the land most—such spots as the deep but soft and easily erodable soils where meadows dip to lake or river, and barrens of steep, unstable scree where tiny plants struggle for roothold.

A considerate person who understands that his feet are small bulldozers will guide them wisely. He won't, for example, spend the evening running around a meadow playing with a Frisbee.

2: HOISTING PACK ON BACK

MANY are the pleasures of a day on the trail, and a hiker may enjoy a rich wildland life never carrying a load heavier than fits neatly in a small rucksack. Especially in the Alps, where huts are closely spaced, and parts of America with an abundance of near-city trails, a person can walk miles and years and always eat supper at a table and sleep in a bed under a roof.

But the day is only half the trail world. Hoisting pack on back has great symbolic importance, signifying acceptance of the other half, the night.

Day is simple by comparison; with a commitment to night come sleeping bag and tent or tarp, cookstove and pots, suppers and breakfasts—and the pack.

Backpackers grow sentimental about the "stone" that holds all necessities and amenities, is bedroom and kitchen and wardrobe complete in one bundle, and delight in the renunciation it expresses of the appliance-cluttered house in the city, the pollution-producer parked at the road, and all the frenetic complications of a society up to its neck in material possessions. To be sure, the renunciation is temporary, but the brief escapes into simplicity—and the anticipation beforehand and the memories afterward—do much to settle nervous stomachs and calm trembling hands.

However, though the veteran feels freedom in hoisting the load,

the beginner, particularly the reluctant one bullied by family compulsion or social pressure, may feel naught but dread. There is, first of all, a fear of the night inbred by millennia of hiding from its jaws that bite and claws that scratch, its things that go bump, in the tightest available cave, hut, castle, house, or apartment. And second, there is a suspicion that the sport is nothing more than the ultimate in masochism. In a world full of painful burdens, who needs an extra?

EASING IN GRADUALLY

Very sad cases are on record of disastrous introductions to backpacking, even when the equipment was ideal and the country beautiful and the weather superb. Such as, the honeymoon couple setting

out for a week in the wilds, the longtime-hiker husband gently helping his never-having-hiked bride into the packstraps, and her toppling to the ground and lying there sobbing. The scene is the more poignant when the roles are reversed.

Generally it is best to learn (remember how) to walk before attempting a backpack. On afternoon strolls, unloaded, then day hikes with rucksack, the use of lungs and legs is mastered, irrational fears allayed.

Having grown familiar with wildland days and accustomed to 10 or 15 pounds, the time arrives to try the "complete home" pack of 20 pounds or so and penetrate mysteries of the night.

Wisdom and nonsense have been written about how heavy a load a human can haul. Again, each hiker must experiment to discover his capacity. A rule with more basis in reality than most is that a person of average strength can carry about one third of body weight, or 60 pounds for a 180-pound man, 40 pounds for a 120-pound woman; of course, these figures are above the comfort range—the man will be happier with 40 pounds, the woman with 25. They also assume the body is not overweight and thus substantially burdened even without a pack. They further assume equal conditions of health; in some partnerships it's the little woman with the strong heart who carries the heavier load, the big man whose weak heart must be protected from *macho* vanity. The body-weight rule does not apply to growing children; however, the average girl at fourteen and boy at sixteen have adult capacities.

The rule perhaps has as many exceptions as applications. Tiny porters employed by expeditions often carry half or more their body weight, as do American backwoodsmen and climbers. ("It's not the stove that bothers me," says the legendary iron man to the awe-struck stranger met on the trail. "It's the darn sack of flour in the oven shifting around and throwing me off my stride.") A frail person, even after attaining top condition, may stagger under a quarter or fifth of body weight.

Then, how far can the stone be toted in a day? Some may never manage more than 5 miles with 25 pounds, while others may easily do 15 miles with 60 pounds.

Finally, how heavy *must* the load be? With moderately careful planning, 20–25 pounds can be adequate for every eventuality of an overnight or 3-day trip. Some experts regularly go for a week in mild-climate, gentle country carrying only 30–35 pounds. Travelers of rough and stormy wilderness, perhaps not quite so attentive to ounces, eating somewhat better and having included gear essential for foul weather and emergencies, find 40 or 50 pounds more common for a 9-day trip—and that therefore 9 days is close to the limit for a hike in reasonable comfort, though shaving grams and gritting the teeth can extend the length to 2 weeks before having to resort to relay-packing or horses.

In summary, the beginner must test his own back, starting with modest loads and short hikes, and gradually increase the pack weight, and the length and duration of trips; this cautious progress is also important when an experienced backpacker is initiating a novice. Maybe that honeymoon would be better spent day-hiking and car-camping, with an occasional night in a mosquitoless motel.

ORGANIZING THE PACK

In olden days the typical pack consisted of a single large bag or a tarp-wrapped bundle lashed to the frame, and the entire contents had to be dumped out whenever any article was wanted. The modern pack eliminates the bother, specifically designed as it is for efficient organization.

Still, the hiker must give some thought to stowing gear; any system will work so long as he remembers what it is. Obviously things used only in camp, such as supper food and cooking pots, belong inside the bag, and those required on the trail or for emergencies in the outer pockets. Aggravation can be saved by always putting each item in the same place to avoid, for example, unzipping every pocket, every time, to find the matches.

Chapters 7–15 discuss what should be carried; a preliminary word needs to be said about what shouldn't. Will that third sweater really be necessary? Will anybody be hungry enough to eat all those canned peaches? Will any possible storm be long enough to get through the *Cambridge Medieval History*?

Considered individually, each item may be small and weigh only ounces and "come in mighty handy once in a while." But a dozen superfluous articles add up to the pounds that can lengthen the final miles of the day to infinity.

When assembling gear, the hiker should give every piece of equipment a hard-eyed scrutiny. The Ten Essentials (see Chapter 15) must be exempted, but all else demands careful consideration, remembering that mile by mile, hour by hour, the stone grows.

LIVING WITH THE STONE

Walking with a pack is the same as walking without one, only more so. The pace is slower, the day's range shorter; rests are needed not only for the legs and lungs but for the aching back.

There are two basic ways to get into a pack: (1) Grab it by the shoulder straps and lift to the knee, slip one arm through a strap, swing the load onto the back, and slip in the other arm. (2) With pack on the ground, sit against it, slip on the straps, then turn onto knees and stand up. To get out of the pack, reverse. When the load is very heavy, rest spots should be chosen so the latter method can

be used. In any event, the hiker must never, no matter how weary, drop the pack hard—that's how frames are broken and bag seams split.

Brief breather rests give more benefit if a boulder or log is available upon which the pack may be set while still on the back, the weight thus momentarily removed from the body.

When the pack is taken off on steep terrain it should be placed with care; nothing is more depressing than watching bed and board bound down the meadows, over a cliff, into a river.

The backpacker has options in scheduling not open to the day-hiker. For example, when the planned camp lies thousands of feet up a sun-blasted slope, the party may prefer to spend the brutal afternoon sacked out by a river, cook supper there, and make the climb in the cool of evening. Similarly, walkers of deserts in springtime typically take a "lunch" break of 4 to 6 hours, dozing in the shade of a cactus. In the Low Sierra in summer only mad dogs and visitors from the rainy Cascades go out on trails in the midday sun; the natives typically travel from dawn to late morning and from late afternoon to dusk; in the long interim they may be seen by suffering foreigners cooking a luncheon stew, snoozing under a Jeffrey pine, splashing in a creek that tumbles down granite slabs.

And when the moon is full and a broad trail follows a high ridge, the party may wish to sleep away the day to hike by night, seeing the world anew, answering coyotes howling all around.

By hoisting pack, the hiker accepts new chores, but gains new freedoms too.

3:

THE day's journey ends, packs are dropped, the hikers are home. If
the weather is mild and night not urgently close and bugs no threat
to reason, the first order of business is mixing a pot of punch, loosen-
ing boots, and sprawling at ease to admire river or lake or ocean,
forest or meadow, glacier moraine or desert oasis. Eventually (immediately in storm or impending darkness) the time comes to stir
about on housekeeping duties, to build a bedroom and a kitchen. But
gently!

Nostalgia for the Arcadia of barbarian ancestors was expressed
years ago by Horace Kephart's *Camping and Woodcraft,* still the
classic manual on remodeling the landscape to suit a pioneer. The
yearning persists, and so urgently that a large bookstore may dis-
play fifty or more volumes on building log cabins, tossing salads of
fern fronds and caterpillars, surviving with a fishhook and sharp
stick, and other lore the frontier child learned as naturally as
breathing. Woodcraft is good sport, and where forests are extensive enough to permit logging they surely can tolerate, in appropriate places, less drastic chopping and whittling. In the doing,
something can be learned about times past, useful in understand-
ing the present.

However, on most trails outside "classroom areas," woodcraft is

dead. Dead because the modern equipment described in Chapters 11 and 12 makes pioneer-style engineering unnecessary. Dead because there are too many wildland visitors and too little wildland.

The goal of the new hiker is not to erect a replica of Fort Ticonderoga as an exercise in ingenuity but to camp so utterly "without a

trace" that following parties must minutely inspect the site to find evidence of his stay.

Here, then, the subject of camping, to which libraries have been devoted in the past, is given a mere several pages—and these concerned less with what the beginner should do than what he should *not* do.

CHOOSING A CAMPSITE

In anthropocentric days of old, when folks were few and room for self-indulgence plentiful, camps were chosen for physical gratification and esthetic delight. Vanities though these may now be judged by wilderness Savonarolas, they still are not entirely contemptible. However, in biocentric days of new, they receive second priority. First comes the land.

FOR THE LAND'S SAKE

In the Golden Age the meager governmental presence in the backcountry was single-mindedly devoted to dogmas of Smokey the Bear. So long as hikers stopped at the ranger station for a fire permit, didn't smoke while traveling or let campfires run away or otherwise conspire to burn down the woods, they were as free as the squirrels. About the only other subject of sermons was letting porkchop bones and whiskey bottles lay where they fell rather than bury them to keep the bears busy. Actually, Golden Agers had a sneaking fondness for the squalor of garbage dumps, which all popular camps were; it was homey. Through the generations, the kitchen middens grew—but slowly, because the backcountry population was so small.

Then came the explosions. Of population. Of garbage. Which were soon followed, to the grief of twenty-second-century archaeologists, by an explosion of disgust, by a Great Big Cleanup Crusade that in a brief decade made the wilds tidier than they'd been since the invention of the tin can. However, resting from labors, garbage crews were dismayed to see that the land was by no means pristine. Campfires were burning green trees and silver snags and brown soil. Boots were crushing flowers, sleeping bags flattening meadows. The water was going bad.

So the crusade has marched on to more comprehensive objectives —preservation and restoration of primeval purity. Thus the present and continuing explosion of management, of regulation. Going, going, where not already gone, is the laissez-faire of the Golden Age, subverted by the population bomb.

As usual during crusades, there's a certain amount of turmoil in American wildlands. Not every slob is submitting tamely to clean living. Not every crusader has the patience of a saint. Though the army of the faithful is united in the one true religion, it is split in a

number of sects. Something like 95 percent of the old bare-dirt camps inherited from the Golden Age are being closed for rehabilitation of the vegetation, hikers directed to new deep-in-the-bushes sites, but not in every case is it agreed that the new camps are less damaging and more pleasing than the old. The regulations in a jurisdiction may be different from the one next door. The regulations in a jurisdiction may be different from one year to the next. Administrators are studying human impacts, debating conflicting philosophies, and experimenting with techniques of managing wildlands and hikers; in some cases they are changing their minds, in others hardening into dogmatism. A perplexed hiker may decide to flee to unregulated lands and fight it out with the loggers and motorcycles.

Yet this, too, will pass. Regulations are not a burden when understood to be designed to provide visitors with the maximum practical quality of wilderness experience while holding impact on wilderness to the practical minimum, to be intended to counsel hikers on how to behave as befits an area "where the earth and its community of life are untrammeled by man, where man himself is a visitor who does not remain . . . which is protected and managed to preserve its natural conditions."

The primary means of achieving the maximum/minimum are restrictions on choice of campsites. The key tools are wilderness permits in National Forests and backcountry permits in National Parks, issued at or near trailheads or by mail. Wilderness rangers (National Forests) and backcountry rangers (National Parks) do not so much police the regulations as host visitors.

In this time of flux a hiker must be very sure to learn the rules of the local game in advance. Arriving at the trailhead stoveless, discovering that wood fires are banned, means a lot of cold gruel. Traveling half a continent to find camping no longer permitted in Shangri-la is the cruel death of a dream. A vacation, a summer, may be shattered by the ranger announcing the whole wilderness is full up until a week from next Thursday, when the hiker is due back at his job in Chattanooga. Following are some of the regulations, and suggestions, current in this or that jurisdiction:

Avoid popular seasons, popular places. Go early and beat the rush, or late, when it's over. Go midweek. Don't go on holidays at all. Go places nobody (perhaps even you) ever heard of.

Limit party size. In some areas twelve is the legal maximum, in others less. A large family may have to get a divorce.

Limit total population. The permits do this. After managers determine the "carrying capacity" of a valley or basin—how many people it can accommodate at any one time, and in any one year, without serious damage—they limit campers, rationing the space (usually) by issuing permits on a first-come, first-served basis, offering latecomers suggestions on alternate destinations.

Beside the trail, concentrate impact. In many jurisdictions, camps are being specifically designated along major trails, and no other sites may be used. Elsewhere managers simply tell hikers to use established camps and to build fires only at existing fire rings. In both cases, a certain amount of "dustbowl" space having been accepted as inevitable to the human presence, campers are confined to the bare dirt, kept off the grass.

Off the trail, disperse impact and employ "no trace" techniques. Though in some jurisdictions no camping is permitted away from trails, in most the cross-country traveler can stay where he likes, though usually without a wood fire. To achieve the "no trace" ideal, recommendations are: camp on tough land, such as in forests, on ridge crests, on rocks, sand, gravel, even snow; do not camp on tender land, such as soft and wet meadows; do not camp near water, lest you pollute the liquid and mangle the shore; carry a collapsible container to minimize path-stomping trips to water; do no cutting, no digging; move camp frequently; if a site obviously has been used before, don't use it; upon leaving, obliterate every trace of your stay.

Preserve the experience. Even if it is legal, don't homestead a scenic shore or overlook, hogging the view. Respect the solitude of others by camping at a distance. Be quiet—the shouter intrudes on the peace of a whole valley. Use clothing and gear of subdued "earth tones" rather than circus razzle-dazzle—a gaudy tent intrudes on the isolation of folks miles and miles away.

Other ethical matters are discussed later in this chapter, in the next, and in Chapter 20. So much talk about virtue may well disgruntle veterans longing for the good old crummy laissez-faire Golden Age. Too bad about them—they shouldn't have had so many children. Perhaps when the population of America shrinks back to 120 million there won't be any more need for ethics.

FOR THE HIKER'S SAKE

Though the health of ecosystems has absolute priority, comfort and convenience still influence choice of camps; the great thing about modern equipment is permitting a good sleep with a clear conscience.

The old woodcrafter rule was that a camp must offer wood, water, and shelter. But the new hiker carries shelter and fuel, and when need be, water and thus can build cozy homes in spots that would have appalled Daniel Boone—a salt flat, a moraine, a glacier.

A camp with water still is better than one without. Aside from that, the main considerations are ground reasonably level (though not necessarily flat), reasonably dry (though ground sheet and/or tent floor plus sleeping pad allow sleeping in snow or a semi-marsh), and reasonably free of large rocks.

During rainy weather it is wise to avoid dips or swales that may become ponds or creeks; knolls and slopes are less likely to be flooded.

During windy weather the lee of a hillock or clump of trees may be sought; in buggy weather the wind may be preferred.

The study of microclimates—why ridges and knolls often are warmer in summer than valleys and basins, why passes frequently are cold and windy while meadows a few yards away are warm and calm, and so on—intrigues a hiker as he gains experience.

When regulations and conscience permit, a party obviously chooses a camp with a view of valley, peaks, waterfall, lake, garden, or whatever may be the local attractions.

MAKING CAMP

In the woodcrafter era preparing for night was nearly as lengthy as proving up on a 160-acre homestead. The hiker with modern equipment can do the whole job in minutes.

The only possible exception is shelter. Any tent is self-explanatory and the typical tarp rigs illustrated in Chapter 12 are simple enough, but the techniques should be mastered in the backyard or during a car-camping trip or short hike rather than, say, at midnight on the tundra in a blizzard.

The first step in making camp, of course, is to set up tent or tarp (assuming shelter is felt necessary) on ground suitable for sleeping, perhaps removing prominent stones and logs that can't be slept around, making sure to replace them precisely later.

No regrade projects should be undertaken, no rock walls or wood tables or earthen dams built. Contrary to old custom, tent or tarp should *not* be ditched. Whenever possible a site should be chosen with natural drainage away from the sleeping area. Otherwise the new rule is to wait until the floods come and then scratch the very smallest channels required, carefully filling them when breaking camp.

Do not build a soft bed by cutting boughs, forbidden in most areas and anyhow unnecessary with the self-contained "sleeping system" described in Chapter 11.

SANITATION

One more facility of the wildland home, the toilet, requires mention, because some hikers don't have the manners of a cat and many who do are puzzled about what to do for a sandbox.

Some backcountry camps are provided with privies and that takes care of that. Where hikers are on their own, three rules must be observed: (1) Pick a spot 300 feet or more from watercourses, whether or not water is running—go up on a hill in the woods or off amid boulders of a moraine. (2) Don't foul a site a following party may decide is a lovely place to pitch a tent or have a picnic. (3) Preserving sod if any is cut, dig a small hole, no deeper than 6–8 inches, in the "biological disposer" soil layer where active ingredients decompose organic material in a few days, and fill in after, replacing sod; if the ground is too hard or rocky (a moraine) or too root-matted (a field of heather) for digging, cover the evidence with leaves or dead bark, loose dirt or gravel.

Be sure to explain all this very carefully to the children.

There remains the problem of toilet paper, which in dry climates may last out the summer, working its way to the surface or being mined by little nest-builders or big salt-seekers, then blowing in the wind, beflowering hill and dale. If the spot is not tinder-dry, a lighted match quickly eliminates most of the paper; otherwise it should be gathered up and taken elsewhere for safe burning. An alternative increasingly favored because it also reduces the logging of forests for wood pulp is use of local vegetation; the only caution is to be wary —very sad stories are told of hikers who grabbed the wrong leaves.

COURTESY

In much-traveled areas, hikers must learn to get along with strangers. It is quite possible for dozens or scores of courteous campers to

live congenially on an acre or two. However, a single thoughtless bunch can ruin the neighborhood.

A major stimulus to the popularity of backpacking is the bedlam of car-camping. See the dark and silent campground. At midnight, the new arrivals. They drive around and around, shining headlights at every site, occupied or not. At last they park—motor running and headlights on. For half an hour they perform the door-slamming ritual, then spread out and begin yelling back and forth. At 2:30 A.M. they go to bed—and an hour later are chopping wood, banging pots and pans, slamming doors, waking up the birds. Shortly they will be thrashing about the lake in motorboats or razzing the trails on motor-cycles.

Backpacking does not offer total escape. For the moment forget (impossible, but try) the motorcycle invasion. See the troop of boister-ous children swarm into camp, and *hear* them—none going more than ten seconds without a shriek, whistle blast, or bugle call. The adults in charge smile benignly, drink covertly from flasks. See the packs of dogs, apparently only loosely associated with human companions, tour the scene, sniffing tents and stealing steaks. Hear the musicians, plucking guitars and singing through their noses far toward dawn. Campers who have been contemplating the solemnity and mystery of wilderness either grit teeth and begin suffering the nervous symptoms they took this trip to cure, or unrig camp and move on, seeking the peace and quiet of a snakepit or avalanche slope.

Noise is not the only pollution. Satan said, "Let there be light!" And lo, the gasoline lantern! Those who illuminate a camp invariably consider themselves benefactors and hang the lantern high so neigh-bors can enjoy the spillover. But the neighbors may wish to become one with the night; when philosophy is lost they may sit in the harsh glare and make plans to buy noiseless, darkness-creating air pistols.

Certainly the sublime appeal of wilderness travel is the freedom to howl with the coyotes, to sweat and break wind, to be a natural animal unconstrained by stifling conventions. But whenever the population of a valley is considerable and a degree of crowding unavoidable, each hiker should do his utmost not to pollute the quiet or the darkness, should strive to be more feline than simian.

In enjoying freedom, do not invade the freedoms of neighbors. Impinge not upon their rights and privileges lest they, in maddened retaliation, impinge upon yours and a lousy vacation be had by all.

4:

EATING

As explorers slashing through Yucatán jungles were astounded to stumble on ruins of temples built by ancient Mayans, so do hikers now, chancing on rotting kitchenry of ancient woodcrafters, marvel at such industry for purposes beyond today's comprehension. To be fair to oldtimers, in their era meals of any kind beyond pilot bread and jam were complicated, and tasty dishes were just barely within the grasp of a talented and experienced engineer-chef. Now and then a grizzled relic still may be observed lashing poles to trees and pounding nails and bending wire and whittling twigs and piling rocks and rigging dinglesticks. His craft was hard-learned and he is loath to renounce it, to admit any beardless youth can eat well with no fuss, no muss. The new hiker ought to be patient with the old crock—he may be somebody's grandfather.

However, except on special occasions in "classroom areas," and only so the past shall not be forgotten (as history buffs dress in costume and refight the Battle of Gettysburg), the backpacker shouldn't manhandle the landscape for the sake of a dinner. Using equipment and foods described in Chapters 13 and 14, the beginner will find meals absurdly easy and quick to prepare, and in a very short while he becomes an expert.

This chapter, therefore, has little to say about cooking and eating and is almost entirely concerned with lightening the pressure of the camp kitchen on tender terrain.

KITCHEN ORGANIZATION

An overnight hike requires no fancier advance organization than dumping cooking and eating utensils and food in packs—only making sure to do so. Discouraging words to be heard ten miles from the road: "But I thought *you* had the pots!"

For trips lasting several days or more, an hour of city preparation reduces time spent ransacking packs in camp. Complete meals may be packaged in poly bags (which also help keep foods dry) labeled Bean Supper, Oatmeal and Prune Breakfast, and so on. Considerable weight is saved by shucking cardboard and paper containers—but not the cooking directions! A simpler method is grouping foods at the trailhead into, say, Soup Bag, Candy Bag, and whatever. Cocoa and sugar and the like should be double-bagged to avoid sticky sweaters.

Meal preparation can be organized any number of ways. In a party of experienced hikers, typically someone rigs tent or tarp while another assembles pots and food and others start the fire (with wood or stove) and haul water—all wordlessly and automatically by individual initiative. Generally each meal should have a single boss; too many cooks kick over too many pots and in the confusion forget to stir the macaroni. Except in the presence of a master chef, the job usually is best rotated from meal to meal.

An inexperienced party, especially with a number of children, ordinarily needs a self-appointed leader or two (such as father and mother) to assign chores—preferably by mild request or suggestion and with instant cheerful acceptance. A regime of shouted commands and sullen obedience is the prelude to eventual desertion of the troops, if not armed mutiny.

FIRE

The backpacker stove (see Chapter 13) has become indispensable because that treasured symbol of the wilderness home, the wood fire, has been banned in much American backcountry, for good reason:

heavily camped areas are wall-to-wall charcoal, fire pits replacing natural ground cover. In popular campsites all the easy wood was burned years ago, and gathering fuel is a pain in the neck. Where the wood is gone but fires still allowed, idiot hatchet men cut green trees —to no avail, since they won't burn, but in the process logging parklands. In high meadows the only wood may be silver snags and logs, bleached bones of trees long dead; in a single evening a party may consume scenery that otherwise would have enchanted hikers for generations to come. Finally, it is disappointing to travel far from city smog seeking clean air and camp in an acrid cloud, coughing and crying from the smoke of a valleyful of fires.

COOKING WITH WOOD

Still, the wood fire is not completely a memory. A stove is always less bother and gives more leisure for sunsets but seldom inspires philosophical reflections, and except in a tent is worthless for warming cold bones. In forests which annually yield a large crop of dead branches and windfall, in high valleys regularly receiving a fresh fuel supply from slope-pruning avalanches, on ocean beaches replenished with driftwood by each high tide—*and where campers are few*—fires are not immoral and may not yet be criminal.

Let it be noted, though, that a hiker's judgment and conscience only apply in the absence of regulations—build a fire in violation and a

party risks a ticket, or worse, a lecture. Land managers, who in the era of empty trails didn't get agitated unless hikers burned whole forests, now have swung pretty much to the far extreme, generally condemning wood fires as the devil's work, at best viewing them as venial sins unworthy of the truly pure. Rules can be discussed with rangers but must be obeyed. And the most nostalgic of unreconstructed anarchists admit that past damage was so great that a time of overreaction, of conservative caution, is wise and proper. Eventually fire may regain some lost dominions, once the debate descends from the realm of theology to ecology.

In any case, even the hiker who always cooks on a stove should have some notion of how to start a fire in emergencies. (The lifesaving value may be overrated, however—rarely can an exhausted person succeed in kindling soaking-wet wood; carrying proper clothing and a light bivouac tarp is more dependable.) As Smokey the Bear keeps warning, no technique is required when dry wood is plentiful. In hard rain and wind the wiliest veteran may be defeated without supernatural assistance.

A few hints may help the beginner; for thousands more, consult the woodcraft literature. First gather a substantial supply of the driest wood available; in rainy weather, look under large logs and break dead underlimbs from living trees. No ax or hatchet is needed, nor should one be carried; if finger-picking fuel ("squaw wood") cannot be found, a fire should not be built and probably can't be, anyway. Some woods burn better than others; this must be learned through experience with local species.

Begin by igniting food-package paper, moss, twigs, or knife sliverings; the emergency fire starter from the Ten Essentials (or a splash of stove gas) may be employed if kindling is damp and wind disruptive. Proceed from small wood to large, never smothering the fire with excess fuel, helping as required by putting the mouth at the critical point and blowing sparks into flames, tiny flames to big. An enclosure of rocks—the traditional "fire ring"—increases efficiency by reflecting heat inward. A fire pan (Chapter 13), required in some jurisdictions, lessens damage to soil.

The kitchen fire should be small; if conscience permits, it may be enlarged later for a social or warming fire, but that's a rare indulgence nowadays. Pots are best suspended on a light metal grate (see Chapter 13), infinitely simpler and quicker than the dinglesticks and crossbars dear to the hearts of woodcrafters.

MINIMIZING FIRE DAMAGE

Whenever possible, an established fire ring should be used to avoid killing yet another patch of plants. If a virgin site is the only choice, virtually every trace of a fire built on bare dirt or gravel can be obliterated when breaking camp by returning fire-ring rocks to exact original positions, and widely scattering ashes and leftover wood. A further step, if the fire was on living soil, is to restore a semblance of virginity and speed regrowth by mulching the spot with duff or humus.

The rules for putting out a fire are rigid and mandatory. Drown the ashes with water or snow and stir until all are cool to the touch. Drench fire-ring rocks (watch out—if very hot, they may explode) until none can possibly harbor a living ember. Make sure no underground hot spots are overlooked; a fire supposedly out may creep beneath the surface in forest duff or along dead roots or buried sticks,

and long after hikers are gone, erupt to the surface and sweep through grass, touch off forests.

The more talk about wood fires, the more reasons for carrying a stove.

GARBAGE

In the 1920s, reformers began replacing the drop-and-toss method of garbage disposal with "Burn Bash and Bury," a rule that sufficed in most American wildlands until mid-century. In such areas as the High Sierra, though, plant communities were destroyed at an alarm-

ing rate by pits dug to bury garbage—pits that often disinterred old garbage. And studies revealed that steel ("tin") cans do not reduce to soil components in less than 20–40 years, or in dry climates 100 or more; if gone they're not forgotten because iron salts leach into and "rust" springs, creeks, lakes, and meadows. The thinnest polyethylene takes 10–20 years to decompose, heavier plastics 50–80. Aluminum lasts 80–100 years, maybe 500; glass 1000 years, perhaps 1,000,000.

Thus a new law: PACK IT OUT.

Adherence wasn't instantly universal. For example, in the 1960s three elderly bird watchers from Seattle were joined by an elderly bird watcher from California for an 80-mile, 10-day walk across the Pasayten Wilderness. The Seattleites felt this section of the Cascades was so empty (then) that B, B & B continued conscionable, and anyhow nobody but a Sierra fanatic would put garbage in a nice clean pack. The fanatic didn't argue, but when companions started off after each meal to bury refuse, mildly asked if he could have it. At trip's end all the garbage plus the double-poly carrying bag were put on a scale. Total weight: *1 pound, 14 ounces.* Seeing that it cost them merely ¾ ounce per man-day, the Seattle bird watchers became fanatics too. And so, now, are all pure-hearted backpackers, everywhere.

PACK IT OUT means PACK IT ALL OUT. On the trail, stuff in pockets every gum wrapper and orange peel. In camp, if cooking on a stove, perhaps hold a discreet little paper fire to burn food packages —but don't bother on any hike up to 5 or 6 days; paper doesn't weigh that much. If a wood fire is built, paper and plastic may be burned— but not aluminum foil, some of which will oxidize but never all; inevitably the ashes glitter. Food packages of foil and paper or plastic are best given a quick burn in a hot flame, and the naked metal fished out before it starts disintegrating. Some hikers still like to scorch cans to remove food residues before stamping them flat for the garbage bag; others wash the cans along with the cooking pots. The final nicety is to spend a half-hour or more meticulously removing tiny bits of foil and unburned paper, orange peels, and egg shells while drowning and stirring the ashes—and meanwhile policing the camp for oddments of debris. Into the bag it all goes for hauling to the road, glorying in the name of garbagemen.

The total nonburnable garbage of four elderly bird watchers from a 10-day hike. Weight including carrying bag: 1 pound, 14 ounces. It's no strain to PACK IT OUT.

WATER POLLUTION

Hikers in settled areas and in wildlands fouled by sheep, cattle, and thoughtless horsemen long have suspected the water and on occasion treated it either by boiling or by adding chlorinating tablets or iodine crystals. Now pollution is a problem even in regions where hikers once trusted every spring, confident that except for occasional indelicacies of wild beasts the purity was absolute. Moreover, recent studies have shown that much "pure" water, clear to the eye, cool to the tongue, is full of invisible wildlife pernicious to the stomach; a lot of the camp dysentery formerly attributed to insufficient washing of dishes doubtless is from natural causes. Therefore, wherever the water flows slow and thin or stands around, perhaps brewing evil, but especially on thickly populated trails, the creeks and especially the lakes, no matter how cold and crystal-clear, should be inspected carefully, and when it is dubious, the water should be treated before use. Iodine-based tablets are the most effective purifiers, though they flavor the water—and must *not* be used by pregnant women.

As with garbage, man-caused water pollution can easily be eliminated from the backcountry if every traveler follows several simple rules.

First, as discussed in the previous chapter, take care of toilet needs far from watercourses.

Second, minimize the human presence in the immediate vicinity of the water supply.

Third, rather than washing dishes in lake or creek, loosing food particles and detergent, carry buckets of water into the woods or up on a knoll and scrub and rinse there.

Fourth, don't put bodies in water unless there's lots of it, as in a big river or lake, and never where swimming is banned, and never soap up—bodies should be washed out in the woods with the pots.

Finally, when other travelers are observed polluting the water, politely lead them into paths of righteousness.

KEEPING ANIMALS HONEST

Nearly all the relatively few dangers from wild animals (discussed in the following chapter) come directly from sloppy kitchens.

Any much-used camp develops a resident population of scavengers. Arriving on wings are "camp robbers"—juncos, jays, nutcrackers, and, at Sierra lakes, gulls. On four feet come wee, timorous beasties that nibble and brazen snafflehounds that gobble. There are porcupines and skunks and raccoons that methodically investigate the scene by night, oblivious to threats. And deer and mountain goats that seek salt, and packrats that devour the armpits of parkas. On ocean beaches there are clouds of crows and gulls ever on the watch for unguarded lunches. And there are bears, too.

When city folk nostalgic for the vanished frontier began visiting surviving enclaves of wilderness they fell in love with the animals and began feeding them. Bears, especially appreciative, decided that if little gifts were good, big ones were better. So was born the Campground Bear, gourmand of the picnic table, slasher of food coolers, smasher of car windows.

Trails continued safe for years, backcountry bears shyly content to tour camps after hikers were gone, lapping up bacon grease and fish guts, excavating garbage. Then camps grew crowded and bears impatiently started taking meals when they pleased, learning that the only human retaliation was yelling and pot-banging, possibly a bit of stone-throwing—which could be dealt with by a bit of teeth-baring and growling.

The population explosion of the 1960s and 1970s was actually a double boom: more hikers, more bears. Where trails still are lonesome (or bear hunters numerous) the olden ways prevail; bears enjoy human foods as holiday treats but not enough to endure loud noises, racial slurs, the chance of a bullet. However, where trails are thronged with people, creating an unnatural ecosystem, camps are thronged with bears. Such notorious bear freeways as the trail from Tuolumne Meadows to Yosemite Valley have an estimated five times more bears than natural foods can sustain. There can be seen red-eyed, feverish hikers staggering from night after sleepless night; ask how things are going and madness lights eyes, tales of woe are croaked: "Seven bears in one night! Can you believe it? *Seven bears!*"

It's difficult in a Seven Bear Night to love wildlife. The defense of bears thus is left to the next chapter. The topic here is defense of groceries and sleep.

The measures necessary depend on the species and numbers and determination of invaders. Local inquiry is desirable; rangers usually know which camps are under heavy attack by what. In olden-day type (lonesome) country, stowing foods in closed pack or tight-wrapped tarp may suffice, though usually not, what with quiet burglars chewing holes in expensive gear; in such situations, better leave the food out and let the two or three mice (darling little critters, watched by flashlight) eat their fill.

But where there are a hundred mice, four squirrels, or one bear, the "sacrificial offering" technique is a snare and delusion—only the Fort Knox strategy works. Maximum defense is recommended whenever enemy strength is unknown; the night is far more restful when the commissary is secure, when no alarums will mobilize groggy militia to repulse squirrels crazed by the aroma of Hershey bars, skunks raving for a granola fix. And bears . . .

Tom Winnett, author-publisher of the Wilderness Press trail guides to High, Middle, and Low Sierra and veteran commuter on bear freeways, teaches in *Backpacking Basics* that bears are (1) too big to crawl in rock crevices and (2) too clumsy to climb rock walls. Thus, if a crevice less than 9 inches wide and at least 4 feet deep is available, the food sack can be pushed in with a stick and be bearproof. Of course, there are still chipmunks. And one must beware of pushing the sack in so far as to be peopleproof. If a ledge is available higher on a cliff than a bear can reach, and if a person can climb there, or push the food sack up with sticks, or lower it with a rope, again only coons and mice will dine that night.

The Ultimate Winnett Weapon is the counterbalance. The technique is simple in camps equipped with "bear cables," and were these and/or "bear boxes" placed in over-beared wildlands, the population would quickly drop to natural numbers via nature's way—pregnant bears, when malnourished, spontaneously abort. But many wilderness managers judge cables and boxes contrary to the Wilderness Act and prefer 500 percent too many bears, contending that this is nature's way of reducing the backpacker population.

A counterbalance is easy to rig if a tree can be found with a branch at least 20 feet from the ground that is 4–5 inches thick at the trunk, and at a distance of at least 8 feet from the trunk is still sturdy enough to support a heavy weight. These distances are necessary in order to suspend a food bag 12–15 feet above the ground and 5 feet below the branch and 8 feet from the trunk. Close wins no cigar—anything less in any direction and the bear cries "Gotcha!" In the real world such branches are rare. It is then necessary to suspend a light but strong rope or wire (carried for the purpose) between two high points, such as trees or rock boulders atop opposite sides of a gulch. In the real world it is not always easy to find such gulches or to climb 20 feet up a tree (two trees); though Professor Tom doesn't say so, presumably a hiker then prays for two hovering angels.

In any event, with branch found or rope/wire placed, the next step is to put all vulnerable food in two large poly bags, which then are placed in two stuff bags. Whether any food is invulnerable is dubious; bears readily open tin cans. Include with the food all cosmetics and toilet articles—soap, suntan oil, lipstick, toothpaste, bug repellent— the perfumes interest bears strangely, even anger them. Distribute the weight so that one bag is heavier. Tie pots or metal cups or jinglebells

to the bags as warning devices should a troupe of bear acrobats pass by on tour.

Now tie a rock to a 50-foot length of strong nylon cord (carried for the purpose) and toss it over the branch/rope/wire. Untie the rock and tie on the heavier food bag and hoist it as high as possible. Now tie the lighter bag on the cord as high as possible—perhaps standing on a chunk of log or atop a human pyramid. Stuff all extra cord in the bag—bears know how to pull strings. Using a stick, push the light bag as high as the heavy one. If due to sag of branch/rope/wire either bag is less than 9 feet from the ground, return to Square One.

In the real world of bear freeways, a hiker must expect frequently to be unable to perform any of the above. The concern then shifts to protecting tents, packs, and bodies that might get between a bear and his supper. Food must not be kept in or near the tent but be placed at a distance. Nothing should be left in the pack; all food and toilet articles must be spread on the ground to facilitate inspection. Pack pockets must be left unzipped to avoid having them ripped open.

So, Mr. or Ms. Bear comes to take inventory. What then? If new at the business, it may be repelled by loud shouts, flashlights, banging pots, derogatory remarks about its parents. If it takes offense? *Don't*

argue. It may have learned it can whup any dozen pot-bangers with one paw behind its back.

What then? Salvage what the bear spurned—they usually mess up more than they eat. Beg handouts from passing hikers. Whine to the ranger. Write letters requesting birth control for bears by installation of cables and boxes. Seek trails where hikers—thus bears—are few.

BUGS AND BEASTS AND SERPENTS

MAN is not alone in the wilderness. Innumerable creatures large and small were there first, are there now, and will remain. A visitor must learn to live with them and respect their rights—enjoying hawks in the sky, deer in the meadows, and others that make interesting neighbors and mind their own business, doing his best to get along with the hostiles and the all-too-companionables.

A few trail-country inhabitants are an occasional danger to human life and limb. Some, notably certain insects and arachnids (or "bugs" as they are ignorantly lumped in common usage and in this book), are mainly a menace to sanity. Far more for good reason are frightened by man, the most dangerous of all predators.

The beginner doubtless has heard horror stories about encounters between man and beast, man and serpent, man and bug. However, he takes vastly greater risks of being maimed or murdered or mentally unhinged on highways leading from the cities (and in the cities) than along the trails. If hikers take the trouble to learn a little about the habits of the natives, the two can share wildlands with minimum discomfort and terror for both.

SERPENTS

"Watch out for snakes," says the guidebook, and so hikers from such poison-free lands as Ireland and Puget Sound and Alaska walk foreign trails a-tremble, leaping high at the sight of every lizard, and lie sleepless in bags, imagining every rustle of bushes to be the approach of evil.

Venomous snakes demand respect but not panic. An estimated 1,000–1,500 persons (in another guess, 7,000–8,000), mostly toddling kids and rambunctious teen-agers, are bitten in the United States each year—a small number, really, considering that millions of rural folk daily live and work amid potentially dangerous snakes. Perhaps a quarter of the bites occur during attempts at capturing or in handling

C'MON ADAM, SNAKES CAN'T HURT YOU!

for religious purposes. About 30 people a year die—a large proportion of the fatalities tiny children. Very few hikers are bitten, and fewer still suffer serious illness, much less death.

Of the scores of snakes common in American trail country, only four carry venom. The coral snake occurs in a portion of the South and Southwest, and the water moccasin (cottonmouth) in wetlands of the South. The copperhead ranges rather widely through the East, and various members of the rattlesnake family are found across the entire nation.

Residents of snake country, though they love to scare dudes with tall tales, are quite casual about the hazard; in the memory of the oldest inhabitants of the Stehekin Valley of the North Cascades, going back eighty-odd years, no human ever has been bitten there; dogs have been, some repeatedly, but only one, a pup, is remembered as dying.

Snakes fear man, and given a chance, will flee his presence; knowing this, the hiker can reduce confrontations with elementary precautions. Be a noisy walker to give ample advance notice of your approach. Watch the path ahead to avoid stepping on a snake or coming near one sunning on a boulder (after a chill night) or cooling in a cave or streambank grass (on a hot day); listen for the rattle that often warns that a rattlesnake is close by, scared, and thus dangerous. (However, since even a coiled snake can strike less than the length of its body, the surveillance need not be extended any great distance.) Do not plunge blindly into thickets or run through boulder fields or scramble incautiously up rocks. For peace of mind, if nothing else, perhaps wear long pants rather than shorts, possibly gaiters.

Authorities generally advise carrying a snakebite kit, but in unpracticed hands of semihysterical first-aiders, the kit can be more dangerous than the bite; the rule is to seek instruction before entering an area where it may be needed.

Enough, here, about timid creatures too much maligned. In many parts of our continent, including most alpine regions, poisonous snakes are totally absent; the relatively few hikers who spend a good deal of time in lands of the serpents will want to study their habits thoroughly, not only to learn to live among them without fear but also for the pleasure of getting to know fellow travelers. Colin Fletcher, in *The Complete Walker,* discusses rattlesnakes at length, crediting as his major source *Rattlesnakes: Their Habits, Life Histories, and Influence on Mankind,* by Laurence M. Klauber. Dr. James A. Wilkerson, in *Medicine for Mountaineering,* is definitive on treatment for snakebite. When new areas are visited, guidebooks should be consulted to find if venom-carriers are present, and where.

BEASTS

Urbanites nourished on fairy tales and frontier lies frequently are uncomfortable in forests, fearing that every thicket conceals a beast ready to pounce. The night, they suspect, does indeed have a thousand eyes—and jaws, and fangs, and claws. Though this may be so in city parks, the wildlands of America contain few animals that threaten man; the menace is the other way around. Several creatures may be cited to suggest how little there is to fear.

Cougars and other cats do not attack man unless cornered, a distinctly avoidable situation; only the rare hiker is privileged even to hear, much less see one.

The same is true of wolves, now tragically scarce, and proven by modern research to be innocent of slanders perpetrated by Little Red Riding Hood and paranoid shepherds. What substance there is for legends of lupine viciousness comes from attacks in the madness of rabies, incidents extremely rare but lingering long in memory and expanding enormously in myth. Rabies afflicts small beasts as well as large and is not restricted to wilderness; a fellow quietly besotting himself at a Manhattan Island bar once was bitten by a rabid bat that flew in from the street. On trail or in city no animal that seems ill or behaves oddly should be picked up, touched, or approached; it may be dying of rabies, plague, or some other disease that can be transmitted by a bite or by infected fleas. Be sure to tell the children.

Elk and moose should be shunned in the fall rutting season, when passion-mad bulls may mistake hikers for competitors and run them out of the country. In spring and summer the cows—and any mother with young—should be given a wide berth so as not to stir maternal hostility.

Skunks? Don't frighten them! Porcupines? An inexperienced dog may require hours of painful surgery pulling quills from jaws. Coyotes? Scary-sounding under the moon, but harmless. Eagles? Occasionally they attack airplanes and nest-robbing ornithologists.

A word about the horse. First, pedestrians should always yield the right of way to equestrians, who often are unstable in the saddle and

53

have scant control of their huge, clumsy steeds. Second, when stepping from the path, a hiker should continue making normal gestures and above all *speak* to the poor dumb beast so it will know it has met an ordinary human, not an alien monster.

SAVE OUR BEARS

The most interesting large animal the ordinary person has a reasonable chance to see on the trail is the bear; eliminate bear stories and wildness would be diminished. However, bison and Indians made good stories too, and look what happened to them; whether bears can survive, for man's sake if not their own, remains to be determined. It can only be so if hikers want them, and help them.

The first rule, elaborated on in the previous chapter, is *never feed the animals, deliberately or otherwise.* A party may consider a bit of food a small price for an anecdote. But only if animals are kept wild and honest can they be kept alive—and the trails safe.

Second, do not fraternize. Forget Jellystone Park and Yogi and Gentle Ben and Teddy—real-life bears are not cute. Forget Smokey —bears are nothing like dogs, never become humanized, at best tolerate and usually hate people. Enjoy them—but from a distance. Stay away from cubs! Though unseen, the deadliest of the species, the mother, is near, ready to take out after photographers.

There are bears and bears. Before entering realms of the Alaska brown and polar bears, a hiker must consult local experts, who often as not advise visiting a lawyer to draw up a last will and testament.

The novice does well to skip grizzly lands altogether; as more hikers crowd Glacier National Park and the wildlands of Canada and Alaska, scenes of most backpacker–*ursus horribilis* encounters, grizzly behavior is more unpredictable, tragedies more common. The veteran who knows the habits of bears on his home grounds knows the risks and how to reduce them—the stranger may do precisely the wrong thing in exactly the wrong place. Rangers constantly study grizzly behavior and try to keep pace with changing patterns by refining rules and closing dangerous camps and trails; heeding their warnings is mandatory but may not suffice; many warnings come only after episodes of blood and slaughter. Recommended procedures currently include: Leave at home dogs, and perfumed cosmetics and toilet articles. Sit this one out if you are a menstruating woman. No solitary hiking. Camp in a tent. No food or garbage or perfumery near camp. Keep all garments and gear clean and free of food odors. Make lots of noise on the trail. But hikers who have obeyed all these rules have been mauled, killed, even eaten. Too much to pay for an anecdote.

Suppose the hiker shuns grizzly country. What about the black bear? To forgo its terrain is virtually to evacuate the trails. And if the black (which in other color phases may be brown, cinnamon, even white) is the smallest of the clan, it's big enough to win any hand-to-paw combat. And if it's the least belligerent, that too is only by comparison—and evidence suggests that blacks all over America are getting more irascible, more aggressive. On lonesome trails where bears are of the old school and dodge man assiduously, the hiker may avoid surprises by making normal noises as he walks, perhaps supplemented by bells on pack or boots and occasional bursts of nervous laughter. But fewer and fewer trails are lonesome, more and more bears are incompletely wild, and as they've grown dependent on human foods they've evolved socially. Every year brings more reports of black bears throwing their weight around, "bluff-charging"—a highly effective tactic, since few hikers call the bluff. More than once, anyhow.

And so, as with the grizzly, defense strategies need revision. When a black bear invades camp, night or day, the technique still applicable in areas of few humans is to yell and holler and bang pots and throw rocks. An inexperienced bumpkin bear will light out for the next county. But the experienced, mod, with-it bear may give a hideous toothy grin, growl, or charge. Is it bluffing? Don't ask. Shut up and run.

When the meeting is on the trail and the bear doesn't flee, that's a very, very bad sign; shouting and rock-throwing are inadvisable unless a run-for-it or climb-for-it sanctuary, tree or cliff, is at hand. Best to stand still or slowly retreat, saying a few pleasant words in a calm and friendly voice. If pursued, throw down the pack—the bear may spend enough time ripping it to shreds for a tree to be found.

If caught, go limp and quiet, do not resist or scream, cover the head with the arms, and pray.

Can hikers and bears share wildlands? The question is open. Remember, the bears were there first.

BUGS

Every long-time hiker has a lurid repertoire of bug stories—the air thick with flailing wings, loud with snapping jaws—infants wailing, wives weeping, strong men teetering on the brink of madness. Wilderness veterans who face tempest and jungle with fortitude quail at the prospect of entering the domain of the Lord of the Flies. However, formidable the insect legions are, rarely can they totally defeat the hiker who learns their habits and employs proper defenses.

In camp a bugproof tent (see Chapter 12) provides a near-perfect haven. For tarp sleepers, as well as for anyone sitting around camp or resting on the trail, a "habitat" can be instantly rigged: a sheet of mosquito netting (or better, finer-mesh no-see-um netting) a couple of yards wide and several long, enough to drape over the entire upper body, weighing mere ounces and compressing to a tiny wad in pack pocket. True peace is never possible while hiking or doing chores, but the target areas can be minimized by covering up with clothing and donning a head net. Insect repellent (see Chapter 15) generally prevents bugs from drilling and biting but doesn't keep them at a respect-

ful distance. The attentive cloud hovers close, landing on untreated clothing and glasses and flying into eyes, nostrils, and open mouth. Chemicals thus don't eliminate the harassment, which is often the worst part of the whole business.

Frequently the only salvation lies in resolute stoicism. Those who yield to paranoia have lost the battle and are not long for the trails. It is necessary to realize that bugs *belong* on earth, that if the Architect had intended wildlands to be perfectly comfortable for man, He would have designed them more like Disneyland.

In extremities some hikers find tranquilizers useful in gaining the proper mental composure; others prefer a shot of rum.

THE CAST OF VILLAINS

By learning to enjoy "bugs" (that is, insects and arachnids and other arthropods), a person enlarges his circle of trail companions; only a very few ever are a bother. Admire the gorgeous butterfly, the spectacular dragonfly, the patient spider, the graceful water skate, the glistening beetle. Ponder the anecdote told by the zoologist G. Evelyn Hutchinson about J. B. S. Haldane. The great biologist "found himself in the company of a group of theologians. On being asked what one could conclude as to the nature of the Creator from a study of His creation, Haldane is said to have answered, 'An inordinate fondness for beetles.' " Illustrating the point in a review of a Hutchinson book, Stephen Jay Gould said: "Since Linnaeus set the modern style of formal naming in 1758, more than a million species of plants and animals have received Latin binomials. More than 80 percent of these names apply to animals; of the animals, nearly 75 percent are insects; of the insects, about 60 percent are beetles." What's good enough for the Lord ought to be good enough for man. Still, folks with a phobia about creepy-crawlies do well to sleep in floored tents.

The experienced hiker has too many problems with genuine menaces to fret about innocents, outlandish and gaudy though they may appear, and adopts the attitude, "If they don't bite, they don't count." It's a frame of mind worth cultivating, saving much squirming and yelping and gallons of repellent.

Ants trouble only the hiker who unwarily spreads his sleeping bag

atop a colony—a typical location being the remains of a rotten log—
and is wakened in the night by the pricking of myriad tiny needles.

Bee-type bugs (honeybees, bumblebees, yellowjackets, hornets,
wasps, etc.) normally let people alone, except to briefly investigate
bright-colored clothing they mistake for huge flowers; together with
flies and mosquitoes they are attracted and thoroughly confused by
damsels and lads who wear perfume. Accidentally stepping on a yel-
lowjacket nest in the middle of a trail can be unpleasant, since a single
warrior can deliver numerous stabs, but the spectacle can entertain
dirty old men when several get inside a female's blouse, or dirty old
women when the drama is in a man's pants. Individuals vary in their
physical reactions to bee stings: some find them no worse than nettles;
others puff up dramatically; in rare cases of extreme allergy the victim
may go into severe, even fatal shock—the proper medication should
always be carried by people who suspect they have a problem.

Midges or gnats often fill the summer evening air in the vicinity of
lowland marshes and lakes.

The chigger, found mainly in the East, is a mite that lives in grass,
digs into skin, and causes an itch.

Annoying these bugs may sometimes be, but none is so dreaded by
hikers as the next characters in this sordid chapter.

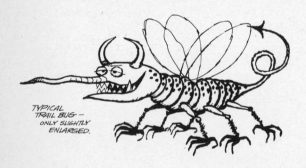

TYPICAL
TRAIL BUG —
ONLY SLIGHTLY
ENLARGED.

Ticks

The tick does not hurt, does not harass, but nevertheless is loathed.
First, because it is nasty, burrowing into flesh and engorging on blood.

Second, because at some times and places (but rarely) it carries Rocky Mountain spotted fever, formerly a much-feared disease with a very high mortality rate but now easily cured by antibiotics. As with the rattlesnake, a mythology of terror has developed and folklore is full of nonsense about the creatures parachuting from trees and screwing into skin.

The tick rarely ventures more than 18 inches from the ground; typically it anchors to brush and grass along routes used by animals, extends hooks, and waits for a host to come within reach; the hooks then clamp tight and the tick climbs aboard and begins to prospect.

Ticks are most plentiful in the springtime of dry lands, when fresh green grass is sprouting and tender leaves are budding and browsers are enjoying salads. Hiker-tick encounters mainly occur in May and June on valley trails leading to alpine regions of Western mountains.

When passing through tick-thick terrain, it is wise to wear long pants treated with repellent. When the hiker is sleeping in tick country, repellent may be applied to all clothing, to sleeping bags, and perhaps tent entries. In the absence of sufficient repellent, hikers may wish to pair off morning and evening to completely inspect each other's bodies. (Please, no giggling.) By this means the danger of disease (which actually is not all that common) can be largely avoided, since a tick normally explores several hours before choosing a drill site, and even if infected, cannot transmit germs for several hours more.

In the early stages of drilling, the entire tick can be gently pulled straight out (not "unscrewed"); then or later, it possibly may be induced to withdraw by touching its rear with a drop of repellent, kerosene, or gas. Once the tick is partly imbedded, the only remedy is to pull off the body, halting the creature's operations by killing it. Perhaps later the patient should visit a doctor to have the head cut out. If localized infection develops, or high fever and severe headache, chills, aching back, and a rash, medical treatment should be sought—in the case of these last symptoms, urgently.

Ticks can roam clothing and sleeping bags and gear several days and thus must be watched for after the party has ascended into high mountains or returned to the city.

Mosquitoes

Except perhaps in parts of the South, the mosquitoes of America do not transmit malaria or yellow fever and the only region where they potentially are a mortal peril is the far North, where by one estimate an unprotected person could lose half his blood in a half-hour. The needle is painless and the itching usually minor and temporary. The central hazard is mental—the maddening whine, the constant cloud, the probing of ears, eyes, nose—moderated but not eliminated by repellent. Mosquitoes probably have stimulated the buying of more tents than rain and driven more hikers into fits and off the trails than all other causes combined.

In lowlands mosquitoes may be met in every season except winter —one or two, a few, or many, depending on the local climate. In alpine meadows and Arctic tundras they achieve the continental climax of mind-boggling when the ground is moist from snowmelt and the air is calm and warm; as pools and humus dry, their numbers diminish; with the first frosts of fall they vanish. Through miserable experience a hiker learns the intolerable times and places and thereafter can schedule trips to notorious hellholes for the off-season.

Mosquitoes have a limited temperature range. In high mountains they ordinarily go instantly to bed with the evening chill, probably to arise at dawn, thin out during the heat of day, and return in force as the afternoon cools. In warm lowlands they may appear at dusk and work all through the night.

A wind keeps them from clustering and thus a camp may be placed on a knoll for the breezes in preference to a sheltered nook nearby. Similarly, a dry hillock may be quieter than a lush vale a stone's-throw distant.

Flies

Scores of members of the fly family infest trail country. Several may be described as representative examples of the range in size and habitat.

The tiny, silent *no-see-um,* mistaken for a speck of dust until it grabs hold, able to pass through most netting as if it weren't there, often gets off an incredibly painful chew but mainly is felt as an overall prickle and itch. No-see-ums generally are confined to lowlands, such as dank river bottoms, which they may on occasion render uninhabitable.

The chief threat is the medium-sized category, represented in some areas by the *black fly,* in others by the *deer fly,* which in a typical manifestation resembles the housefly. In "fly time" every square yard of trail may harbor hundreds of sharp-eyed, sharp-toothed, loud-buzzing villains, and to calculate the numbers in an entire valley is to submerge sanity in a vision of infinity—an infinity of evil. Driven by

heat to fiendish hyperactivity, flies attack most furiously precisely on those sweaty, gasping uphill drags when the hiker moves slowest. Now and then a kamikaze plunges into ear, nose, eye, or wide-open mouth—to feel wings and legs scrambling around in the throat, to gag and retch, is the ultimate initiation.

But all is not lost. The unbearable fly time usually lasts only a few weeks of summer, ending with the first heavy frosts, and the fly empire, though extending from low valleys to meadows, usually is impossibly crowded only in the upper forests. Moreover, flies vanish in the wind and evening chill; even the cool microclimate next to a waterfall may allow a peaceful lunch when the forest world all around is pure hell. Finally, since flies patrol at random in search of a victim, the interior of a lean-to (or a tent with one closed end) has only one-quarter the number of the surrounding woods, since from three directions they bump into walls. Even an open-ended tarp cuts the population in half, and a closed tent is perfectly secure.

Deer flies ordinarily diminish or disappear in parkland and meadows, which apparently by family agreement are the domain of the *elk fly,* which ranges upward into snow and rocks but luckily occurs in dozens rather than thousands. These enormous beasts, which take such big bites that they seem to be slicing off steaks, can be slapped with relative ease—though for final destruction one may have to take a club and beat them to death.

CRIMINALS

Despite occasional raids by frontiersmen living off the land, snatching bacon from unguarded camps and jacking up cars to steal the wheels, hikers used to feel safe from crime in the hills. Largely this was because hikers used to be such a ragtag lot that when dressed up in surplus gear after World War II as the Khaki Gang they actually thought themselves rather dashing. But burglars weren't impressed. It was when hikers got rich and pretty that they got into trouble. In

1978 more than 8,000 felonies, mostly theft and vandalism, were reported in National Parks.

As tourism and backpacking brought the campground bear, so the $100 pack and $200 tent and $10 freeze-dried porkchop brought the trail thief. There are amateurs unable to resist the sleeping bag airing on a tree. And there are professional bandits, indistinguishable from other backpackers, who case a basin, spot the nobs, and when camp occupants go on a flower stroll, dart in and out, pack stuffed with $1000 worth of geodesic tents, Gore-Tex parkas, and freeze-dried strawberries.

What to do? Above all, as with bears, don't let crime pay. Starve the crooks. Camp in secluded spots with subdued gear that doesn't scream for attention. In crowded areas, leave camp unattended as little as possible. When going off on a day jaunt, carry costly bags and parkas and the like some distance and hide them in the bushes.

The trailhead is the major danger zone, the operations area of interstate gangs including spotters who loiter around parking lots chatting with folks about where they're going, for how long, and watching who locks what in which trunk; lookouts posted down the road and up the trail with CB radios; fences in distant cities; and guns.

These gangs will go out of business at some future time when they open a hundred cars and net nothing but moldy tennis shoes, stinking T-shirts, rotten bananas, and warm root beer—or when all gear is so prominently and indelibly marked by the owner that no fence will touch it. A hiker who owns a car with mag wheels, thousand-dollar carburetor, and tape deck–stereo–AM-FM radio should buy a second car, a battered relic with retreads and broken windows, for driving to trails. Valuables must never be left in the car, must always be carried on the trail; picklocks open doors and trunk as fast as a key, and the pro knows all the clever hiding places for cash and credit cards. If the hike is in the course of an extended highway tour, store extra gear in a nearby town; many motels provide such service.

The ultimate solution, of course, is abject poverty. Nobody ever stole from the Khaki Gang.

6:	DANGER!

BEFORE this invitation to wildland pleasures continues, a word from the devil's advocate.

There is misery on the trail, and pain, and death. Questions for the new hiker: *Do you know what you're getting into?* Are you aware of the risks? Are you willing to accept those you cannot invariably avoid? If so, welcome to the wild bunch. If not, think about it, please.

A number of discomforts and dangers are discussed in other chapters; they will not be repeated here, nor an exhaustive catalog of perils presented in the tradition of seeking to scare the innocent half to death. However, a germ of fear must be implanted, hopefully to grow to a mature respect.

BEGINNER-KILLERS

If a person brooded incessantly on all the ways there are to be maimed, he would never get out of bed—until he began worrying about burglars, earthquakes, and bedsores. Certainly no one would ever stride blithely along a trail if at each step he were watching for snakes and bears, falling trees and mountains, flash floods and lightning bolts.

Paraphrasing the last journal entry of Scott of the Antarctic, at the death camp on the return from the Pole, "we take risks, we know we take them. Therefore, when things come out against us, we have no cause for complaint." To live is to be insecure. But to die from ignorance is a shame.

Over the years a hiker encounters numerous hazards, common and uncommon. Encyclopedic coverage of the threats in every realm of hiking terrain from snow to deserts is given in *Outdoor Living: Problems, Solutions, Guidelines,* edited by Eugene H. Fear, as well as in his similar *Surviving the Unexpected Wilderness Emergency.* Certain perils seem to have a particular affinity for the inexperienced, and several are especially notorious among rescue experts as beginner-killers.

WEATHER: HYPOTHERMIA

Except in desert country, where sunstroke and dehydration are the killers, the vast majority of weather-caused fatalities—among veterans as well as novices—result from hypothermia, whereby the body loses more heat than it can generate. (Older names were "exposure" and "freezing to death.")

A hiker needs only get rain-drenched and wind-blasted a few times to pay close attention to the forecast before leaving on a trip, and constantly watch the sky while in wildlands. Eventually he learns the characteristic weather patterns of home hills, develops some skill at interpreting clouds and winds, and can guess with better-than-random accuracy the prospects for coming hours.

But every summer, somewhere, a beginner sets out in morning sun so warm that only a loony would carry an extra sweater or parka. He admires the pretty billow on the horizon—too far away, surely, to be a threat. But in afternoon the cloud arrives, and he wishes for that sweater and parka, yet still no need to worry, the car is just a couple of hours distant. Then begins rain (or snow), driven by a gale. Muscles become clumsy, thinking tangled. He stumbles and sprains an ankle, or misses the path and is lost in

mist. Unless rescuers find him in time, the rest is silence.

A common misconception is that hypothermia is a danger only at below-freezing temperatures. The accompanying table shows that a wind of 20 miles per hour at 40°F cools the body as effectively as still air at 18°F. *Wind chill* can cause hypothermia at temperatures far above freezing.

Moisture cools somewhat by wetting the skin but mainly by reducing the insulation value of clothing; the thermal conductivity of water is 240 times greater than that of still air. Hypothermia is not confined to high ridges but can occur in low forests from *water chill*. The combination of wind and rain is particularly lethal.

WIND CHILL

To find the approximate effective temperature (cooling power) of wind-driven air compared to that of still air, read downward from the still-air thermometer readings of the top line to intersect the wind speed in the left column.

Skin-Effective Temperature
(degrees Fahrenheit)

Wind		50	40	30	20	10	0	−10	−20
Wind	0 (still air) _ _ _ _ _ _ _	50	40	30	20	10	0	−10	−20
Speed	10 _ _ _ _ _ _ _ _ _ _ _ _	40	28	16	4	−9	−21	−33	−46
(miles	20 _ _ _ _ _ _ _ _ _ _ _ _	32	18	4	−10	−25	−39	−53	−69
per	30 _ _ _ _ _ _ _ _ _ _ _ _	28	13	−2	−18	−33	−48	−63	−79
hour)	40 _ _ _ _ _ _ _ _ _ _ _ _	26	10	−6	−21	−37	−53	−69	−85

Well-equipped hikers, faithfully carrying the Ten Essentials (see Chapter 15) rarely die from hypothermia; when they do, it is usually because they ignore the sky, their inner voices, and push forward rather than retreating or holing up.

GRAVITY: FALLING AND BEING FALLEN UPON

Chapter 17 discusses rough-country travel and warns against attempting cliffs and snowfields properly left to trained climbers. Such ill-advised adventures by daring beginners fill pages and pages of the annual reports of rescue groups. The reports also devote considerable space to falls from trails; in steep terrain the tread is often wide and safe, yet inches away is a cliff and to stumble over the edge is perhaps to tumble dozens or hundreds of feet.

How do hikers fall off trails? By rushing when they should be creeping. By fainting from heat exhaustion. By not carrying a flashlight and by staying too long on sunset-colored ridges and then, while blindly descending dark woods, missing a switchback.

Another danger of gravity is that piece by piece, year by year, mountains are disintegrating. Far more common than spontaneous rockfall, though, is the peril of heavily traveled trails where carefree and careless hikers kick rocks loose to plunge onto people below.

GETTING LOST

Hikers who know the techniques of finding and keeping the route, as introduced in Chapter 16, are rarely lost longer than overnight. Moreover, those who carry the Ten Essentials have a survival rate of virtually 100 percent.

Even ill-trained, ill-equipped novices generally do not become seriously lost if the party always remains together in confusing terrain. They are, for one thing, less likely to miss the way, and if they do, reinforce one another physically and spiritually. It is the lone traveler who succumbs to panic, the prelude to tragedy.

If lost, what then? Rescue experts emphasize that the problem is not being lost but staying alive long enough to be found.

First, as soon as confused, *stop;* don't plunge onward, getting more thoroughly lost. Sit down, rest, have a bite to eat. Think calmly. Do not let fear lead to panic. If two or more persons are lost together, discuss the situation—and do not henceforth become separated! The annals abound in incidents where every member of a lost party was eventually found except the one who went for help.

Second, mark the location. Chances are the trail is not far away. Conduct short sorties in all directions, returning to the marked spot if unsuccessful.

Third, shout—and listen for answering shouts. Or blow a whistle if one is in the emergency kit—an excellent idea—as whistling can be sustained much longer than shouting. (Three blasts at a time, three of anything being the universal signal of distress.) Friends or strangers may answer, their shouts guiding the way back to the trail.

Fourth, prepare for night well in advance. Conserve strength for the cold, dark hours. In bad weather, look for the snuggest available shelter under trees or overhanging rocks. Build a fire if possible, not only for warmth but because searchers may see the flame or smoke.

The hiker lacking considerable experience in cross-country navigation should, if first efforts fail, concentrate not on finding the way but on letting rescuers *find him.* Above all, this means staying in one place. The hard cases are those who go and go as long as legs work, leaving the area being combed by the rescue party, eluding searchers as if playing hide-and-seek—at last, from injury, hypothermia, starvation, or a combination, dying alone.

GOING FOR HELP

Most provinces of North American trail country are now served by rescue systems coordinating land administrators, regional and local police, military and naval forces, news media, helicopters, and unpaid volunteers from outdoor clubs, Explorer Scouts, and/or units of the Mountain Rescue Association.

Though the average hiker ordinarily is never asked to join a rescue (for which only experienced and trained wildlanders are wanted), he must always be prepared to undertake the very important task of summoning experts. Thus, before setting out on any trail, he must know how to activate the local system—usually by contacting the nearest ranger or policeman.

When a member of the party has been lost, injured, or become ill, what's to be done? It depends. How large is the party?

A lone hiker, disabled, can at most shout and wait and pray. Something for soloists to think about. (In empty country a broken leg or inflamed appendix can be fatal.)

In a two-man group the victim—perhaps unconscious or delirious and requiring constant attention—must be left alone by his companion seeking help. Something for two-pal, girl-boy, and daddy-son parties to think about. (In rough terrain, walk as if in a minefield.)

With three in the party the victim can be constantly tended while a messenger runs for the ranger. With four, two messengers can go, thus eliminating the chance of a single one becoming lost or hurt and compounding the problem.

Before leaving the scene of the accident (or illness or loss), the messenger should gather (preferably write down) data the rescuers will want: nature and location of the accident, extent of injuries, the number of people on the scene and their resources of equipment and experience, names of party members and phone numbers of next of kin.

Wherever they exist, hikers should scrupulously observe sign-in/sign-out regulations, which in effect make the rangers backup members of the party who will automatically come looking if the return is delayed. Where such procedures don't exist, often rangers or law officers regularly check trailheads. Their task would be eased if every car had a note taped to the windshield saying where the party is and when it expects to return, but this would also ease the task of burglars. Nevertheless, a note with the names and addresses of party members, and a whom-to-notify phone number, doesn't aid thieves and does help authorities solve mysteries. On any trip in an area lacking sign-in/sign-out provisions, the schedule and route should be left with relatives or friends so rescuers can be alerted if the party is late getting back. Such precautions have sustained the life of more than one walker lying helpless, alone, but not without hope.

RESPECT

Probably no long-time rough-country wanderer can look back on his travels without wondering how he survived. He recalls the time he tripped on a root and his pack flew over his head and he teetered on the trail edge looking straight down at a boiling river. And the time he was strolling a ridge under a fantastic cloud and suddenly hail pelted and rocks buzzed and lightning blinded. And the time he waded into a meltwater flood and in an instant the torrent threw him against a boulder a hundred feet downstream. And the time he swam to the middle of a cold mountain tarn and found his legs and arms going limp from hypothermia and only while sinking for good was able to crawl ashore. And the time he was walking a broad trail through forest and a mild breeze arose and with that final delicate push a huge snag killed in a fire fifty years ago crashed to the ground right in his path. And the night of the big storm when he huddled in his tent while torrents pressed down the roof—and the next morning he crawled out to find that a few feet from his bed the meadows were obliterated under tons of boulders and gravel.

And so on, and so on, over the campfires the tales are told, the memories renewed. At last one veteran asks old companions of the hills, "How did we ever *make* it this far?" And they all laugh nervously, for they all should have died many times when they were young and raw and fearless. And maybe they are silent a moment, remembering the companions who didn't make it. Including those who missed this campfire only by months or days—because veterans, too, sometimes die.

All well and good for the surviving veterans—they have buried friends and now know fear that is healthy, and when scared, say so loudly and proudly and not for years have fretted about being called "chicken." They quote the maxim from the Alps: "When a climber (hiker) is injured, he apologizes to his friends. When a climber (hiker) is killed, his friends apologize for him."

But the beginners? They may be driven by social pressure to run when they know it would be wiser to walk, to continue toward the planned objective when they know it is time to retreat. Or they may be dumb slaves of internal compulsions—a fear of not measuring up to manhood (common among boys), of not meeting a husband's expectations (the bride syndrome), of becoming old (the middle-aged-athlete syndrome).

A hiker, no matter how inexperienced, almost always realizes when he is in great danger. He *knows* when the terrain is so steep that a fall could be mortal. He *knows* when the wind is so ominous that a bad storm is building.

Beginners die on the trails because they do not have the guts to be cowards. They have been led to believe that man has conquered the earth and that to quail when confronted by the naked force of amoral, uncaring nature is to break faith with the pioneers, to deviate from the American Way.

Hiking tends to build humility. And respect. Qualities that not only improve the soul but enhance chances to walk wildlands for years with only an occasional disaster.

Part Two

EQUIPMENT: INTO THE THICKETS OF THE CATALOGS

7:

ASSEMBLING THE OUTFIT

IN THE olden days of 35-odd years ago it was easy to buy equipment for hiking and backpacking—there was so little to choose from. And with gear then available at prices and weights ordinary folk could afford and tolerate, there was general resignation to shivering when it was cold, getting wet when it rained, eating strictly from hunger, and eventually developing back trouble.

Nowadays? A whole new world. Carrying loads lighter and more comfortable than oldtimers believed awaited them in heaven, the modern backpacker travels and sleeps warm and dry in all but the worst conditions, quickly prepares tasty meals, and walks proudly erect, every resemblance to the shambling, stooped apeman erased.

Yet as in so many other aspects of contemporary life in superconsumer nations, with physical luxury has come mental confusion and psychic distress.

See the novice enter a large backpacking shop. His heart leaps with joy at the gorgeous array and he wanders in a happy daze, visualizing himself already in a wilderness camp, wiggling toes in viciously handsome boots, cooking a savory dinner on an ingenious little stove, easy-on-the-back pack beside lightweight, storm- and bug-proof tent, within which is spread comfy sleeping bag.

BOOT DEPARTMENT

Getting down to cases, he tries to select a pair of boots and finds dozens of models, all brutal enough to delight Attila the Hun—but which do his feet genuinely desire? He moves to the packs and each is a masterpiece of engineering—but which will bring his back true happiness? He switches to sleeping bags, dashes to stoves, flips to parkas, dabbles at food, giggles at hats.

Desperate, he runs from the shop empty-handed, wild-eyed, and trembling, seeking the nearest tennis court, running track, skateboard course, or hang-glider cliff. Or cracks wide open and compulsively fills a shopping cart, only later discovering he has equipped himself not for weekend walks in nearby woods but for an expedition to Karakorum, and is now bankrupt.

Veterans, too, suffer from the Gear Sweats. Many a creaky old crock stubbornly defends his medieval torture rack because he secretly fears humiliation amid mysteries of body-contoured aluminum packframes, wears the same style boots he did in 1940 because he is ashamed to confess he doesn't know a storm welt from a scree collar.

The new is not necessarily better than the old but it is invariably more complicated. Yet let no beginner, no veteran, abandon hope. The catalogs are no more impenetrable than jungles of slide alder, vine maple, and devil's club.

GETTING ORGANIZED

Perhaps every reader of these pages has spent a little time on trails, if only strolling in city parks. However, the most difficult case will be assumed, that of a person who has always lived amid concrete and plastic and now by some supernatural flash has decided to go hiking and is so ignorant as hardly to know the flowers from the birds.

The transition from sidewalks to trails can be organized in the following steps.

FIRST, DECIDE WHAT YOU WANT TO DO, AND WHERE AND WHEN

If day hikes on broad paths are the maximum ambition, that's one thing. If the goal is roaring wilderness on week-long backpacks, that's another.

Will most trips be in lowland forests or in high mountains? On ocean beaches or in deserts? Cold and wet country, or hot and dry, or hot and wet? Entirely in summer or partly on the fringes of winter?

Each sort of hiking, each hiking area, and each season requires more or less special tailoring of the basic outfit.

SECOND, SEEK ADVICE

Backpacking shops and the backpacking departments of more generalized stores are now so ubiquitous that most people can readily visit one to try on a boot and shoulder a pack and crawl in a bag and ask a clerk's advice. Many shops publish catalogs, indispensable guides to the latest miracle inventions and staggering prices; even if a person doesn't wish to buy by mail order, reading prepares for in-shop visits.

Magazines keep abreast of the state of the art and provide addresses of shops that issue catalogs and of family enterprises that handcraft cunning curios in the basement. Oldest of the pertinent magazines (since 1954) is *Summit,* P.O. Box 1889, Big Bear Lake, California 92315. Founded in 1974, *Backpacker* (65 Adams Street, Bedford Hills, New York 10507) has the largest circulation. Aimed mostly at the climber are *Off Belay* (15630 SE 124th Street, Renton, Washington 98055) and *Climbing* (Box E, Aspen, Colorado 81611).

Other magazines of regional circulation, as well as journals of climbing and hiking clubs, are useful for close views of individual trail provinces and expert commentary on equipment locally appropriate. Some newspapers run backpacking columns.

Then there are books. How many backpacking manuals a person can read without permanent impairment of literary taste is a question, even though so far as content goes, most of the dozens published in the past decade are fair-to-superb and only a few are outright penitentiary offenses. Reading (or scanning) more than just a single manual can save a beginner from being led deviously into eccentricity. A novice of the Appalachians does well to listen to an Appalachian veteran wise in the perils of 100 percent humidity and black flies and lurking moonshiners. And to learn the technique of the midday nap and crossing a river on an air mattress, consult the veteran of the Low Sierra and other deserts. For rain you're already in the right book.

By joining an outdoor club, a beginner can be tutored in locally favored gear. With common sources of supply has come, in recent years, substantial continent-wide and earth-wide uniformity, but there remain regional and national differences. As a further benefit, if the club has an environmental conscience, the beginner can instantly start doing his share to preserve trail country.

A novice with a trail-wise friend quite naturally and simply receives counsel and absorbs quirks.

One should not be bashful about striking up conversations with strangers met in wildlands; often they will be delighted to lecture at length on their equipment—and lecture, and lecture, and lecture.

THIRD, PREPARE A CHECKLIST

Starting with the very general checklist at the end of this chapter, and advice from anywhere and everywhere, prepare a personal list of needed gear.

FOURTH, DRAW UP A SCHEDULE OF PURCHASES

But before spending a nickel, ransack the closet, basement, attic, and kitchen. Unless the immediate goal is to join the ranks of the beautiful people in the catalogs, much clothing too shoddy for city wear (old trousers, shirts, sweaters) or acquired for other outdoor activities (shorts, windbreakers) serves for hiking. A decent enough camp kitchen can be improvised from home utensils and tin cans. Work shoes may suffice for the first hikes, or sneakers for any and all short hikes.

Don't buy anything until it's needed for the next trip. Such as, if planning a series of day trips before trying a backpack, delay purchasing a packframe and sleeping bag to the last minute and use the time to examine options.

Some articles can be rented from some backpacking shops—another way to postpone decisions, as well as to experiment with various styles of boots, packs, tents, snowshoes, and so on.

Buy inexpensive items for stopgaps while carefully considering large cash outlays. For example, make do with a tarp that costs a dollar or two while studying the intricacies of tents.

However, avoid false economy in major purchases. Don't pay $20 for a pack that looks sharp in the drugstore but falls apart on the first hike; instead, spend $60 for one that will last for years. And don't waste $18 on a "down" sleeping bag that spits chicken feathers every time a cock crows.

The schedule of purchases obviously depends on financial resources. With no trouble at all and in a matter of minutes, a big spender can run through $1,000 acquiring a complete, first-class outfit. However, by scrounging around the house and charity-operated thrift shops, buying second-hand equipment and cheap fill-ins, renting and borrowing, a rough-and-ready basic outfit can be put together for less than $200, maybe $150, spent over several months; the ideal outfit can be assembled piece by piece, as the budget allows, in following hiking seasons. Families have more of a financial problem, but that's not news.

WHERE TO BUY

In the Golden Age, the 1930s, places to buy trail gear were as few as the items available, and hikers resembled fishermen, loggers, sourdoughs, or Boy Scouts, and mostly that's what they were.

For a brief period after World War II, when surplus stores flourished on every corner of America, the trails seemed to have been conquered by a vaudeville version of the Mountain Troops, the legendary Khaki Gang. There were army boots and army pants, army sleeping bags and army tents, army canteens and parkas and sweaters and mess kits and field rations. And from the South Pacific there were jungle hammocks, camouflaged ponchos, and bug juice so potent that it shriveled the skin. And for combined operations, navy life-raft sails and air-force goggles. From the standpoint of the backpacker, that really was the only war ever worth having, though some military surplus from subsequent wars continues to dribble into the civilian market.

Mountain shops, the early ones founded by climbers unable to get needed ice axes and dehydrated spinach from regular sporting-goods stores, grew in numbers until by the 1970s few cities near mountains or trails lacked one or several. However, increasingly their climber customers were outnumbered by pedestrians using no hands. Where they gained the name "backpacker" is uncertain—perhaps in the

Sierra, to distinguish them from the burros. The neologism was resisted in the Pacific Northwest. There, unless folks hired a packer and horses for a "pack trip," they simply "went hiking." If overnight, obviously they carried packs, and where else than on backs? "Backpack" seemed as redundant as "footsock" or "headhat." But the term prevailed and the sport has overwhelmed mountain shops, which thus in this edition are rechristened "backpacking shops," under which are included the backpacking departments of more comprehensive stores.

These specialty shops are logical headquarters for the beginner, even though not all are staffed exclusively by experienced mountain bums, as once was the case. That's why this book was published—to provide genuine bum advice.

Further, it must be noted that many shops have succumbed to the tyranny of the majority, expressed in the first law of merchandising: "What people don't buy, you can't afford to stock." Where once shops catered to tightwads and indigents who proudly strutted around the glaciers in fifty-cent war-surplus parkas, now their inventories appeal to well-heeled hikers who flit from fashion to fashion and don't always know what's good for them. Difficult to believe but true, today it's virtually impossible to find a mountain/backpacking shop that still sells dehydrated spinach.

83

As for other retailers, department stores lacking specialty departments may carry such things as sleeping bags and tents of good quality at bargain prices—if the hiker knows gear well enough to recognize a bargain. Fast-in/fast-out emporiums often advertise hiking gear at fantastic prices. The canny hiker may find real steals—loss leaders or genuine military surplus. But the novice must beware of fantastic trash.

Many small trail items are sold by supermarkets, drugstores, hardware stores, etc.

Thrift shops run by Salvation Army, Goodwill Industries, St. Vincent de Paul, local churches and charities, offer outstanding buys in used clothing and kitchenware, and the like. The beginner on a lean budget should tour the thrift shops immediately after ransacking the basement and before starting heavy spending. Even this late in the inflation spiral a person can obtain wool pants, shirt, and cap for less than $5. Parents with fast-growing kids should spend a lot of time at thrift shops. So should conservationists-environmentalists striving to "waste not, want not, despoil not."

Anyone with a sewing machine, knowledge of sewing basics, and spare time can save up to half the normal cost of such expensive articles as parka, pack, sleeping bag, and tent by assembling kits. Frostline was the pioneer, but now several firms are in the field; look for their ads in hiking magazines. A wealth of money-saving do-it-your-selfery is in two books, *Make It and Take It,* by Russ Mohney, and *Lightweight Camping Equipment and How to Make It,* by Gerry Cunningham and Margaret Hansson.

Hikers near factories may find stunning bargains in "seconds" (items with minor flaws), overruns (in excess of what could be sold to retailers), returns, damaged goods, or seasonal merchandise. Much is sold only at factory outlets, but some is scattered around the nation and appears at department stores on budget floors and in end-of-month sales and warehouse clearance, at "surplus" stores, and at the June weekend Big Specials of your local Handy-Dandy Super-Thrifty Drugs.

Increasingly common are exchange shops featuring used gear; bring what you can't use, trade for what you can.

Warning: Putting price tags on backpacking equipment is like keeping track of the earth's population—memorize a figure, blink your eyes, and it's gone up, up, and away. And as long as the population rises, so will prices. Hikers recently coming upon the first edition of this book, published in 1972, have been disabled by convulsions of laughing, then sobbing. One is reminded of Germany in 1923, when workers were paid twice a day so their wages could be raised fast enough to buy potatoes. Nevertheless, in following chapters prices are noted for many articles. These are not exact and are intended merely to suggest the approximate range, but were advertised by one retailer or another at the time of writing.

BASIC EQUIPMENT CHECKLIST

As noted above, the beginner should prepare a checklist of equipment to be purchased or otherwise assembled. The list, regularly revised to reflect experience, has continuing utility, perhaps being posted in whatever corner of the house serves as the "hiking center" and consulted when the person is getting ready for trips to make sure nothing has been forgotten.

No hiker, not even a raw beginner, can be satisfied by someone else's checklist, no matter if it was drawn up by a forty-year veteran of thousands of miles of trails. Each person must do his own, based on conditions in his regular hiking terrain and on his personal idiosyncrasies.

The following list is limited to basics and does not include the myriad nice little items like binoculars, candles, pliers, reading material, playing cards, and the hundred other things individuals may come to consider indispensable for safety or pleasure.

For short afternoon walks in summer sunshine on broad trails, no equipment is really necessary—nor any clothing where local authorities are tolerant and the climate benign, as in Hawaii.

For full-day hikes the items listed below for "Day Trips" are generally essential; those in parentheses may be essential in some areas, under some conditions. (See Chapter 15 for a discussion of the Ten Essentials.)

For backpacking, additional gear is listed under "Add for Overnight" and a few more things under "Add for Special Situations."

Day Trip	Chapter Reference
Boots	8
Socks	8
Underwear	9
Shirts and sweaters	9
Parka	9
Trousers or knickers	9
(Shorts)	9
Headwear	9
Rucksack	10
(Child carrier)	10
(Water bottle)	13
Food	14
(Sunglasses)	15
Knife	15
Matches, firestarter	13
First-aid kit	15
Flashlight	15
Map and compass	15
(Whistle)	15
(Sunburn lotion)	15
(Insect repellent)	15

Add for Overnight	
Packframe and bag (or softpack)	10
Sleeping bag	11
Sleeping pad	11
Ground sheet	11
(Air mattress)	11
Tarp or tent and accessories	12
(Grate)	13
Stove and accessories	13
Cooking pots and accessories	13

(Collapsible water carrier)	13
Eating utensils	13
Garbage bag	4
Food containers	13
(Bear wire and cord)	4
Repair kit	15
Toilet articles	15

Add for Special Situations

(Gaiters)	8
(Poncho)	9
(Down vest or sweater)	9
(Rain pants)	9
(Mittens)	9
(Ice ax)	17
(Hiking rope)	17
(Snowshoes)	19
(Cross-country skis)	19

8:

BOOTS

EVERYONE should go barefoot now and then. A meadow delightful to the eye is equally so to the naked sole, feeling grasses cool in the morning dew. And a stream is only closely known when toes are probing swift, cold water seeking fingerlike grip on pebbles. Glacier-polished granite, squishy black muck, powdery dust, beach sand, pine needles, snow, all gratify the sensual foot.

But if feet can bring pleasure, so too are they exquisitely sensitive to pain. And since civilized folk lack the built-in leather normal among closer-to-the land people, and the sore-footed hiker is no hiker at all but a semi-invalid, the average backcountry traveler limits barefoot strolls to special occasions, and for the general run of the trail armors his feet against the rough earth.

An amazing variety of armors will more or less do the job. On paths near tourist centers, millions of miles are walked annually in sandals, thongs, even high heels. And not a few hikers have roasted their boots by a campfire and retreated to the road with feet lashed up in sweaters.

None of these are recommended, but they demonstrate the possibility of going a long way with very little. The novice walker needn't worry much about foot protection. Any shoe comfortable for padding around sidewalks and lawns serves for short jaunts on good paths. But once a person decides hiking is his game, it's probably time to think boots.

Ah, but *which* boots? A large backpacking shop may have a quarter-acre of boots-boots-boots marching up and down again. Novices wander among them in dazed confusion. Others in the hinterland stare at catalogs, baffled.

Actually, a choice can be made quite easily, in person or by letter, by telling the shop staff the trails contemplated; from their experience they can narrow the options to several models. This method is best for the first boots. Possibly all. But sooner or later a person may want to know his boots inside and out. Especially if his feet hurt.

Beginners should skip the next section of this chapter, which tells more about boots than they need to know. For hikers preparing to buy their second or third pair, following is an unravelment of the secret code of the catalogs.

THE INS AND OUTS OF BOOT CONSTRUCTION

THE FUTURE: UNKNOWN

All prices go up and up, but some faster and faster, notably the price of leather as a finite number of cows strive to cover feet proliferating by the millions, the billions, the googols.

After the leather supply is entirely reserved for emirs, what then? Manufacturers wish they knew. Vinyl is being used for uppers of inexpensive work boots, nylon cordura for fancier ones. Canvas is making a comeback. A variety of synthetics and plastics (already used for ski boots) are under study, in various combinations. Something new there eventually must be. The cows can't do it all.

THE PRESENT: LEATHER

Nevertheless, nothing yet has been found to match leather's combination of comfort and durability and flexibility and breathability and waterproofability—a "second skin." As long as they can, hikers are likely to grit their teeth and pay the price.

Leather in the boot upper, where quality is supremely important, may be bragged up as "shoulder leather," or "Russia [heifer] leather," or "Swiss grade AA," or "Galluser leather." Having no idea what they mean, the ordinary person must take it on faith that if he's paying a pretty price, he's getting a pretty good leather.

Leather of lesser merit is used for insoles and midsoles; it may even be "reconstituted"—that is, a cemented composition of ground-up scraps.

For comfort, inner liners may be *calfskin* or supersoft *glove (glove-tanned* or *garment-tanned)* leather, also commonly used for the above-ankle portions of the high boots once standard on American trails and still with a few adherents.

Tanning

Since the hide would quickly rot without treatment, it is put through as many as nineteen mechanical and chemical operations while being cured, or tanned, into leather.

In *chrome tanning* or *dry tanning,* the most common process in America and most of Europe for making the leather in city shoes and also boots, the hide is tanned with soluble chromium salts, giving a hard finish with a dry look, and treated with waxes to replace natural oils.

In *oil tanning* and *vegetable tanning,* favored by a number of Italian manufacturers and some American, the hide is tanned either with oils or with vegetable material ("bark tannins") derived from plants and woods, giving a soft, supple finish with a wet, oily look.

In the relatively uncommon (for boots) *combination,* or *vegetable-chrome,* tanning, agents are combined.

The advantages of the methods are a matter of arcane debate. Excellent leathers are produced by all three, and the main reason a hiker should know what his boots are is to give proper treatment for water-repellency and leather maintenance, as discussed below.

Double tanning, by whichever method, is just what it sounds like—a doubly good job.

How Is It Sliced?

As worn by the animal, the hide varies in thickness from one part of the body to another. In preparation for boot (or other) use, the hide may be sliced in as many as half a dozen layers of different thickness, or *gauge.* Thin-gauge leather is characteristic of light-duty boots, heavy-gauge of heavy-duty.

Leather made from a layer including the outer surface of the hide *(grain side)* is called *top grain.* This is the best slice for boot uppers, for obvious reasons the toughest and most water-resistant. The inner surface of the hide is called the *flesh side.*

Any slice not including the outside of the cow is called a *split.* Splits are fine for insoles and midsoles but inferior for heavy-duty uppers, being hard to waterproof and very stretchable. When used for an upper, split leather is called *suede,* a poor choice for slogging wet trails but excellent for dry paths, especially in hot climates, because it is lightweight, porous, and easy-breathing.

Which Side Outside?

The cow wears its skin with the grain side outside, the flesh side inside. Hikers, when they appropriate the hide for their feet, may do the same, or may not.

In a boot upper, top-grain leather with the grain side outside, the "right" way, is called *smooth* or *smooth-finish* or *smooth-out* leather. Partisans say this tougher and more water-repellent surface is the proper one with which to confront the wilderness. Critics say the tough outer layer is quite thin, readily breached in rough travel; once penetrated, it allows water to pour through the soft underlayer.

A top-grain leather with the flesh side outside is called *rough-out* or *flesh-out* or *reversed* or *reverse-tanned* or *rough-tanned* leather. (The term "suedelike," sometimes encountered, is misleading; to be sure, flesh-out leather looks the same as suede, but the latter is a split.) Partisans say that to preserve its water-repellency, the tough outer layer of hide is best kept from contact with the wilderness and that the flesh side, though it scuffs and abrades easily, is never weakened structurally and wears away only bit by bit.

Experts argue back and forth. They agree, though, that the quality of a hide is more significant than whether it is used rough-out or smooth-out; first-rate boots are made both ways. The important distinction is whether a leather is top-grain or split.

Natural or Prettified?

A bootmaker using a quality hide is frequently so proud of it that he retains as much as possible of the original appearance. In such *full-grain* or *natural* leather no buffing has been done to smooth the surface and thus conceal healed scratches or small pits caused by tick and fly bites. The natural look is not only considered the most beautiful by connoisseurs but maintains the full inherent strength, durability, and breathability. The color of boots made from full-grain leather usually is not uniform throughout due to variations from hide to hide.

A *corrected-grain* leather is not necessarily inferior in strength and may be of excellent quality. However, the manufacturer has chosen to hide blemishes to obtain a uniform appearance. For example, in a *pebble-grained* leather the surface has been stippled by tiny gouges.

A smooth or rough-out leather is usually *dyed* only very lightly (or not at all) to retain the natural look. Most suedes and some other leathers are dyed black, gray, green, blue, red, brown, or whatever. The dye doesn't harm the leather and may appeal more to stylish walkers than the color of a cow.

STRUCTURE OF THE BOOT

The complications of leather-making are nothing compared to those of boot-designing. Mathematically speaking there could be—and to the layman there sometimes seems to be—an infinite number of combinations of features.

The maze may best be charted by systematically exploring each region of the boot.

The Upper In General

One school of experts holds that the best way to build a boot upper is from a *single piece* of leather, thus keeping seams—lines of potential weakness and leakage—to a minimum. Another school defends *sectional* (from two or three pieces) construction, saying that (1) the upper can more easily be made to conform to the foot, (2) smaller pieces of prime leather can be utilized and thus the expense is less for the same quality, and (3) seam leakage isn't that much of a problem anyhow. Neutrals don't get very sweaty about the matter, admitting that most climbing boots have one-piece uppers, most hiking boots sectional, and that perhaps this means something, but insisting that either method will work fine for either purpose. Certainly, a lot of stitching on an upper by no means indicates a bad boot.

A *double-stitched* upper has two lines of stitching at every point, thus reducing chances of all stitches being cut at once. Triple-stitching gives that much more insurance.

The least complicated and costly design of an upper is the venerable *shell* boot, unlined and unpadded, with a single layer of leather between foot and outside world. Many hikers like such a simple style, old but good, preferring to add their own padding, as situations warrant, with insoles and socks; hot-country hikers particularly despise the alternative padded boots, calling them "sweat boxes."

Most modern boots have some lining, reinforcing, and padding. The more there is, the more the foot protection, insulation, comfort—and weight and expense. For light hiking, less is better; for hard pounding in cruel terrain, more is essential. Where lies the golden mean? In a different place for each use. One observation may be made: just as the average American tends to buy more automobile than he needs, so does he buy more boot than he needs; economists call this "conspicuous consumption"; psychologists see sex in it.

The *lining* may be complete, partial, or nonexistent. Usually of pigskin, calfskin, or some other soft, supple leather, the lining lets the foot glide smoothly in and out and minimizes chafing.

Most boots have *padding* in the ankle area; others are padded elsewhere, perhaps throughout, though rarely to the toe. The padding material, inserted between the outer wall and the liner, may be foam, rubber, or felt. (To be avoided for ordinary hiking is the *insulated* boot designed for extreme cold.)

Reinforcing at heel and toe is discussed below. There may also be *side-reinforcements* of leatherboard or other material above the ball of the foot and from the ball backward toward the heel. Reinforcements where needed for foot support and protection, designed whenever possible for softness and flexibility, are characteristic of the best boots. Cheaper boots may give protection and support with stiff materials, uncomfortable and difficult to break in. Quality boots with a good deal of reinforcement may have a *hinged instep,* a small cutout from the leather of the upper that allows the boot to flex.

The Upper Part of the Upper

Hiking boots come in overall heights, measured from the top to the welt, where the sole joins the upper, of from less than 6 inches, or barely covering the ankle, to 9 inches, or partway up the calf. A height —say 5½ inches—that protects and supports the ankle is the minimum for any extended walking and suffices for good trails. Where stream crossings, mud, or snow are expected, a height of about 7½ inches is preferable to keep moisture from coming over the top. Some hikers of well-watered mountains go even further, up to 9 inches; this height is objected to by others as making the boot difficult to get in and out of and perhaps constricting the muscles of the calf, especially in uphill walking. The excess leather in high boots also tends to stretch out of shape and either bunch or buckle behind the ankle, sometimes pressing on the Achilles tendon.

Many boots have a gap-closing device at the top to prevent water or snow or pebbles from slipping down inside. Most common is an elastic fabric, perhaps padded, that fits snugly against the leg. Among the names for the device are *scree shield, scree collar, scree gaiter, snow protector,* and *cuff.* Half or less of all hikers find this feature effective; the others feel it doesn't work at all (though few think it detrimental) and prefer to do the job, when necessary, with a separate gaiter, discussed below.

The collar may include a roll of foam padding to comfort the Achilles tendon; in a *Komito collar* the padding is on the inside only, just as comfortable and far more durable. With some boots the tendon is further pampered by cutting the leather of the upper low in back and adding a soft panel of garment leather.

The Back of the Upper

Some climbing boots have a *hinged heel (flexible rear hinge);* a section of the upper is cut out and replaced by a softer leather that lets the boot flex slightly.

All heavy-duty and many medium-duty boots have a *heel counter (heel cup),* a piece of leather or rigid fiber inserted inside, cupping the heel to help anchor the foot to the boot sole, thus minimizing heel lift. Added protection is also given the heel.

A *heel cap* (sometimes called *outside heel counter*) is an extra piece of leather stitched to the boot exterior to guard against abrasion.

The Toe

Boots in the American pioneer tradition have a completely *soft* toe, easy on the foot—until it runs into or is fallen upon by a rock. So frequent are foot-rock encounters that toes on nearly all modern hiking and climbing boots are more or less *hard,* ranging from being slightly stiffened by a piece of plastic inside to total bombproofing by counters of leather, leatherboard, or plastic. The result may be described as a *toe counter* or *guard, hard toe, box toe,* or whatever. Rarely a boot may be found with a *toe cap,* serving the same purpose as a heel cap.

The *moccasin toe* still has fans. Because the structure is soft (and difficult to make hard), the hiker's toes are cozy. Moccasin toes and high-top uppers generally go together on boots of the old, old design still beloved of woodsmen who tramp mainly soft forest duffs.

Tongue and Closure

In the tongue-and-closure area the boot designer has three concerns: (1) preventing water from seeping or pouring through the gap, (2) providing the foot expeditious entry and exit, since donning and doffing wet or frozen boots can be an excruciating test of muscle and will, and (3) being kind to delicate flesh. In the upward progression from easy, dry trails to rough, sopping terrain, increasing attention must be paid the tongue and closure. The expedients adopted by designers are countless; they all, however, represent one of two basic approaches.

The *gusseted tongue* bars water by placing an unbroken barrier between foot and wet world. On simple boots the barrier may be nothing more than a small strip of soft leather attaching the tongue to the boot upper, the tongue being described as *sewn-in;* the barrier strip, and sewing, may extend to the top or only part of the way. On more complex boots the barrier is a considerable mass of flexible leather that opens out in a *bellows* to let the foot in and out, folds neatly when laced. In a variation, the boot has two tongues, a soft inner one for comfort and an outer gusseted tongue.

The *split tongue* permits the boot to be opened very wide so the foot can gain easy ingress when the leather is frozen rock-hard; it keeps out

Tongue and closure. Left: *Hiking boot with gusseted tongue (plus inner tongue).* Center: *Light climbing (heavy hiking) boot with overlapping split tongue (plus inner tongue).* Right: *Trail shoe with simple split tongue.*

water (though perhaps never so absolutely as a gusseted tongue) by creating, with the help of laces, devious passageways that discourage inward-creeping moisture. Many a split-tongue design has two tongues, a soft inner (often partly sewn-in) and an outer which actually is the boot upper, split down the middle. The most elementary example of the split tongue is on city oxfords and light-duty trail shoes, where the halves of the upper are drawn together over the inner tongue by laces. On heavier-duty boots the split halves of the upper overlap. A few boots have a third tongue outside the split tongue for more complete baffling of water.

Having thus cast light into the swampy darkness of the tongue situation, it is now necessary to murk it up again by saying that there are many combinations of gusseting and splitting, resulting in a variety of hybrid designs.

On light-duty trail shoes the tongue proper may be a single thickness of leather. On heavier-duty boots that require tight lacing, the inner tongue is *padded* to cushion the foot against pressures of laces; it may also be *contoured* or *hinged* for easy flexing.

Lacing

Completing the closure is the lacing, which may be by eyelets, D rings (also called swivel eyelets), hooks, or a combination.

A very few boots, including light trail shoes as well as some traditional American designs, have *all-eyelet* lacing, with eyelets formed by grommets set directly into the upper. The advantage is that grommets virtually never fail until the boot is ancient, and even then the holes seldom enlarge or split out, since before this can happen, the metal pieces must break loose. The disadvantage is that lacing is tedious.

More common are boots having *eyelets partway up, then yielding to hooks*—the latter much quicker to lace and unlace. An alternative to the grommet-type eyelet set in the upper is the *swivel eyelet,* a D ring attached to a clip riveted to the upper; this combines easy lacing with maximum water-repellency and insulation. *Speed lacing,* most common on older ski boots, employs closed hooks; a single quick pull tightens the laces from bottom to top.

Lacing systems. Left: *Swivel eyelets and hooks (the leather is smooth-out).* Center: *Grommet eyelets and hooks (rough-out leather).* Right: *All-eyelet lacing (suede leather).*

Incidentally, most hikers do not realize that hooks, rings, clips, and grommets can quickly be replaced in any shoe-repair shop and many backpacking shops. There is no need to accept the loss of metal fixtures fatalistically and go about with half a lacing system, the boot flopping on and off the foot.

As for *laces,* leather retains a few adherents but stretches when wet and thus loosens. Nylon is more popular nowadays for its greater durability; soft-woven, unwaxed laces hold knots best.

A *built-in lace lock* is a common feature of rock-climbing shoes, where extremely tight fit is essential from instep to toe. It is mentioned here only because some rock shoes resemble lightweight trail boots.

Some climbing boots have a lacing system that allows the boot to flex at the ankle, and/or *flush lace hooks,* where the metal is inset to avoid snagging during intricate rock-climbing moves.

A tip about lacing: The beginning walker, or any walker at the start of the season, may find his tender shin abraded by the top of the boot, especially the knot. The remedy is to lace to the top, then lace back downward two or three rows and tie the knot there. This gives support the full height of the boot but removes the knot from the tender spot, as well as from the knot-loosening activity of the ankle; it also reinforces the heel and helps keep the entire lace system secure.

Another tip: If toes feel cramped, lace the lower area of the boot loose, then tie a knot and lace the upper area tight. Or in a different situation, such as downhill walking, lace tight down low, especially at the toes, tie a knot, and lace loose up high. In summary: experiment.

One final tip: If lacing stiff boots tight enough is difficult, try the *cargo knot.* Bring laces to the middle of the boot, wrap them over each other, and thus, when cinching, reverse the normal direction of pull and gain a mechanical advantage.

Insole

The bottom of the boot is where the hiker meets earth, thudding against hard places, slithering on slippery places, and thus where he seeks cushioning and traction. It is also the area of most complicated boot engineering because of problems in attaching the upper to the soles and keeping them firmly together.

The sole has three parts: insole, midsole, and outsole.

The next-to-foot insole (inner sole) is usually leather, sometimes cellulose. Ordinarily it is covered by a thin synthetic *sock liner* that gives low-friction foot entry. Some boots have *cushion* insoles, foam rubber covered by lining leather.

On a *channel* insole, typical of better, stronger boots, the stitching of insole to midsole is done in a channel cut in the insole leather.

Midsole and Shank

Boots meant for soft paths sometimes do not have a midsole; the insole is attached directly to the outsole. On bumpy ground such boots let every sharp pebble stab the foot. When foot collides with mean and nasty earth perhaps 10,000 or more times a day, midsoles are badly wanted for stiffness, support, and cushioning. The heavier the construction, the more the midsoles: perhaps from a minimum of one in front increasing to three under the heel, to a maximum of three leather and one rubber throughout.

Many experts favor leather midsoles, saying they help shape boot to foot, absorb sweat, breathe, are flexible, and break in quickly. Others lean to rubber, stiffer but cheaper and giving a firmer bond to the outsole, plus more cushioning. Combinations of leather above and rubber below are common. In addition, some boots have a cork or foam *filler* between midsole and insole, again for cushioning.

All but the simplest boots have a *shank* to support the arch, protect the instep, and keep the foot straight. Since the softer the sole, the more comfortable the foot movement, light-duty boots generally lack any shank and are easily bent double in the hands. Medium-duty boots with a medium shank can be bent a little, and heavy-duty boots with a heavy shank not at all.

The shank extends from the heel either one half (best for most hiking) or three quarters (for heavy hiking) or the full length (for rough climbing) of the boot. In descending order of strength are shanks of tempered spring steel, plastic or fiberglass, reconstituted leather, laminated wood, and stiffened nylon. Some shanks are combinations.

Boots with sturdy shanks and many midsoles, and thus nearly or completely rigid, always have a *rocker bottom,* shaped to curve up slightly or considerably at toe and heel to permit an approximation of the normal walking configuration of a naked foot.

Outsole

Until World War II just about every American hiker and climber gained traction on trail, footlog, meadow, and snow with nailed soles. For the hiker there were hobs, rosebuds, and slivers, plus needle-sharp logger's calks (pronounced "corks") in the instep. For the scrambler and climber there were Swiss edge-nails favored by a scattering of oldtimers—but for the masses (all couple of thousand or so) the tricouni nail, or "trike."

Then the Mountain Troops came home from Italy wearing the "Bramani," a legendary boot that weighed a ton, sold for nickels and dimes at surplus stores—and was fitted not with an iron-studded bottom but with rubber lugs. A passionate debate began throughout

North America. Trikes were attacked as "heat sinks," conducting the heat of the foot out of the boot. They were defended as infinitely superior to lugs on hard snow, footlogs, heather, steep grass—indeed, in virtually every terrain except rock and well-maintained trails.

Here and there may still be found a mountain shop whose cobwebby back room has tricounis to please those ancient pedestrians who stubbornly prophesy a return of the Iron Age. And maybe they're right, but the debate waned in the early 1960s and since then the lug has held almost universal dominion on American, as well as European, trails and peaks.

It is not an uncontested dominion. In the 1970s, lug boots began to be denounced as miniature bulldozers, their black fangs chewing up fragile soils, ripping tender plants, digging erosion gullies. Preservationist friars glorying in the name of "tenny-runner freaks" began preaching that hikers with heavy boots are so armored that they bruise the earth unwittingly, that those with light shoes walk softly for feet's sake and thus spare the land. Sensitive folks are torn. Damaging wilderness pains them. But so does falling down a lot.

Clearly, the friars are partly right. On level or gentle trails in the dry season, and when packs are light, a firm enough grip on the ground is provided by gravity alone, and the proper footwear is the sneaker or a very light boot with a *textured (ripple) rubber* sole.

However, when trails are steep and muddy or snowy or otherwise slippery, and packs are weighty, a sole merely textured entails a slower pace and the tedium of constantly picking oneself up and applying Band-Aids. Must, then, each man kill the thing he loves, lugs being the blunt instrument? Not necessarily. The alternative is to walk with a light foot: place boots with care not to erode, not to stomp; stay on maintained trails; stick to tough terrain—hard rocks and resilient forests and expendable snow—rather than soft meadows. Actually, much of the destruction attributed to boot soles is due to the proliferation of feet, which in large numbers trample and gouge with lugs or without, with boots or without. The blossom beneath a bare foot is just as crushed.

Despite growing alarm about the heaviness of feet, textured soles are hard to find in high-quality hiking boots. Virtually every model

Left: *Vibram rubber-lug sole, Montagna style.* Right: *Molded lug sole, all one piece.*

stocked by backpacking shops has a rubber-lug (really a high-carbon neoprene, which is synthetic rubber) sole. Though Galibier, Pirelli, and several other brands are about the same, Vibram dominates the market. Vibram soles come in twelve different neoprene compounds of varying hardness and in several designs, ranging from the comparatively shallow, soft, and flexible Roccia typical of lightweight boots to the Montagna with deeper tread and harder rubber. For extra cushioning there is the light-brown Honey Vibram.

Some very light boots and children's boots (and a few heavier boots) are of cemented construction (discussed below) and have a shallow *molded lug sole.* Molded lugs are difficult to replace, but a repairman can grind them down and bond on a new sole.

The longevity of lugs is determined not by the number of years the boot has been owned but by how many miles the hiker has walked —and where. Lugs may last a decade in travel on soft humus, four or five years with a moderate admixture of rockslide, or one summer on naked moraines. In the mid-1960s, when the "European climbing boot look" was a campus fad, Vibrams were subjected to punishment for which they were never designed; city sidewalks literally eat lugs alive. But in the 1970s, sexiness became suaver and the boot yielded to the running shoe.

Attaching Sole to Upper

The attachment of sole to upper is, for the layman, the most mysterious aspect of the boot; listening to dogmatic experts merely compounds confusion. For openers, then, let it be declared that every customary method of attachment, whether or not it involves *welting* (stitching of sole to upper) has distinctive virtues (and vices) and is good for certain uses.

Cement construction is least expensive. The upper is folded under a light insole and a one-piece rubber outsole cemented on. No midsole, no welting. The boot is very flexible, gives little support, and usually cannot be resoled. Many light-duty trail boots are cemented. The comfort on soft paths, and the economy, are attractive.

Somewhat similar is *injection molding,* familiar in modern ski boots and used on a few trail shoes and superheavy mountaineering boots. Molten neoprene applied under pressure takes the place of welting or cementing.

With the *inside-stitching* method, also called *Littleway construction* (or *Littleway welt*), the upper is folded under and sandwiched between insole and midsole, the outsole is glued to the lower midsole, and the layers are fastened together by a double row of lockstitching, concealed within the boot and thus protected from moisture and abrasion. (A boot so made can be recognized by the absence of exterior stitches.) Advantages of Littleway are that the sole can be closely cropped to be nearly flush with the upper, the boots are more waterproof than outside-stitched ones, and they are less expensive to build and repair. Disadvantages are that the stitching of midsoles to insole makes the boot relatively stiff and that the *last* (the foot-shaped form of metal or plastic around which a boot is built) must be removed before final stitching. As a result, the upper may not fit the boot so well and may require an extended break-in period. The better trail boots, an increasing number of hiking boots, and a few climbing boots are of Littleway construction.

The term "welting," though sometimes applied to Littleway, ordinarily is reserved for *outside-stitched (welted)* boots, of which two types are common.

With the *Norwegian welt (European welt),* currently used on nearly all climbing boots and many if not most heavy-duty hiking boots, one line of stitching angles inward, securing insole to upper, and a second (sometimes a third) line is vertical, securing

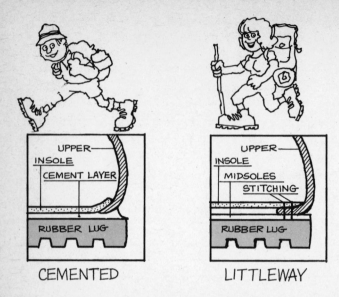

UPPER
INSOLE
CEMENT LAYER
RUBBER LUG
CEMENTED

UPPER
INSOLE
MIDSOLES
STITCHING
RUBBER LUG
LITTLEWAY

midsole to the outward-turned upper. (A Norwegian-welted boot can be recognized by the two or three lines of stitching visible on the ledge atop the sole, though the inward-slanting line may be difficult to see.) Advantages are: because the last remains in the boot until construction is complete, the insole conforms around the last without distortion, assuring a good fit; replacing midsole and outsole is easier than with a Goodyear welt (though not as easy as with a Littleway); and—according to proponents—it is the strongest and most durable way to build a boot. Disadvantages are the expense of manufacture and the vulnerability of the outside stitching to wear and leakage.

With the *Goodyear welt (U.S. welt, true welt),* found on most men's street shoes and many American-made boots, the upper is stitched directly to a raised rib on the insole and to a narrow piece of leather (called the *welt,* just to complicate terminology) which goes completely around the boot exterior at the junction of sole and upper. The welt is then stitched to midsoles. (A Goodyear-welted boot can be recognized by the single line of stitching on the ledge atop the sole.) Advantages are that the method permits

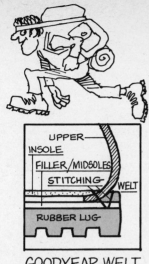

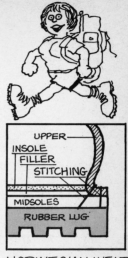

GOODYEAR WELT NORWEGIAN WELT

rapid machine production and thus lower cost. Disadvantages are that when repairs are needed only the outsole can be easily replaced.

(To further foul up this welt business, some mountaineering boots have, in addition to the above, a *storm welt,* an all-around exterior piece of leather sewn to upper and midsole as an extra guard against leakage.)

In conclusion, price of a boot typically ascends in the progression from cemented to Littleway to Goodyear welt to Norwegian welt. Despite the quarreling among manufacturers, good boots—for their intended purposes—are made by all these methods.

VARIETIES OF BOOTS

The novice who has heeded earlier warnings begins reading here, having at most skimmed the preceding section. Fascinating as anatomy may be to the deep student, the ordinary hiker doesn't want to know about a boot's shanks and welts but only: *Does it feel good?*

Marrying boot to foot is discussed later in the chapter. Before making a commitment, though, one must shop around, and the essential preliminary is choosing the general category. Manufacturers and retailers pretty much have adopted semistandard terminology. Boots suitable for hikers typically are described by some such system as (1) trail shoes or "light hikers," (2) hiking boots or "medium hikers," and (3) climbing boots or "heavy hikers."

The categories are partly differentiated by *price,* which reflects quality of materials and manufacture, but principally the amount of foot protection. That is, every added midsole and stiffener and pad, every such feature as shank, heel cup, hinged instep, and so on, pushes up the price.

Every added feature also adds *weight,* an even more accurate indicator of category. Let the novice be warned: heavy-duty boots are really and truly heavy, and carrying unnecessary loads on the feet is devoutly to be avoided; the U.S. Army Research Institute of Environmental Medicine has determined that 1 pound on the feet demands as much energy as 6 pounds on the back; what with a boot being lifted more than 1,000 times a mile, after a while even toenails seem a painful burden.

Despite emphatic advice of clerks and pundits and friars, hikers tend to over-boot, wasting money on bludgeons built for bashing glaciers and talus, and wasting energy dragging them along plush trails. If anything, one should err on the side of lightness. Buy enough boot but not too much.

What *is* enough? Two factors rule: the terrain to be walked and the load. In lands of dry trails (say, the High Sierra in midsummer) or soft forest duff (say, Ozark ridges), sandals may nearly do; lands of rain and snow and brush and moraines all jumbled up (say, the British Columbia Coast Range) may rebuff General Patton tanks. The second factor is of equal importance. If the feet must support only the 120 pounds of a small person with day-hike rucksack they can skip nimbly about to dodge danger and need only modest protection. But if a 200-pound body and 60-pound pack are above, there'd better be a lot of substance below, guarding blundering feet of the tottering tyrannosaur.

Representative hiking boots. Top: *Trail shoes, or "light hikers," weighing 3–4 pounds for an average-sized man's pair.* Center: *Hiking boots, or "medium hikers," 4–5 pounds.* Bottom: *Climbing boots, or "heavy hikers," 5–6 pounds.*

SNEAKERS

Are boots really necessary? The question increasingly is asked in reaction to over-booting, renunciation of over-lugging, and rebellion against overspending. New attention is focused on that old companion of summer, the "tennis shoe" or "sneaker," nowadays joined by the "running" or "training shoe." Many current models are meant mainly to complement the pretty skivvies of tennis court and jogging paths. And many cost as much as boots. And most stop below the ankle, failing to support a crucial linkage. However, if already owned for other purposes, they are adequate for good dry trails with light loads—or, if scrupulous attention is paid to where the foot is put, on worse trails with heavier loads.

Such shoes are no bargains if bought specifically for hiking, but similar footwear offers low cost and weight and substantial protection. Examples are few at the present time; more can be expected in coming years.

The Sierra Sneaker, an English "trail boot" popular for years (under other names) in Europe and Japan, has a thick rubber sole with lugs, padded insole and ankle and tongue, a rubber toe counter, and a canvas upper. The price is about $23, the weight (in man's size 9) 3 pounds 2 ounces.

The Maine Hiking Shoe of L. L. Bean has cushioning, ankle and heel and arch support, and an upper of army duck vulcanized to crepe rubber soles in a ripple pattern. Price about $15, weight about 1 pound 11 ounces.

Bean's French-made Wilderness Boot is similar but sturdier and has a lug sole. Price about $30, weight about 2 pounds 4 ounces.

TRAIL SHOE

Also called "light hiker," "lightweight hiking" or "lightweight trail" boot, or "wafflestomper," the trail shoe serves well for well-maintained trails and light loads (body plus pack).

The leather is often suede, occasionally top grain, construction is cemented or Littleway, midsoles are nonexistent to few, the shank

Special boots. Left and center: *Shoe-pacs with leather uppers and rubber bottoms, for the wet and the cold.* Right: *Sierra Sneakers, a light and sturdy no-leather trail boot.*

half-length at most and not too stiff, padding and reinforcing minimal, the lug a Roccia. The boots are flexible and comfortable. Protection is about that of a good sneaker.

Trail shoes range from around $35 to $60, a few as high as $80 and some very light wafflestompers as low as $20. Weight per pair in an average man's size is about 3–4 pounds; in an average woman's size about 2½–3½ pounds.

HIKING BOOT

The hiking boot, called "medium hiker" or "medium-weight hiking and climbing" or "lightweight climbing" boot, is the proper choice for heavyweights (body plus pack) who travel trails with much water and muck and rock, now and then venturing off into moraines, scree, snow, brush, and steep flower fields.

Leather is top grain, construction sometimes Littleway but usually Norwegian or Goodyear welt, midsoles are thicker and shanks (half-length to three-quarter) stiffer, and padding and reinforcing more extensive, making quite a rigid boot but giving a high degree of protection. The lug typically is Montagna. The top may be low (less than 6 inches) for average terrain, or high (up to 9 inches) for wet country.

Hiking boots range from around $60 to $90, with some at $100. Weight per pair in an average man's size is about 4–5 pounds; in an average woman's size 3½–4½ pounds.

CLIMBING BOOT

The hiker who does considerable off-trail brawling through brush, boulders, and snow has climberlike needs and thus may be interested in the "heavy hiker" or "medium-weight climbing" boot. The price range is $90 to $150. Weight per pair in an average man's size is about 5–6 pounds; in an average woman's size 4½–5½ pounds.

Few hikers want this much. None wants the "heavy-duty" or "heavyweight climbing or mountaineering" boot that weighs up to 7 pounds or more per pair and costs from $100 to $250.

WOMEN'S BOOT

The female foot tends to be smaller, and even when not, narrower than the male. The European shoe-size system doesn't differentiate between sexes; the American system has a size-and-a-half offset—a man's 6 is a woman's 7½. But this equation is not exact because women's sizes are made on narrower lasts. A woman with wide feet thus may be happier in a man's size, and a man with narrow feet in a woman's size.

Though many models are offered in sizes for both sexes, usually the construction is the same in both and throughout the range from large to small. However, as size diminishes, the boot components become crowded, have less space to move around and loosen up. Thus in any model the size 5 is much stiffer than the size 10, the problem compounded by the smaller person having less weight to throw around to loosen things up. For that reason some models specifically are designated "women's boots," using lighter construction for equivalent support. The sexual connotation is unfortunate; if they were renamed "suave boots," perhaps clerks would not have to sneak them in for small-footed males uncomfortable in *macho* models.

CHILDREN'S BOOT

A major objection to children is that they grow (and grow, and *grow*) and *out*grow boots at a ruinous rate. Hard-pressed parents often outfit offspring in sandals that fit the budget, on the theory that kids can stand anything. In fact, little feet are at least as tender as big feet. Kinder parents buy proper boots to start and then, to stay out of bankruptcy court and on the trail, hand them down from one child to the next or pass them around a circle of friends in similar straits.

As with adults, sneakers suffice for light walking.

Stepping up to the trail-shoe category, the "patrol boot" and "work boot" found in department stores and the like generally sell for about $20 or less. The customary ripple-rubber, or crepe, sole is adequate for most trails.

A giant step up is a true hiking or climbing boot identical to those for adults, scaled down to serve from cradle through early adolescence. Various sizes of various models run around $25 to $40. Such boots may in the long run be less expensive than cheaper expedients. Some backpacking shops give a generous trade-in if they have been treated carefully; after the initial blow, parents can keep kids in first-rate footwear by modest annual or biennial expenditures. (At such shops thrifty parents first ask to see the *used* boots.)

BOOTS FOR THE WET AND THE COLD

The birder who slops around in swamps and tidal marshes, up to the ankles all day in water and muck, may switch from his regular trail boot to a *shoe-pac*. A typical example is a "marsh boot" (or as L. L. Bean calls it, "Maine Hunting Shoe") with a 10-inch leather upper welded to a rubber bottom, a full-gusset tongue, weight about 3 pounds, price about $35. These sweat (not as much as all-rubber boots), and so the feet get wet, but sweat wet is warmer than swamp wet.

Good for the wet *and* the cold, as in slushing through melting snow on springtime trails, is a shoe-pac of rubber bottoms and leather uppers plus felt liners. Weight ranges up to about 5½ pounds, price to about $50.

Also for the wet and cold is the *insulated boot,* made of leather to breathe but heavily impregnated with silicone to be waterproof, seams latex-sealed, rubberized-compound lug sole permanently bonded to the upper, and foam insulation. Various models weigh 3–5 pounds, cost $60 to $90.

HANDMADE BOOT

A generation ago the dream of every hiker-climber was the ultimate in comfort, durability, and swank—boots lovingly crafted by hand to fit his personal feet.

The demand for handmade boots has dwindled now that backpacking shops offer so many ready-made models. However, hikers with foot problems may find that no ready-made, nowhere, nohow, is anything but a bone-mangler, a blister factory, a torture chamber.

Custom bootmakers remain active in most parts of America containing trail country, and many backpacking shops can recommend a nearby craftsman. The alternative is to try the Yellow Pages.

The cost may be $100, $150, or $200, depending. However, custom boots often last years and years. And if the choice is between hiking foot-happy and hiking footsore, any price is cheap.

BUYING BOOTS

The best way to buy, of course, is to visit a shop, browse around, consult the staff, and try on boots, many boots. The trying on cannot be overemphasized because boots are manufactured for that anatomical rarity, the "average" foot; actually, if people went around with faces veiled and feet bare, they would recognize each other as readily by individual peculiarities of feet as they do now by those of faces.

After the in-shop trial of an hour or less comes the in-house trial, at home, of several days. If that proves satisfactory, the out-of-doors breaking in can begin; if not, back to the shop for an exchange— usually for full credit if the boots are "like new."

Some backpacking shops rent boots, allowing a novice to go hiking while struggling over a decision.

In selecting the proper *length,* it is important that the toes do not extend all the way to the front of the boot; if they do, they will bump, especially in downhill travel, and soon become sore and blistered; also, the toenail will be jammed into the cuticle, causing pain and perhaps loss of the nail. As an approximate rule of thumb, with the boot unlaced and the toe pushed to the front (touching but not jamming), a person should be able to slide one finger down behind the heel. If the finger is snug, the fit borders on too tight; if two fingers can be inserted, the fit borders on too loose. When the boot is laced tight a person should not be able to push the toes against the front (stand on the slope of the shoe-shop stool to test toe room).

Variations in feet are such that a boot that fits well from the ball of the foot forward may not fit rearward to the heel (the instep area); length of the arch (from ball to heel) can be more critical than length of the total foot.

In selecting the proper *width* for the ankle area, a visual inspection should be made to ensure that there is, when laced tight, a gap of at least ¼–⅜ inch between the tongue and hooks; otherwise the tongue will run against the hook posts and allow no space for tightening.

The width elsewhere must be judged by feel. The boot should be comfortably snug, allowing toes to move, yet holding the ball of the foot firmly to the sole, and permitting little if any lateral movement or "slop." Some slight up-and-down motion ("lift") of the heel is nearly unavoidable and does no harm in itself; however, with improperly adjusted socks the foot may rub back and forth and blister. Boots stretch in use, becoming somewhat wider (though not longer) and thus the width in the shop should be a bit on the tight side.

When trying on boots, wear two pairs of socks, one light and the other medium (so say some experts) or a single pair of heavy socks (so say others). Remember the stretch that will come with use; if a hiker plans to wear two pairs of heavy socks on the trail and does so in the shop, within a year he will have to wear three pairs.

FITTING BOOTS TO ODD FEET

Many hikers, perhaps a majority, cannot find any boot that fits well precisely as it comes off the shelf. These are the people with narrow

heels or flat arches, or long skinny feet or short fat feet.

For those with wide bridges or toes and narrow heels, the only hope may be handmade boots; an extra pair of socks may hold the heel securely and keep it from going up and down at each step, but more often than not the solution creates a new problem—constriction of the toes.

Other foot peculiarities may also require custom boots, but various simpler alternatives suffice for most situations. For example, hikers with narrow heels may use a *heel cushion,* or *lift.* Those with narrow feet may add one or more *insoles,* which not only remedy fitting problems but give extra cushioning. *Arch supports* are invaluable to some hikers, especially with lightweight boots. Another common device is the *tongue pad.* Finally, a boot can be stretched slightly at critical points by any shoe-repair shop.

Some backpacking shops are equipped with machines that make customized *full footbeds.* The hiker stands in a heated, softened foam as it cools and hardens (yet remains flexible) to a perfect match for the foot bottom. Inserted in the boot, the footbed firmly locks the foot in place. No sliding around, no friction. These footbeds—very durable, and reshapable in the machine should they distort in prolonged use—are not to be confused with off-the-shelf types that last mere hours on the trail. But neither are they to be confused with corrective devices prescribed and fitted by podiatrists—a person with serious foot trouble must go to a doctor, not a machine. However, they may bring bliss (at a price—perhaps $50) to the hiker whose feet feel fine except in a boot.

Adjusting the number and weight of socks is done by all hikers at various times on the trail as their feet swell or shrink.

BREAKING IN BOOTS

If a boot doesn't feel basically "right" in the store, it will never feel good on the trail, and therefore one should not put too much trust in the corrective action of breaking in the boot. If the boot is fundamentally incompatible with the foot, never the twain shall be happy together, and the boot is going to win all the arguments.

Leather forms around the foot to a certain extent as the body heats it, so simple shell boots tend to conform to feet; padded, stiffened, supported boots stay pretty much the same. People with very average, very tough feet never have to worry about breaking in a boot—if they've chosen properly. The breaking in takes place in the first few miles of the first hike, with no pain, no blisters. However, the begin-

ning hiker, especially, is well advised to try his new purchase on a short walk or two before committing his feet to a long trip where disabling blisters could be serious.

Boots constructed of cheap materials or designed for very heavy duty are so stiff that two or three fairly long and strenuous hikes may be needed before they feel broken in. If they are still a misery, face it, they're a lost cause. Trade them in for a new pair.

Beware of drastic measures recommended for an instant perfect fit. Breaking in a boot by soaking it in warm water may, indeed, help shape it to the foot—but at the cost of weakening the inner structure, composed of various materials that dry at different rates, shrink differentially, and in the process pull apart. Water is not good for a boot. Wilderness water carries on a war of attrition; the "instant break-in" hits like a blitzkrieg.

Still worse are such methods as soaking the boots in alcohol, which is lethal.

ORDERING BOOTS BY MAIL

Many American hikers and climbers cannot conveniently visit a boot supplier and must order by mail. Fortunately, a number of shops are skilled in selecting boots for distant feet.

The first thing the purchaser-by-mail must realize is the futility of trying to find an exact equivalence between his street-shoe size (or the size of his current boot, if any) and that of the proper size in the desired style and brand. The boots stocked by backpacking shops are made on several continents, in half a dozen nations. They are made on the American last and on the very dissimilar European last, British last, and Italian last. Also, every manufacturer has his own sizing system and no two are precisely the same.

Suppliers rather uniformly give the following instructions for ordering by mail:

1. Send street-shoe size and width. These don't tell what boot size is right but provide a starting point.

2. Do not order by boot size unless you have previously tried on the *exact* style and brand of boot you are ordering, in which case give the size, style, and brand.

3. Using your larger foot (nobody has feet exactly the same size), put on the socks you intend to wear in the boots. Stand (with weight evenly distributed on both feet) on a piece of cardboard or stiff paper and trace a heavy line around the foot, making very sure to *hold the pencil absolutely vertical at all times.* (Some suppliers recommend tracings of both feet.)

4. Cut out the foot tracing, write your name on it, and enclose it with your order.

Suppliers generally add that a first choice of model should be stated plus one or two acceptable alternates. Most boots come from distant points, and stock of any given size or style may become depleted in periods of heavy purchasing, with no chance of quick replenishment.

When the boots arrive they should be checked carefully for proper fit, following the methods described above. Wear them *around the house* until satisfied; if not, return them. If the boots prove unsatisfactory after a hike or two, they will still be accepted as trade-ins by shops that deal in used boots.

BEING KIND TO BOOTS

Being kind to boots is being kind to the feet and the pocketbook. Mistreated boots vent their spite on tender flesh. They may, if badly abused, die prematurely, taking revenge on the bank account.

The boot once was part of a cow; now it must be treated as part of the hiker. The boot cannot cry out in pain, as could the cow, as can the hiker, and therefore must be guarded from harm all the more zealously.

Often the questions are asked, typically at funeral ceremonies of a $125 pair: What's the normal life expectancy of a boot, and why is it so short? Ancient pedestrians spin yarns of the wondrous past when the simple shell lasted nigh as long as a man. The problem with the newfangled marvel, they say, is too much of everything. Having all those innards of different materials shrinking and swelling at different rates during wetting-drying, heating-cooling, it literally pulls itself apart. The death of the sophisticated contemporary boot is usually not a tragedy of circumstance, but of character. That's the theory of the ancient pedestrians.

Experts yawn. They insist that circumstances of use mainly determine longevity. "Use" comprehends more than pounding trails, includes storage in camp, car trunk, closet. Whether a simple shell or a 68-piece boulder-banger, a boot's welfare depends on protection from excessive heat and too much wetting—or rather, the drying that follows the wetting. What usually kills a boot is one method or another of cooking.

HOW TO COOK A BOOT

Two traditional ways to destroy boots are (1) "drying them out" by a campfire and (2) sitting around a campfire, boots on, "warming up the toes." Throughout the backcountry are scorched corpses; one wonders how their owners got home—barefoot, or with feet wrapped in sweaters and bits of tarp?

Though the cow is long dead and its hide tanned, it is still a skin and will suffer from any heat the living animal didn't enjoy. The test is simple: while sitting by the campfire, put fingers on the boot; if uncomfortably warm, the leather is being cooked.

A slightly slower but equally effective way to cook a boot is putting it too close to the car heater on the way to or from a trip, or storing it by a furnace or hot-air vent or atop a radiator.

The mud treatment is also popular. If after a hike unclean boots are

tossed in a corner, the mud dries and in so doing dries out the leather and the cement holding the boot together—especially around the sole, where mud is usually caked. The leather crystallizes, the cement fails, and the boot falls apart in another hike or two.

If boots come off the trail muddy, they should be brushed at hike's end with a whiskbroom kept in the car for the purpose. At home they should be washed immediately with a stiff brush and cool water, the interiors sprayed with disinfectant to prevent mold and then stuffed with crumpled newspapers or paper towels, which absorb moisture exhailed by wet leather, help hold the shape, and stop deep wrinkles from setting in. After a day or two, change newspapers. Placing boots in a ski-boot rack or press while they are being dried and/or stored prevents curling. When boots are dry they should be treated with a leather-conditioning and waterproofing compound—the next subject on the agenda.

CONDITIONING AND WATERPROOFING THE BOOT

The process that began when the cowhide was tanned to leather must be continued throughout the life of the boot. Since the cow no longer can circulate natural juices and oils in the skin, the hiker must supply substitutes. If he does not, the leather sooner or later lets water flow through freely. It also, in drying, becomes stiff—a blister machine. Eventually it cracks, the upper and sole separate, and the time has come for another anguished funeral.

The hiker must know how the leather of his boot upper was tanned (if the clerk doesn't know, ask him to find out) in order to apply the proper conditioning and waterproofing preparation. It is often said that the wrong compound may do more harm than good. However, different shops and bootmakers give conflicting prescriptions. And they change their minds. A hiker must be a person of strong faith.

Compounds come in liquid and paste and aerosol forms but the crucial characteristic is the active ingredient; the two most common in America have long been oil and silicone. The general rule is *oil on oil-tanned, silicone on chrome-tanned* leather.

Oil-Tanned and Vegetable-Tanned Leather

Oil-tanned and vegetable-tanned leather may be treated with liquids (Red Wing Shoe Oil, Huberd's Neatsfoot Oil) or greases, which are merely thick oils (Huberd's Shoe Grease, Red Wing Shoe Conditioner).

The compound should be applied liberally to uppers, worked in vigorously, especially around seams, and allowed to dry, preferably overnight, before use.

Oil should be kept away from the welt-sole area; it softens the natural-fiber stitching (synthetic-fiber stitching is used on uppers) and thus reduces resistance to abrasion.

Biwell

An exception to some of the rules above and below is a long-time European favorite, Biwell, a hybrid of fish oil, wool fat, carnauba (wax from a Brazilian palm tree), and white spirit (alcohol). It penetrates leather deep and prevents cracking but neither weakens stitching, as do all-oil compounds, nor dissolves cements, as do the solvents in some silicone preparations. Biwell is excellent for oil/vegetable-tanned leather and can also be used on chrome-tanned—though only after the original wax-silicone dressing has leached out, opening pores for entry by the oil-fat-wax. Because it is absorbed rather than remaining on the surface, as does Sno-Seal, Biwell is not rubbed off by plants and snow. Because it goes deeper than Sno-Seal, Biwell is superb for reconditioning old, abused boots.

Chrome-Tanned (Dry-Tanned) Leather

Chrome-tanned leather is best treated with Sno-Seal, a wax and silicone mixture; the wax holds the silicone in place and thus gives longer-lasting water-repellency than such liquid or spray preparations as Red Wing Silicone Dressing and Dow-Corning Silicone for Leather.

Chrome-tanned leather requires particularly tender care; the silicone should be applied as soon as the boots are purchased and very regularly thereafter. *Oil or grease must never be used;* they enter the pores, filling air spaces and reducing insulation. Plain wax can also be used; it remains on the surface, providing waterproofing, but is more difficult to apply than a silicone mixture. Now, the exception: when boots are getting along in age, a switch to Biwell may extend their life.

Suede Leather

The best treatment for this thin, porous leather is very frequent application of a liquid or aerosol silicone compound.

Special Areas of the Boot

What's good for the upper may be bad for the cemented-together layers of the sole. Oil adversely affects the adhesive bond; the solvent which is often the vehicle for silicone (especially in sprays) may temporarily dissolve the cement and permanently weaken the bond. The recommended treatment for the sole area is shellac, a wax and shellac mixture (Leath-R-Seal), or wax (Kiwi Polish).

Areas particularly vulnerable to water intrusion, such as welt and seams, may also be treated with Leath-R-Seal or Welt Seal. Sno-Seal Seam Sealer can be used on clean leather which has not had other materials applied.

Again the Biwell exception: having little oil and less solvent, it can be applied safely anywhere.

Rock climbers often coat toes and seams with epoxy to protect leather from abrasion.

Incidentally, the inside of the boot should not be neglected—a light rub with the compound used for the outside helps keep the leather soft and supple.

SOCKS AND GAITERS

SOCKS

Socks provide insulation, padding, and skin comfort—they do, that is, if they are the proper socks, in the proper amount, for any given foot in any particular situation.

Hikers who wear knickers usually prefer knee-high knicker socks. For others, the socks should be high enough to extend an inch or two above the boot to avoid creeping-down-in and bunching-up.

As for size, the general rule is: size 8 sock for men's shoe size 3–4 and women's 4–5; 9 sock, men's 5–6 and women's 6–7; 10 sock, men's 6½–8 and women's 7½–9; 11 sock, mens' 8½–10 and women's 9½–11; 12 sock, men's 10–11½; 13 sock, men's 12–13. If two or three pairs are to be worn, the outer pair might well be a size larger.

As for material, ordinarily most of the total should be wool, which insulates, absorbs sweat, and is warm when wet. However, due to lack of stretch and low abrasion resistance, all-wool socks quickly get holes; nylon reinforcing of heels and toes or a percentage of nylon through-out greatly increases durability. Hot-country hikers like all-cotton socks—when wet, they stay wet, but on a desert that's good.

A wool-cotton mix costs less than all-wool and has some of the nice feel of all-cotton. Tender feet may appreciate a light inner sock of silk (which wears out fast) or nylon. Acrylic socks, rough on the flesh but cheaper than wool and insulating well, may be worn outside others. "Wick" socks of polyester, olefin, or orlon-wool-nylon don't absorb moisture; foot heat causes water to wick along fibers toward the outer air. The theoretical result is dry feet. But not in a swamp. Or snow.

A technique for the cold and the wet, as in snow slogging, is the "plastic sock." A person dons in order: (1) a light cotton sock for comfort; (2) a plastic bag that retains sweat, causing "dishpan feet," but warm, but warm; (3) wool sock or socks, protected by the plastic bag from wetting by sweat and thus retaining full insulation; (4) a second plastic bag to protect the wool from wetting by outside water; (5) the boot. Important note: When exercise ceases, the sweat-wet inner socks grow cold and so do the feet; a change to dry socks is essential—possibly to avoid frostbite.

The sock combination depends on the boots being worn—and on personal preference. One common choice is two pairs of medium-weight, dominantly wool, nylon-reinforced socks. Another is one pair of heavy socks and one light or medium weight. And so on. Some hikers always, or sometimes, wear three pairs. Some wear a single pair, perhaps filling out the boot with insoles.

Even for day trips, perhaps a person ought to carry an extra pair of socks in the rucksack; during the hike water literally may be squeezed from the foot, which shrinks enough to slide around in the boot. Many hikers, when beginning a long descent, stop to add socks to tighten the fit and avoid downhill blisters. Contrarily, the feet may swell on a hike and feel crowded; it is then proper to remove socks or substitute lighter ones.

On overnight and longer trips the hiker should have at least two extra pairs in the pack to adjust padding, change to dry socks, and replace those that wear out. (On the other hand, a climber once wore only one pair of socks, and the same pair, for forty-five straight days on Yukon glaciers. Eventually, seeing his extras weren't needed, he threw them away to save weight.)

The choice of socks is a matter of personal taste, developed by learning to know one's feet. The only general rule is to have enough to meet any changing situation.

When socks get wet the normal instinct is to dry them by a campfire; the wilderness thus is littered with charred wool. If enough time is available, and care is taken, socks can be dried by a fire, but it's a lousy way to spend an evening. Many hikers dry socks by wearing them to bed—not recommended if they are soaking wet. An alternative is to spread them on bushes in the sun, if any. Another is to tie them to the outside of the pack while traveling.

Hikers with tough feet often say the heck with it and wear the socks wet. Hikers with tender feet cannot be so casual and must carry an abundance of spares; wet socks are especially productive of blisters.

Care should be taken to avoid wrinkling and bunching of socks in the boots, since lumps make blisters. For the same reason, socks with holes should be discarded.

GAITERS

No matter how tightly constructed the boot, no matter how carefully treated with waterproofing compounds, there is always the gap at the top. When a hiker wades a creek, the stream may pour directly in. When he travels in snow, crystals creep inside and melt. When he walks through wet grass or brush, moisture soaks the top of the socks, which then wick water down to the feet.

The built-in snow or scree guard described earlier may close the gap adequately—or may not. For extra protection the gaiter is available in several designs of differing materials and weight.

The long gaiter, 16 to 18 inches, extending from the laced area of the boots to the upper calf, is for deep, soft snow.

The short gaiter, 6½ to 9 inches, also called an *anklet,* suffices for the average hiker, assuming he worries that much about wet feet.

Gaiters with uppers of Gore-Tex (see Chapter 9) stay dry and keep trousers and socks dry.

BEING KIND TO FEET

The hiker blessed with tough feet can break just about all the rules of boot selection and sock use and never suffer more than an occasional blister. Less fortunate souls can follow all the rules meticulously and spend their outdoor lives hobbling in pain. A brief experience of trails tells a person where he falls, and those who find themselves afflicted with tender feet must pay close attention to the rules at all times, and devote special effort to getting their feet, along with the rest of the body, in condition for lengthy hikes by first taking a number of shorter walks.

If boots are chosen properly for the kind of travel planned, and also the proper mix of insoles and socks, sore feet and blisters should be a rarity.

Unfortunately, people do make mistakes, such as using a running shoe for a boulder-hopping, snow-plugging brushfight. Also they become careless, especially when tired. And finally, a beginner, or any hiker early in the season, may go through a period of developing calluses in the appropriate places—a blister being nature's way of saying here is where the foot needs a callus.

The most important rule in foot care is not to neglect warning signals. If a hot spot develops, stop instantly. Straighten crooked socks, switch socks from left foot to right, dump out pebbles, or perhaps pound down a nail that has punched through the insole. If the trouble stems from the foot sliding around in the boot, tighten laces or add another pair of socks. And while making whatever adjustment is called for, put a bit of adhesive tape or, better, moleskin or molefoam, on the hot spot. Some hikers, having learned precisely where they always blister, tape up beforehand.

Another preventive measure especially favored by hot-country travelers (a desert in summer sun can fry eggs—and soles) is stopping periodically to wash or air the feet and apply talcum powder or medicated foot powder.

One more: clip toenails short before a hike.

And another: if boots have been in the closet long, don them before leaving home so that on the drive to the trailhead they warm up, are moisturized by perspiration, and thus loosen a bit.

If despite all adjustments and care (or because of the lack of them) a blister develops, first aid is required. If the blister is small, cover it with moleskin or molefoam or a Band-Aid and a layer of adhesive tape. If it is large and full of liquid, insert a needle (sterilized in a match flame) at the base, drain liquid by pressing the blister gently, apply antiseptic, Band-Aid, tape, and, over all this, moleskin or molefoam.

Never "tough it out" on the trail to avoid delaying companions. The party will not appreciate the thoughtfulness if it afterward is immobilized in camp with an invalid. Blistered hikers have had to be evacuated by helicopter or packhorse—even to medical care when the blisters have become infected.

Tramping long trails, picking up boots and laying them down thousands of times a day, is brutal for citified feet. It therefore is very nice indeed to have dry socks for wearing around camp within boots laced loose and sloppy. Despite the extra weight, some hikers carry canoe moccasins or other light footwear to give surcease.

Nothing is more delightful than to stick hot, sore feet in a cold stream at the end of a hard day, hold them there to the point of numbness, then pull them out and screech and howl at the tingling rush of returning sensation. A further advantage is that the process cleans the feet, not a bad idea every few days.

The hiker absolutely must have awaiting him in the car a pair of light shoes or moccasins plus clean, soft socks. No matter how deep an affection is developed for boots, trusty companions of the trail, the feet go into delirium when at last they escape from prison.

9:   CLOTHING

SO THE story goes: a lone youth once hiked across the Olympic Mountains from Hood Canal to the Pacific Ocean with no equipment or food and wearing nothing but tennis shoes and swimming trunks. He shivered a lot and was scratched and bitten and sunburned, yet spent little time wishing for more clothes—he was too busy chasing frogs and pulling rotten logs apart for the grubs.

Though naked adventure cannot be recommended except for folks seeking a mystical experience or a totem, the journey has lessons for the overdresser, which the novice backpacker usually is. Typically, for example, the Tenderfoot Scout's mother, fearing the lethal effects of a weekend unprotected by roof, walls, and central heating, burdens him with three sweaters, a muffler, and a union suit.

Let it be noted that no Tenderfoot was ever killed by extra sweaters. Overloaded surely and likely humiliated, but never drained of life, as many have been by wind and rain. Tennis shoes, shorts, and T-shirt are a fine, free costume for an afternoon stroll in the sun, but if the rain comes down and the wind comes up, misery is certain and tragedy possible. Every year rescue parties carry back hikers who set out from the parking lot in sunshine, unprepared to cope with the tiny cloud that suddenly became a big storm.

How much clothing is enough, and how much is too much? It

depends on the trip—short afternoon, long day, overnight, full week; in forest, desert, highland; winter, summer. It also depends on the person, since some people have metabolisms and built-in insulation (fat) that make them comfortable sitting in a snowbank in a blizzard while others have a trembling fit when a cloud momentarily covers the sun. The following summaries suggest what is sufficient for the *average* person in typical *summer* conditions in country with some potential for *turning wet and cold* on short notice.

For a several-hour *afternoon walk in good weather,* wear shorts or any other pants; T-shirt or any other shirt; and perhaps wrap a wool shirt or sweater around the waist.

For a *full-day hike,* add to the above, to be carried in the rucksack if not worn: long pants, wool shirt or sweater, parka, extra socks, and some sort of hat or cap.

For an *overnight or longer hike,* add another wool shirt or sweater or equivalent, for a total of two; and possibly mittens.

This much suffices for *most* hiking country, for *most* people, in *summer conditions.* It is too much for desert country. It is not enough for climbing country, winter conditions, or cold people. However, having said that much, it now must be said that practically nothing has

been said, because there are pants and pants, parkas and parkas, hats and hats. There is no alternative but to start at the beginning and painstakingly explore the various portions of the body and discuss what can be done to cover them up, and with what.

KEEPING WARM, KEEPING DRY

Too cold. Too hot. Too wet. Too dry. Every hiker much of the time is one of these, or two, and on some trips all four, though rarely all at once. "Too dry" is alleviated by dumping water in the body or the body in water. "Too hot" is corrected by shade, wind, water, rest, or taking off clothes. "Too cold" and "too wet" are more difficult because on the trail both are ordinarily dealt with by putting on clothes, but the clothes keeping the body warm may not keep it dry, and those repelling wetness pouring from the sky may retain wetness breathed from the pores.

In olden days a prerequisite of hiking was stoic acceptance of semi-simultaneous cold-hot-wet-dry, and that's why there were so few hikers and so many mystical experiences. Now, though, man having been to the moon without getting his toes frostbit, Americans expect to be comfortable everywhere, are confident that if nature in a surly mood intrudes on an idyll, science will rush to the rescue. Indeed, the trouble today is not so much nature as science. Too many marvels. What's a person to do—buy six marvelous parkas and a wheelbarrow to cart them?

Probably not. But in narrowing the choice to a single parka, one may grow disillusioned, having set out expecting too much. As the Shropshire Lad said upon awaking after a night when Ludlow ale gave all the universe a glow of promise, "Then I saw the morning sky— heigh-ho, the tale was all a lie. The world, it was the old world yet. I was I. My things were wet."

Still, there truly are marvels, some as new as Gore-Tex, others old as sheep. The task is to meet a problem with the best solution. To do so it is necessary to study, first, the materials of wildland clothing and, second, how they are assembled.

CLOTHING FABRICS

Each material has characteristics useful in certain situations. It may entrap dead air and thus provide insulation, thus warmth. Or it may let air circulate freely and thus let perspiration breathe out. It may be "hydrophobic," refusing to absorb water and thus being water-repellent; since water has twenty times the thermal conductivity of air, "dry" tends to be "warm." Or it may soak up water and thus not feel clammy. Following are descriptions of common materials, and what they do and don't.

WOOL (Underwear, Socks, Pants, Shirts, Sweaters, Hats)

Wool's tightly curled fibers trap air efficiently, providing warmth. Moreover, they do so when soaking wet; though the conductivity of the water then reduces insulation value by half, the garments are still comparatively warm and therefore are strongly recommended in rainy-cold country where hypothermia danger commences at the car door.

Wool tears easily, so in outer garments takes a ripping from brush and rocks; it resists abrasion poorly, so wears through at sock heels

and shirt elbows. It also feels scratchy. Both faults are eliminated by an admixture of other fibers, such as nylon, making a fabric tougher and softer than pure wool. However, persons allergic to wool—and many are—must keep it away from the skin or, in extreme cases, off the body altogether.

Warmth and comfort are greatest in 100 percent all-new (virgin) wool. Reprocessed wool, from old garments chopped up, bleached, dyed, and recarded, has shorter fibers and is not so soft or durable.

Wool is woven for shirts and pants to bulk and snag less, knitted for sweaters to insulate more. Sweater wool may have natural oils left in for water-repellency, in which case the garment shouldn't be dry-cleaned, at least not until the neighbors insist.

Angora wool, from rabbits, is soft and snuggly but tough. And costly, as are fine wools from other critters.

COTTON (Underwear, Pants, Shirts, Parkas, Hats)

Not produced by the petrochemical industry, cotton is less expensive and less polluting than most fabrics; unlike petrochemicals, it can mildew and rot. The cloth feels nice, keeps off sun and breezes, and insulates well when dry. It drinks water greedily, which can be good or bad: next to the flesh it absorbs sweat without getting clammy,

131

appreciated in warm weather; once wet, it insulates scarcely at all, and should the temperature drop, freezes hard as a rock. Water-repelling compounds (Rain Chek, Scotchgard) can be applied by the hiker and are soaked up as avidly as water; in a steady rain only a few extra minutes of dryness are gained, but every little bit helps.

Ventile is made in England from long-staple Egyptian cotton with fibers up to 2 inches long, nearly triple the length of regular cotton; it is woven extremely tight, then treated with Zepel. When wet, the fibers swell, closing the already small intervening spaces, yet still permitting perspiration to breathe out. For decades Ventile was the classic parka material, warm and water-repellent and strong, though heavy. However, the cost has become so incredibly high and and the competition so fierce that its popularity has dwindled.

SYNTHETIC/COTTON BLENDS (Pants, Parkas)

Blends combine cotton's comfort and good looks with greater strength and wind-resistance.

60/40 cloth is 60 percent cotton threads running in one direction (the "fill") and 40 percent nylon threads running at right angles (the "warp"). When introduced in the 1960s, the fabric was an instant smash hit, but the growing scarcity and expense of its long-staple Pima cotton (named for Pima, Arizona, where it was originally grown from Egyptian seed) have sharply reduced use.

65/35 cloth is an "intimate blend," each thread in both warp and fill having polyester (65 percent) in the core for strength (greater than that of 60/40), and cotton (35 percent) on the outside for comfort.

Both fabrics breathe freely, and both, due to the cotton, accept water-repelling compounds, the 65/35 more uniformly. However, since neither can be made notably water-repellent, they mainly are used for "wind parkas" and not treated at all.

Durable, water-repellent, and less expensive is *80/20 cloth,* polyester outmassing the cotton.

The above are mostly employed in parkas. Pants of cotton/polyester (usually Dacron) are light, strong, easy-breathing, and more durable than pure cotton. Blends known as *stretch cloth* (a typical one is 62 percent polyester, 33 percent cotton, and 5 percent "stretch spandex") bend with the body for comfort and allure.

NYLON (Parkas, Sleeping Bags, Tents, Everything)

"Better things for better living through chemistry," promised the radio announcer of the 1930s, delivering the DuPont commercial. And lo, three wars ago, all it took to transform any GI into a Clark Gable was a box of Hershey bars and a pair of nylons. Came peace-

time, and ski hills were terrorized by the "black flash" parka. And so it went. Nowadays, take away a hiker's nylon and what have you got? Scarcely enough to preserve modesty.

The stuff comes from the chemist's kitchen as chips. These are melted and extruded through microscopic holes to form round, hard rods that are twisted together in yarn that is woven into cloth. Many different cloths are made, depending on the size of the holes, and thus the rods or filaments, the number of filaments in a strand of yarn, and the tightness of weave (the "thread count," or number of strands of yarn per inch), and such processes as "calendering" (usually done to prevent down from working its way through the fabric), where the fabric is drawn between heated metal rollers to soften and squash the yarn.

Nylon is easy to manufacture and treat and thus comparatively inexpensive, stronger than cotton for equivalent weights, abrasion-resistant, and durable. It dries quickly and usually wears out for other reasons long before rotting. It also stretches when wet and is weakened by ultraviolet radiation; these are matters of some significance for tents but not for clothing. Due to the slipperiness of the filaments, cut edges of fabric fray easily.

When only wind protection is wanted, the fabric is untreated. Fending off rain is more complicated. Because the synthetic threads are impenetrable by liquids (and that's why pure nylon feels clammy when wet), compounds must be "painted on" to fill interstices between threads; this is a factory process requiring machinery and heat and is beyond a hiker with paintbrush and a pot of goo—a "windbreaker" cannot be converted to a "rainbreaker."

The usual compound is polyurethane, applied in up to five layers depending on the degree of water-resistance wanted, least for clothing, most for tents. A light coating constrains the cloth's stretch and thus makes it liable to rip. A heavy coating actually increases fabric strength, the added layer being stronger than the nylon. In a typical five-layer (tent) treatment (Super K-Kote) the outer layer is thinned with silicone for flexibility; ultimately it peels or abrades off, but without drastically reducing water-repellency—four layers remain. The bending and twisting of normal use eventually separate fabric and coating, but not for a very long time. By then the coating probably is wearing thin all over and water flows freely through and there's naught to be done about it—recoating is impossible at home and impractical in the factory. (However, small rips and holes can be patched by cementing on bits of waterproof cloth.)

Seams are the leaky spots and a hiker periodically should paint on a seam-sealer. Experiments are in progress with a "sewing machine" that welds rather than stitches; if they are successful, the parka of the future may be seamless and virtually waterproof.

Such nylon fabrics as cordura and pack cloth are discussed in Chapter 10. Following are those most common in clothing (and sleeping bags and tents).

1.9-ounce uncoated ripstop; 70 denier yarn, 112×100 thread count. (These numbers mean that a square yard of fabric weighs 1.9 ounces, that a single strand of yarn 9,000 meters long weighs 70 grams, and that the *warp*—the strands held taut on the loom—has 112 strands of yarn per inch, and the *fill*—the strands woven at a right angle to the warp—has 100.) There are other ripstops, such as 1.5-ounce, 128× 86. The distinctive feature is that about every ¼ inch in both warp and fill the threads are doubled, forming reinforcing squares that stop rips from spreading. For comparable weights the fabric is stronger than others and for a time was the fad sensation of the outdoor scene. It continues popular for many purposes, such as tents, while fading away in others. One objection is that adding a light coating for water-repellency prevents stretching and nullifies the ripstop feature; for this reason ripstop parkas are usually uncoated, for wind protection only. Symptomatic of how things are going on the trails nowadays, a main complaint is that the fabric is unesthetic.

2.7-ounce coated taffeta; 70 denier, 103×84. (Uncoated is lighter.) A high-count taffeta such as this achieves the tear-resistance of ripstop with a modest increase in weight and has the same (medium) abrasion resistance. However, a chief reason for its taking much of ripstop's former domain is the softness and quietness of the plain-weave fabric, widely used for parka linings, rainwear, tent floors, and much else.

3.4-ounce uncoated taslan; 70 denier, 110×90. The yarn is "air-bulked"—spun in a stream of swift air, giving a rough texture that has "surface interest." At 3.4 ounces the fabric is correspondingly more resistant to abrasion and tearing than 2.7-ounce taffeta, but a key appeal of "taslanized" (also called "sueded") cloth is luxury and style.

2.7-ounce uncoated trinyl; 70 denier. An intimate blend of 50 percent polyester, 25 percent cotton, and 25 percent nylon, the fabric has low abrasion resistance and tear strength but is popular for sleeping-bag linings and fashion outdoor wear. It's soft and pretty.

1.5-ounce uncoated nylsilk; 50 denier, 168×110. Abrasion resistance and tear strength are low but the cloth is lightweight and tight-weave, made soft and silky by calendering. Nice for sleeping bags and high fashion.

1.5-ounce uncoated antron; 70 denier, 160×92. Medium abrasion resistance, low tear strength. Woven from a "trilobal" yarn that refracts light, giving a sheen that looks just darling.

1.2-ounce uncoated tricot; 20 denier, knitted. A very light fabric originally used for swimwear and sleeping-bag baffles, now employed as an inner protective layer in some rainwear and Gore-Tex laminates. The knitting makes for comfort and entrapment of perspiration, preventing clamminess. The low strength is no handicap in customary uses.

POLYPROPYLENE (Underwear)

Wool and cotton underwear can get wet and heavy, but a thin, knitted polypropylene cloth is nonabsorbent and ever-light, wicks sweat away from the body, and "feels dry all the time."

PLASTIC (Parkas)

No rain can come in and no sweat can breathe out. The fabric is thin and light, and on the trail has a life-expectancy measured in hours, if not minutes, but if protected from tearing or puncturing in the pack is good for standing around camp. In cold weather the plastic stiffens and cracks easily. But it's cheap.

RAINGEAR (Pants, Parkas)

Where the breathing out of perspiration is a trivial concern compared to the saturation of the surrounding world (as in walking ocean beaches in winter storms and half-swimming brushy trails after a deluge), the closest practical approach to total waterproofing may be sought. Several combinations are employed.

Rubberized cloth, neoprene combined with cotton, is strong and watertight and heavy, rapidly crumbles and cracks when exposed to sunshine, and is cheap.

Vinyl-coated cotton with welded seams is heavy, bulky, and costly but strong and durable; the vinyl outside completely stops the storms from seeping through, and the cotton inside feels nice.

Polyurethane/nylon laminate with welded seams is used in garments by Macbean and also by Peter Storm (Bukflex). The outside layer of nonwoven polyester coated with polyurethane repels rain; the inside layer of light, absorbent nylon tricot prevents clamminess. Comfortable, durable, expensive.

PILE (Sweaters)

Though new on the American backpacking scene, pile is no passing fad; use over many years by Norwegian fishermen, then European hikers, has provided as rigorous a field test as could be wanted. Sheep are getting stiff competition for the sweater business.

Pile is not a single material but a category. There are all-nylon piles (Helly-Hanson Fibrepile, REI Mountain Hard Pile), all-polyester piles (Patagonia Pile, Patagonia Bunting, REI Mountain Soft Pile), piles half acrylic and half poly (Macbean Pile), piles 85 percent acrylic and 15 percent poly (Patagonia Fleece), and other mixtures, other trade names. Thicknesses and weights and finishes are many. Some have the fuzzy or fleecy side outside; in rough use these "pill" and look scruffy, admired by folks who march to a scruffy drummer. Other piles have the fuzzy side inside, the outside treated with urethane for a smooth, hard finish. Others are smooth inside and out. American wildland use has not yet been extensive enough for a consensus to develop on which is best for what.

The secret of pile is the knitting of a synthetic fiber on a heavy base into many fine loops that trap air with extreme efficiency, resulting in a material giving the same insulation as wool for half the weight. In wet weather the superiority is even greater, because pile absorbs only

2 percent water by weight, compared to wool's 40 percent, so both feels dry and wicks moisture away from the body. Finally, it's machine-washable in cold water.

All in all, though too bulky for hiking pants, pile is widely considered to have made wool obsolete in sweaters. With a lining (or used with a shell parka), a pile sweater is windproof; laminated with Gore-Tex, water-repellent. Indeed, the lower cost of such combinations put pile in direct competition with insulated parkas.

GORE-TEX (Gaiters, Shirts, Parkas, Sleeping Bags, Tents)

In 1969, employees of W. L. Gore Co. playing with gobs of polytetrafluoroethylene (PTFE for short, better known as Teflon) discovered that when it is pulled rapidly in opposite directions while in a plastic state, tiny holes open in the material and adjacent molecules align in the direction of pull. Proceeding from laboratory taffy-pulls to serious inventing, in 1975 they produced Gore-Tex, 82 percent air, with 9 billion holes per square inch, yet very strong even when rolled in sheets merely .001 inch thick. The magic of the stuff derives from another boggling number—the pores are just .2 micron (.000008 inch) in diameter. Because in liquid water (rain) the molecules cluster in aggregates 20,000 times larger than that, the moisture can't pass through but rather beads on the surface. However, the "excited" molecules of gaseous water (perspiration) stay in groups small enough to slip through. The rain stays out (and so does the wind) and the perspiration breathes out, while permitting body heat to stay in.

According to U.S. Army standards, a fabric must resist a water-entry pressure of 25 pounds per square inch (psi) to be considered reasonably water-repellent. (Nothing is "waterproof" if enough pressure is applied.) Army tests show Gore-Tex resisting 65–80 psi, compared to only 2 for Ventile and 60/40 cloth. (Bukflex handles 90–110 psi, Super K-Kote Fabric 120, and PVC/cotton 160.)

Breathability is less amenable to testing or definition, as the variables of temperature and humidity and metabolism and work are so numerous, but an accepted standard for comfort for a person at rest is a breathing (water-transmission) rate of 350–600 grams of water per square meter of cloth per 24 hours (measured under laboratory conditions). A rate of 2,000–3,000 grams prevents condensation of perspiration in most hiking. (In hard work at high temperatures, no fabric can breathe fast enough.) According to the W. L. Gore Co., the laboratory rate for Gore-Tex laminated to 1.5-ounce nylon is 2,800, compared to 5 for PVC/cotton and 10 for Super K-Kote and 20 for Bukflex. (Ventile handles 4,900, 60/40 cloth 5,200, 65/35 cloth and 1.9-ounce ripstop 5,800.)

As the figures show, other fabrics keep rain out or let perspiration breathe out, but don't do both. Gore-Tex is unique. Further, it's inert (as witness the use of PTFE for vascular grafts), nonflammable, nonaging, and weather-durable.

Strong though the material is, a thin membrane is too fragile to be used alone and is always laminated to other fabrics, resulting in a variety of materials. A Gore-Tex laminate may be lined with nylon taffeta or taslan, cotton poplin, or pile. Or it may be sandwiched between a knit liner inside and another fabric outside.

The long-awaited ticket to the Promised Land? Despite continuing improvements in the basic membrane and thousands of people-years of trail use, a minority of suspicious veterans who've watched many a wonder flash across the sky still whisper "Sweat-Tex." (When it comes to tents they do more than whisper.) Certainly, dazzled hikers often ignore the fine print of ads and expect never again to be wet, imagine that the miracle fabric will part the Red Sea.

Nevertheless, the expert consensus is that in clothing (and sleeping bags and bivvy sacks) Gore-Tex really works in all but rather extreme conditions of heat/humidity/work—if given proper maintenance. It is *not* for the sloppy and scruffy. Seams must be sealed annually with Seamstuff or the like. If body oils, sunburn cream, insect repellent, or plain crud contaminates the membrane, the dirty spots let rain in; the corrective treatment is sponging with rubbing alcohol. General accumulation of grime leads to overall leaking; the material should be kept clean by regular washing with Ivory Snow and cold water, double-rinsing to remove soap; dry-cleaning is forbidden. Damage to the membrane also causes leaks; the treatment is to dip the garment in a tub of water to find the leak, then dabble on seam-sealer.

The high price of a Gore-Tex garment is deceptive; considering what it replaces and outlasts, in the not very long run the cost may well be less.

ZIPPERS AND THREAD

A *coil zipper,* two continuous nylon rolls sewn to cotton/polyester tapes, is light, strong, and "self-healing"—that is, when the zipper goes off the trolley, a return to the terminus puts it back on. It turns sharp corners well and thus is preferred for arch-shaped tent doors and panel packbags.

A *toothed zipper,* the teeth molded directly on cotton/polyester tape, resists separation better. Nylon is the usual tooth material, except the YKK brand, which uses Delrin, a light, tough thermoplastic that doesn't get brittle in extreme cold. Metal zippers cheaply made tend to ice up and jam, but those used by Kelty (the only major company to do so) are of such high quality as to be remarkably trouble-free.

The best *thread* for sewing outdoor gear is cotton-covered polyester; cotton isn't strong enough and nylon stretches too much.

UNDERWEAR

In ordinary summer hiking, enough warmth is provided by outer clothing; underwear is purely for comfort and whatever feels good at home is fine on the trail. Especially in hot or dry country, fabrics all or mostly cotton are usual. Cotton/polyester *fishnet,* with a very open weave that lets the skin breathe free but sops up sweat, is comfortable worn alone on hot days, though modest souls ordinarily wear something over, on the bottom at least. The skin develops a fishnet pattern that some folks abhor; others love the distinctive sunburn.

When the temperature drops, the wise move is to shed cotton, which clings with all its sweat and triggers the shivers; better to wear shirt or sweater next to the skin, despite scratching. Excellent underwear for wet-cold weather is wool/cotton fishnet that traps dead air and holds body heat.

"Long johns" are the warmness champions, but most models are too heavy for walking or even carrying to camp. However, the Stil-Longs, Stil-Top combination weighs only ½ pound per bottom and per top. Made of 85 percent merino wool, soft and cuddly, plus 15 percent nylon for strength, they are mainly for chilly camp evenings, and are considered essential by many a person with icicles for bones, perpetually on the brink of hypothermia. They serve elsewhere very well, too. On a windy ridge a hiker in shorts may slip into Stil-Longs, then re-don shorts for modesty. In cold, rainy, wet-brush terrain the Longs may be worn under rain pants. As the central-heating thermostats are turned down all over America, long johns surely will reappear in city and suburb, most of whose residents don't remember when fall colors were the reminder that the time was near to change to winter underwear.

People engaged in strenuous exercise in cold weather—running, cross-country skiing—like long underwear (or undershorts) of thin, light polypropylene. Whereas wool soaks up sweat and grows steadily swampier, the poly always feels dry.

VAPOR BARRIER

In these pages, as throughout the literature of conventional wisdom, much ado is made about "breathability." But abroad in the land are heretics who sneer at "the great breathability myth," who declare that perspiration is no enemy but a friend, who denounce the Three

Fallacies of the Breathers: (1) sweating means wetting; (2) skin is meant to be dry; and (3) sealed fabrics cause condensation.

They counterpose the "vapor barrier," so intricately based on the laws of thermodynamics that the full exposition is best left to *Pleasure Packing*, by Robert S. Wood, and the catalogs of Jack Stephenson, which picture his unusual equipment.

To understand the principle, consider attempts of the body to maintain an ambience resembling the primordial seas. Man's remembering skin likes the relative humidity of the air immediately next to it to be about 70–95 percent, and to maintain that level respires, during rest, about 1 pint of water a day in *insensible perspiration* (gaseous water, invisible vapor). But in cold weather the air cannot be brought to the desired humidity; the body keeps pumping out vapor and still the skin dries; a person isn't sweating yet mysteriously develops a fierce thirst. If, in addition, hard work is being performed, producing excess heat, the body tries to cool itself by pouring out *sensible perspiration* (liquid water, sweat); if this is "breathed out" in accordance with dogma of the established religion, heat is conducted away from the body by the water at a terrific rate, 20 times faster than by air; as a further complication, the insulating materials of garments are wetted.

The heretics concede that breathability works well enough in ordinary hiking in ordinary spring-to-fall weather, or at least does little harm. However, they say that during hard labor in extreme cold there's no room for nonsense; the hiker must seek a better simulation of the primordial seas, and the way is by erecting a vapor barrier, as follows: The hiker dons (1) fishnet undershirt for sweat absorption and skin comfort, then (2) an impervious vapor-barrier shirt, essentially a large plastic bag weighing a few ounces, and finally (3) sweater and/or parka for insulation. The heck with "breathing." Insensible perspiration ceases because humidity inside the barrier quickly rises to a cozy 100 percent. Sweat can't get out to wet the insulating garments, can't conduct precious heat from the body. In sum, it is claimed that the light and simple shirt adds 25 percent to the insulating value of the total clothing assembly—besides preventing that assembly from getting wet from the inside.

It is not necessary for the entire body to swim in the primordial; a vapor barrier for the trunk, which produces half the sweat (the other half equally divided between the legs and the head/hands), suffices. A winter mountaineer may well carry a vapor-barrier shirt as survival gear.

The principle is extended to sleeping bags. Proponents say that the sleeper within an impervious vapor-barrier liner doesn't risk drowning in his own juices, in fact feels merely a bit damp by morning. Again, insulation is protected from wetting by perspiration. And no frost forms on down bags. The condensation of insensible perspiration on tent walls is reduced (mouth and nose continue to breathe, even if bags don't). The "comfort zone" is increased 10° –15°F—a bag comfortable at 30°F can serve down to perhaps 15°F. Finally, the Breathability Myth having been debunked, there is no reason a person shouldn't put a waterproof outer cover on his bag and laugh at the rime falling from tent walls, the rain falling from the sky.

Now, back to the conventional wisdom.

SHIRTS AND SWEATERS

At different times during a single day the hiker may have two opposite problems: retaining warmth generated by metabolism when wind and rain and snow are striving to steal it away, and getting rid of excess body heat when all the world around is bathing him in energy from the solar furnace. One minute too cold, the next too hot, often the hiker is beset by extremes and must make frequent adjustments to stay in the narrow comfort zone between broiling and shivering.

Second only to the head-and-neck area (discussed below), the torso, especially the front, is the most critical portion of the body in controlling the human thermostat. For complex physiological reasons, if this section can be kept warm (cool), the rest of the body will tend to feel warm (cool).

Though applicable elsewhere on the body, here the *layer system* has special value. The essence is to depend on several thin layers of insulation, and the dead air they trap between them, in preference to a single, massive layer, such as a logger's mackinaw or any other heavy coat. With such materials as wool, cotton, polyester, and nylon, the layer system gives the most warmth for the least weight and also allows fine tuning of the heat control, rather than a simple on-off, totally hot or totally cold. (Insulated garments are another story, told below.)

The hiker may set out on a chill morning with torso covered by undershirt, a light cotton shirt, and a wool shirt. Once he is warmed by walking, off comes the wool shirt. During a long rest, as sweat cools, he may put the wool shirt back on. If the day turns cold, he may add a sweater, and if wind comes up or rain down, a parka. Thus, by carrying several light garments, he can vary torso coverage from bare skin up to four or five layers.

Some hikers tinker too much and drive companions crazy by incessantly stopping for addition or subtraction. Veterans tend to enlarge their comfort zone; that is, they endure excess warmth or chilliness for the moment, knowing that a few minutes later the balance may shift the other way. Also, they depend as much as possible on varying a single garment—for example, a wool shirt. As ventilation is needed, the sleeves are rolled up and the front unbuttoned. As warmth is wanted, down come the sleeves and the front is closed up. At a rest stop, when sweat turns icy, they start hiking again rather than putting on a sweater.

In warm weather there usually should be an inner layer of cotton —undershirt, T-shirt, running shirt, old dress shirt, or light turtleneck shirt. In the cold, however, polyester is better.

For any hike beyond the shortest stroll a person should carry, if not wear, a medium-weight wool shirt. A full collar and a neck button keep the neck warm. The tails should extend well below the beltline to avoid goose bumps on the midriff. The prices of fancy wool shirts know virtually no upper limit, but decent ones can be bought for $25–$35—or a fraction of that at thrift shops.

For any long hike a person should have a medium-weight sweater or a second wool shirt large enough to fit over the first. A heavy sweater is to be avoided—if more warmth is desired, better to carry two light sweaters (or an insulated sweater). The sleeves should be

*Lightweight pile sweater,
jacket style.*

wrist-length and the bottom should extend below the beltline. Though the pullover is most common, some prefer a buttoned-front jacket style for the ease of getting in and out and of varying the warmth/ventilation. A turtleneck protects the neck but can become uncomfortable unless it has a partial front opening.

Pretty wool sweaters cost all sorts of money but serviceable ones weighing 1–1½ pounds cost $20–$40—again, much less at the thrift shop. A pile sweater, twice the warmth for the same weight, is transitional to, even competitive with, insulated garments. Depending on the design (pullover or jacket) and special features (zippers, hood, handwarmer pockets), weights range from ¾ to 1½ pounds, prices from $25 to $50 or more.

In cold but dry weather a light nylon *wind shirt,* weighing about 3 ounces and wadding up to fit in a pocket, adds as much warmth as an extra sweater.

145

PANTS

Since the main centers for controlling the human thermostat are the torso and head, pants are often worn less for warmth than protection from sunburn, nettle stings, poison ivy and oak, and mosquito bites; this, however, is not so in cold country, notably high mountains, where every part of the body must be insulated in a storm or a freezing night.

For first walks and any short walks a beginner can't go far wrong by wearing on the trail any old slacks or shorts that happen to be around the house. The important thing is that they be cut full enough to allow easy action, not binding the hips or knees during long strides.

For long day hikes and backpacks the hiker must pay more attention to selection. No single garment does everything, everywhere.

Clothing sufficient for a pleasant-day, several-hour walk not far from road or camp: shorts, light cotton shirt, and wool sweater in case of chilly moments.

SHORTS

Probably more people hike more miles in shorts than all other bottomwear combined. It's not a garment demanding a lot of thought. Cotton or polyester/cotton are the standard materials. Six-pocket "cargo" designs are convenient for ready access to items frequently used. "Bavarian" and "Sierra" and "rugby" and bib styles have adherents. But unless a person lives most importantly in the eye of the beholder, he generally wears whatever comes to hand, such as cutoffs. Running shorts walk well and are cheap, light, and comfortable; nylon ones dry in a hurry.

For any trip except the briefest in good weather, the hiker who wears shorts must carry long pants in his rucksack—for cool nights, sudden storms, and emergencies. Long pants may also be carried to prevent a disabling sunburn, especially during prolonged snow travel, though pajama bottoms are just as effective and much lighter.

Some people wear shorts even in a hard rain, keeping trousers dry in the pack. Indeed, they may take off pants when rain begins, or when entering wet brush or fording a stream, and don shorts. However, congenital hypothermics who fear being rained to death may add long johns or rain pants.

Lederhosen are costly and rare, durable, very hot in hot weather, very cold in cold weather, and—so sexists say—cute on the right figure.

KNICKERS

Nowadays knickers are worn mostly by climbers. They rarely bind at the knee, and opening the bottom strap and buckle and rolling down the knicker socks permits ventilation almost as good as shorts.

The best for all-around wear is wool or wool/nylon, with a hard whipcord finish and double seat and knees, selling for about $40–$60.

TROUSERS

Most hiking trousers are cotton, warm when dry, cold when wet. Blue jeans were common on trails years before they became stylish

Hikers dressed for a day hike in cool weather: knickers and wool shirt, trousers and wool sweater. Storm clothing is in rucksacks.

in polite society; the price runs about $20. Cotton work pants, equally good though not à la mode, sell for $10 or so.

More elaborate are "trail pants" (or "mountain pants" or "bush pants" or "canvas pants") of cotton/nylon or cotton/polyester, priced around $5 in army surplus and $25–$35 in civilian models. Again, the six-pocket "cargo" design is convenient.

Trousers (and shorts, too) of polyester/cotton/stretch spandex hug the flesh and move with it, providing comfort, durability, a dressy look, and a sharp drop in the cash balance.

In country liable to be wet and chilly on short notice, all-wool or wool-blend trousers are just about essential. A high-quality, rugged fabric—wool/nylon or hard-finish whipcord wool—is tough and durable; price, $50 or more. Not particularly stylish but warm and inexpensive and deservedly popular are plain all-wool trousers. An excellent buy—usual price, $10 or so—is army surplus. Thrift shops offer the real bargains. An old pair of men's suit pants may be obtained for a dollar or two and, perhaps with patches added at the knees and seat, give miles of service on the trail long after they are too crummy for civilization.

RAIN PANTS

Hikers in well-watered country sometimes carry lightweight rain pants to keep trousers and socks dry; rain chaps, which slip individually on the legs, have the same purpose.

Very light plastic pants costing several dollars tear easily when snagged and self-destruct with the first long stride. Polyurethane-coated nylon pants, costing $15, are durable enough for busting brush. Gore-Tex pants, ½–¾ pound, $30–$50, are wind pants as well as rain pants.

Except for Gore-Tex, rain pants do not breathe, so when worn during steady walking, they wet the legs from the inside as thoroughly as rain would from the outside. They therefore are best suited for camp use or loitering along an ocean beach in a winter storm or punching through saturated brush where every step is a showerbath. However, because rain water is colder than sweat, a person subject to fits of the chillies may don rain pants in any hard rain or strong wind.

HEADWEAR

The most critical portion of the body for regulation of the thermostat is the area of the head and neck; the brain receives 20 percent of the body's blood supply, 25 percent of its oxygen, and the head, having little fatty insulation, may account for up to half the body's total heat radiation. If head and neck are cold, the whole body will shiver, and if they are warm, one may feel quite comfortable even with bare legs on a frosty night. It is wisely said, "If your feet are cold, put on a hat."

Similarly, in scorching sun an overheated head can lead to dizzy misery, even heat stroke.

Finally, in hard rain, if head and neck can be kept dry, one does not feel totally drenched and blinded and lost in the swamp.

It is perfectly all right to choose headwear for style or personality as long as the choice gives the necessary protection. At least one climber has attained the summit of Mt. Rainier wearing an opera hat and causing a sensation, but he had a stocking cap in his pack.

For Rain

The *rain hat,* sou'wester style, though designed specifically for ocean conditions, such as walking beside the surf in winter, also provides sun protection, just as other headwear also provides rain protection.

The high-crowned, broad-brimmed Akubra Bushman has character.

The *umbrella,* on American trails thought eccentric, long has been popular in Europe.

For Sun

The natty *mountain hat,* ordinarily worn by guides because tourists expect it of them, guards the head against rain and hot sun, as do the *crusher,* the *glacier hat,* also known as the "Aussie tennis hat" (not to be confused with the "Allagash" or "Aussie bush hat"), the baseball cap, and the cowboy hat, with or without rattlesnake band.

For sun protection on deserts and scorched hills one may wear a *handkerchief hat,* knotting a large handkerchief or bandanna at all four corners to fit comfortably on the head. It may periodically be dipped in streams, rubbed with snow, or saturated from the canteen for additional cooling. A hat of terry cloth holds more water longer.

A bandanna may also be used to protect the neck, a particularly excruciating place to have a bad sunburn.

A *sweatband* on the forehead keeps sweat from running into the eyes.

For Warmth

The most warmth is provided by a wool *balaclava,* or *toque,* which covers the whole head and neck except the face; a "K-2 cap" with polyester insulation, snap-up earflaps, and elastic for a snug fit; or the detachable hood of an insulated parka.

Next best (and cheapest) is a wool *watch cap* or *stocking cap* which can cover the upper head only, be rolled down over the ears, or even onto the back of the neck. The "Danish fishermen's" hat or "Cascade Hiker" is similar.

The *beret* is almost as good, perched jauntily atop the head or pulled down over the ears; the British green beret has a sinister commando look, the French beret a boulevardier air.

Any headwear not extending to the neck may need supplementation by a *scarf* (or bandanna) or *neck band,* a simple wool collar. A wool scarf wrapped around both neck and head, babushka style, is superb in hard rain driven by high wind.

Some hikers are content with naught but an *ear band.*

MITTENS

Few hikers ever need to protect their hands more than can be done by sticking them in pockets. However, those who spend much time in high hills or winter, and especially if they must keep hands out of pockets, such as to carry an ice ax, should have mittens. The best are pile inside, nylon outside, warm, windproof, water-resistant, quick-drying, and only $10 the pair. Gloves may be mandatory for dense

A sampling of headwear for various situations and personalities. Top: *Glacier hat, up-downer (modified Sherlock Holmes), and crusher.* Center: *Stocking cap, K-2 cap, and balaclava.* Bottom: *Sou'wester rain hat, beret, and handkerchief hat.*

brush thickly thorned but are not recommended for the cold—fingers are much warmer snuggling in mittens.

PARKAS

Hikers who always travel dry, calm country never need a parka, and some roam even roaring highlands from youth to age with nothing outside shirts and sweaters. But some people go barefoot, too, and

152

some die of hypothermia. When rain drenches down, wicking body heat out through garments, or when wind simply blows through, a parka may give more than mere comfort. Having his life saved only once every several years may make a hiker feel that the weight is worth it.

Except for those with filler (discussed later), parkas give little insulation (warmth) in themselves. Mainly they are protectors of warmth-giving insulation—they are rainbreakers (primarily) or windbreakers (primarily). As the tale will reveal, only one parka does both jobs well.

Following sections first discuss these two roles of the parka, then take up the various features of parka design.

RAINBREAKERS

Rainbreakers are of three general sorts: roomy shelters for much or all of the body and the pack as well; "true" parkas; and foulweather jackets.

The waterproof poncho, a portable tarp, is mainly worn while puttering around camp in the rain, but sometimes also during downpours on the trail.

The *poncho,* essentially a tarp to be worn while walking, is big enough to be worn over a pack and protect the entire body except the lower legs. Depending on the fabric, ponchos weigh from less than 1 to nearly 3 pounds and range from $10 or so for heavyweight army-surplus rubberized cotton to $20 or more for coated nylon.

A poncho is splendid for standing around or doing camp chores in a downpour; in strenuous hiking it becomes a portable sauna. The design is cumbersome, and in anything but the simplest maneuvers, fouls on brush, pack, cooking pots, feet, and other hikers. Comes a high wind, and the poncho flaps and flies and tangles and obscures.

The *cagoule,* essentially a tent to be worn while walking, is a full-cut, calf-length garment meant to be worn over bulky clothing, as in bivouacking during a wintry climb. Some stormy-country hikers like them for standing around camp. Representative examples of coated nylon weigh 1–1½ pounds, cost about $50.

A "true parka" rainbreaker or *rain parka* slips on over shirt and sweater (or insulated parka) and keeps them dry. For a while. Until perspiration wets them from the inside. A simple shell of coated nylon, jacket style, weighs less than ½ pound, costs about $25; more elaborate, ¾ pound, $40. Add a cotton/polyester liner for warmth, and a rain parka becomes a *storm parka,* 1½ pounds, $55.

Foulweather jackets of vinyl-coated cotton or polyurethane/nylon laminate (Macbean, Peter Storm's Bukflex) are as "waterproof" as clothing gets. A jacket may weigh from 1¼ pounds to more than 2; added to rain pants (see above), the resulting *rainsuit* is more practical for digging clams in an ocean blow than tramping miles in wildlands. Jacket prices range from $45 to $75.

All the above are nonbreathers. The only rainbreaker that is not is *Gore-Tex* (see below).

WINDBREAKERS

The thin shell of the typical rainbreaker prevents molecules of rushing air from directly battering a hiker's inner clothing, but doesn't seriously impede loss of heat from the insulating layer to the cold, cold wind. To do that a parka must be more than a simple shell. But then, while breaking wind, why can't it break rain? To an extent it can, but usually not very well, because whatever is done to keep rain out also keeps perspiration in. (With that one exception.) Therefore, the traditional pattern has been to make parkas that do a lot about rain and little about wind, or the reverse.

Cotton long was the standard material of wind parkas, and Ventile the classic best. But cotton is now used less and less and Ventile has virtually vanished—when a Ventile parka can be found it may weigh 2½ pounds and cost $100, or $150, and be infinitely more appreciated by an expeditioner at 26,000 feet on a Himalayan icicle than a trail-tramper in the Great Smokies. Such water-repellency as a cotton parka has derives from characteristics of the fibers and from Scotchgard or Rain Chek or other compounds sprayed or painted on by the owner.

After cotton, the championship was held for a time by *ripstop nylon,* uncoated, which lingers on in a few examples of lightweight windbreakers.

Currently pre-eminent are polyester/cotton blends, 60/40 cloth and 65/35 cloth, uncoated. These yield what often are called "all-weather parkas," excessive praise. However, they exclude a wind as long as it's dry, and if treated for water-repellency, stand off a mist for hours and shed a moderate rain for 15 minutes, time enough for a hiker to get under a tree or poncho or tent. Examples weigh 1½–2 pounds, cost $60 to $120.

And then there's the exception, *Gore-Tex,* the miracle double-threat that costs more but does so much more that it saves money and weight by replacing two garments. Depending on features of design and the materials of the laminate, a Gore-Tex parka weighs 1 to 1¾ pounds, costs $65 to $150.

There are also Gore-Tex wind-rain pants, wind-rain climbing bibs, wind-rain gaiters, wind-rain cagoules, wind-rain-warmth pile sweaters, wind-rain-warmth insulated garments, and perhaps before long, Gore-Tex cats and dogs, for very hard rains.

Representative jacket-style parkas. Left: *Windbreaker, polyester/cotton lined with nylon taffeta.* Center: *Rainbreaker, coated nylon taffeta lined with polyester/cotton.* Right: *Rainbreaker-windbreaker, Gore-Tex laminate with nylon taslan on the outside, nylon taffeta lining on the inside.*

PARKA DESIGN

Front-Opening or "Jacket" Parka

Of the two basic parka designs, the jacket style, with a complete front opening, is best for backpacking. A full-length zipper allows easy getting in and out and also good ventilation. In a warm, misty rain, for instance, one may wish to wear the parka to keep head and shoulders dry but open the front to avoid sweat saturation.

Since zippers sometimes fail and a wide-open parka is worthless in a storm, for high-country (or winter-ocean) travel the front should have a *storm flap* with a back-up system of snaps. These reinforce the zipper and replace it in event of failure and can be used in its stead for more ventilation.

REPRESENTATIVE PARKAS RECOMMENDED FOR HIKERS
(All are front-opening, or jacket design)

Material	Use	Approximate Weight (pounds)	Approximate Price
Plastic	Rainbreaker; for very careful, infrequent use; untrustworthy in emergencies	⅜	$5
Coated nylon-taffeta shell	Rainbreaker; mainly for around camp; emergency use during storms on good trails or in brushless terrain	½–¾	$25
Coated nylon taffeta, lined with cotton/polyester	Rainbreaker; for extended, strenuous activity in cold, wet country	1½	$55
Laminate of nylon tricot and polyurethane	Foulweather gear; for lobster fishing, rain forests in winter, and ocean beaches in sideways rain	1¼	$70
Polyester/cotton (65/35, 60/40) lined with nylon taffeta	Windbreaker; for extended, strenuous activity in rough, brushy, cold country in all sorts of bad weather except steady rain	1¾	$60
Gore-Tex lined with nylon taffeta	Rainbreaker, windbreaker, and warmthkeeper; for extended, strenuous activity in all sorts of country in all sorts of bad weather	1¼	$80
Gore-Tex with nylon taslan outside, nylon taffeta inside	Ditto the above, but more abrasion-resistant	1½	$95

Pullover Parka, or Anorak

The second basic design, the anorak, has no front opening that might allow penetration of rain or wind. The price paid is that the garment must be donned and doffed over the head and ventilation is difficult. Such parkas are better for climbers than hikers.

Various Parka Features

As with boots, packs, and sleeping bags, parkas exhibit a bewildering variety of features. Here only a few of the most significant will be noted.

The lightest parkas are *single layer* throughout. Others have complete *double-body* construction, such as 65/35 cloth outside, lined with nylon taffeta. Double-body construction gives a thermal barrier and thus more insulation—and weight. Some parkas are of double construction only in the upper half and the sleeves.

The *hood* may be an integral part of the parka or detachable. The best hoods cover the lower face when tightened by the drawstring. Some fold into a back-of-the-neck pocket secured by drawstrings.

Cuffs may be elastic, to hold the garment to the wrists. Many have buttons, snaps, or Velcro ("sticky tape") for adjustment, and a gusset in the sleeve for ease in pulling over gloves or mittens.

A *drawstring waist* is useful for cinching the parka around the midriff, holding it tight to the body in storm winds. Similarly, a *bottom drawstring* brings the skirts close to the hips.

There may be no *pockets,* or two slash pockets for handwarmers, or patch pockets, or any number of pockets inside and out, zippered or snapped or with Velcro closure, for carrying items to which convenient access is desired.

Some parkas have two overlapping layers of fabric in the upper back, the two not sewn together, to allow some ventilation through the gap. Some have *underarm zippers* that permit ventilation of these torrid zones.

Since seams and stitching are most likely to leak, and since the upper part of the parka takes the brunt of rain, the better parkas intended mainly for rain protection either have one-piece construction to avoid all seams and stitching at the shoulders or else place all seams on the sides and under the sleeves. In wind parkas the seam location is of no consequence.

Whatever parka is chosen, the skirts should come well below the waist. It should also be *full cut* to allow room inside for sweaters and to permit easy mobility. A tight parka steams up fast, tears easily with sudden movements, and causes claustrophobia.

INSULATED CLOTHING

A long time ago folks in cold country who couldn't afford six sweaters but were chilly with only two began stuffing the space between with straw, moss, lichen, leaves, or dog hair. From this expedient evolved double-wall garments filled with wool, cotton, or kapok. Finally arrived (actually, very early among goose-raising peasantry) down—and then polyester—and climbers on Himalayan peaks began surviving nights in the open without carrying sleeping bags. Because they were wearing them.

Just as the "climbing-boot look" became the campus rage, the "quilted look" grew so fashionable it was celebrated in a *New Yorker* cartoon. Not merely expeditionary mountaineers were quilted but little old rose gardeners; Yves St. Laurent offered a quilted cocktail dress in basic black.

The wearing of insulated clothing in mild climates may seem as preposterous as going disco in army boots. But there are hikers who live ever in the shadow of hypothermia, who could crawl in the furnace to share the cremation of Sam McGee and shiver the fire to death, who never before the Quilted Age were truly cozy on windy evenings of bleak tundra or moraine. Nor should hikers with built-in furnaces reject insulated garments out of hand—they weigh tremendously less than wool counterparts of equal warmth, though not so much less than those of pile. Further, down garments compress to tiny wads when crammed in nylon stuff bags and take minute space in the pack—and here down has it over pile and polyester as well as wool.

The insulating characteristics of down and polyester are treated in Chapter 11, "Sleeping Bags." With clothing as with bags the question arises, which is best? That depends.

The case for down: Warmer and thus better for sheer cold unmixed with liquid water. Softer, feels nicer. Breathes easier. Stuffs tiny. Lasts years. *The case against:* Collapses when wet and then gives virtually zero warmth and takes days to dry; fussy protection is essential, as by use with a rainbreaking outer parka and tight tent. Mildew is possible. Some people are allergic. The initial cost is higher.

The case for polyester: Insulates somewhat even when drenched, is quickly dried by wringing it out, and thus is better for country that is rainy, drizzly, misty, or clogged with snow (on ground, in sky) that infiltrates clothing and tents and turns liquid; also better for hikers who carry no rainbreaker and/or sleep under a tarp. Nonallergenic. Initial cost lower. *The case against:* Aside from less warmth and more bulk, wears out much faster and thus in the long run costs more.

To these two fillers now must be added a third, still another in the contemporary parade of miracles. Or so it will become if it is not shaved by Hume's Razor. This new prodigy is offered by the 3M Company (an unlikely nest of heresy), which challenges the received belief that insulation is directly proportional to thickness. The company says tests show ½ inch of its *Thinsulate,* made of extremely thin fibers that trap air better than thick ones, insulates as efficiently as 1 inch of down. More field-testing and debating will determine whether here is yet another turning upside down of the backpacking world, so often turned upside down in recent decades. Further tinkering also may be required—at present, for equal warmth, garments of Thinsulate cost more than polyester, weigh more than down.

Thinsulate aside, insulated clothing falls into five basic categories: polyester fill with outer shell of (1) nylon taffeta, lightweight, for comfort in careful use, as standing around camp, or (2) 60/40 or 65/35 cloth or ripstop nylon, sturdy, for more rugged duty; and down fill with outer shell of (3) nylon taffeta or (4) 60/40 or 65/35 cloth or (5) Gore-Tex. The shells of (1) through (4) are at most rain-repellent; that of (5) is everything Gore-Tex is cracked up to be.

Representative insulated garments, jacket style. The filler may be either down or polyester. Most have detachable hoods. Left to right: Sweater, parka, vest, Gore-Tex jacket.

Sewn-through construction (see Chapter 11), giving that famous quilted look and permitting perspiration to exhale freely, is best for most clothing. Box, double-quilt, and overlapping construction use more filler, add weight and cost, and are mainly for intense cold.

The pullover (anorak) design is less good for backpacking than the jacket design with zipper or snap front.

The simplest insulated garment is the *vest,* sleeveless, covering the trunk only. Maximum freedom of movement is combined with much warmth; in cold country, though, some other garment is needed to cover the arms. Approximate weights and costs: polyester, 1 pound, $35; down, ¾ pound, $60; Thinsulate, 1 pound, $45.

The *sweater* (or *sweat shirt* or *shirt*), a jacket extending to midhip, intermediate in weight and price between vest and parka, has nearly disappeared from the market. One reason is that the upper part of a set of *underwear* is similar and costs a bit less.

The *parka* extends farther down the hips. Approximate weights and costs, complete with hood (usually detachable): polyester, 2–3¼ pounds, $50–$70; down, 1¾–2 pounds, $80–$120; Gore-Tex/down, 1½ pounds, $125; Thinsulate (no hood), 1½–2 pounds, $50–$100.

Heavier parkas, as well as insulated socks, booties, underwear lowers, pants, mitts, dickeys, coveralls, and face masks are for sports colder than ordinary backpacking.

10:

CANDY bar and apple in pockets, cup on belt, sweater around waist, camera over shoulder—off and away the happy hiker strides.

Good enough for an afternoon stroll. For a long day, though, or a short one if much lunch or children's clothing or camera or birding gear are hauled or mushrooms or pretty rocks gathered, stuffing pockets and draping the body interfere with free-action walking. The answer? A pack.

Also, at any distance from the road the hiker must carry the Ten Essentials (see Chapter 15), used infrequently but then *essential.* They weigh little but won't all fit in pockets. Again, a pack.

Finally, if the trip is overnight, most pilgrims expect supper, bed, and breakfast and won't want to walk with sleeping bag under one arm and sack of groceries in the other. Yes, a pack.

Yes, but *which* pack? After the boots-boots-boots trample a novice, the packs-packs-packs do the flattening. The assortment in shops reflects the importance of the pack—with boots, sleeping bag, and tent/tarp ranking among the Big Four Basic Decisions. It further reflects the restless creativity of manufacturers burning to achieve the Grail. Or Grails, since no pack is ideal for everybody and everywhere. And even if one were, no two manufacturers would agree where to look for it.

Harangued from all sides by bickering prophets, which way should the hiker go? The first consideration: *What's the pack for?* Short walks, full-day rambles, occasional overnights, every-weekend year-after-year long-distance hauls—the needs differ. As they do for trail-tramping, peak-climbing, snow-sliding. Even foreign travel.

Then, *how's the bank account?* The hiker with money-lumpy pockets can fill his basement with special packs for special purposes, choose the top of the line and maximum gingerbread, and keep up with all the fads. But poverty-stricken youths and parents impoverished by numerous offspring must spend carefully and not very often, seeking compromises between cost, versatility, and durability.

With these questions in mind and a resolution to keep cool, the novice is ready to address the three categories of pack: The *rucksack* is mainly for day hikes but in larger models handles overnight gear decently. The *packframe and bag (external frame)* can do day duty well enough but is chiefly for overnight and longer. Occupying a shifty in-between position is a hybrid, more or less inaccurately but quite generally called the *softpack* (or *internal frame*), with distinctive virtues for special situations.

RUCKSACKS

Lumping together all the transport devices traditionally labeled "rucksacks" is as informative as calling all the passengers on the Ark, including Noah, "animals." The pussycat and the elephant are

Rucksacks on a day hike. That on the left can be used in a pinch for overnight trips, sleeping bag carried under the top flap. The one on the right, with a back-opening panel, has only enough capacity for day loads.

related, but which would a person put his howdah on? And which would he want in his easy chair? Scanning the hundreds of sizes and shapes, the novice may well ask, "Who needs *this* aggravation?"

Many hikers don't, content on every occasion with the packframe-bag. However, those who ease gradually into trail country by taking day walks before venturing overnight are wise to buy an inexpensive rucksack, delaying purchase of a packframe-bag until they've studied the choices. The rucksack has continuing utility when backpacking commences, such as for short explorations from a basecamp; to elimi-

Representative rucksacks. Left: *Two-compartment teardrop, a day pack for light loads.* Center: *Day pack for medium loads.* Right: *Pack for heavy day loads, also usable for overnight hikes.*

nate an extra item, it can do double duty as stuff bag for the sleeping bag. Moreover, rucksacks are no longer confined to trails but are put to good use in hitchhiking and cycling, in toting books around school and groceries home from the supermarket. Finally, the bigger designs may be quite rational alternatives to a packframe-bag for overnight hikes.

Rucksacks weigh from ¾ to 3 pounds, cost from $15 or less to $50 or more, have capacities from several hundred to a couple of thousand cubic inches. An eyeball inspection quickly separates those suitable for trips of various lengths.

DAY PACK

Pouches that fasten to the belt with loops and *belt bags (waist packs, fanny packs)* that strap around the waist supplement pockets for short walks, holding a few ounces to several pounds. Photographers like them for gadgetry.

The simplest true rucksacks, refined versions of the carriers peasants lugged up and down Alps for centuries, are bags, with one or two outside pockets, shoulder straps, and perhaps a waist strap *(belly band)* to control bouncing and flopping. The two basic shapes are the old *egg,* so called because that's what it looks like when stuffed full, and the newer and more popular *teardrop,* tapered to be larger at the bottom to put the weight more directly on the hips. With either shape the load hangs directly from the shoulders, painlessly enough if weight is under 10 or 15 pounds. As with all rucksacks, gear must be stowed thoughtfully to prevent sharp edges from stabbing the back; clothing or a sheet of foam rubber can provide padding. Such a pack weighs about ½–1¼ pounds and sells for $15 to $45.

DAY OR OVERNIGHT

The hiker who can't spend a day on the trail without three flower books and two cameras, spare clothing for a child, a nine-course lunch, or a watermelon should avoid a little, limp-cloth rucksack which, when crammed full, forms a hard round ball that beats a tattoo on the spine. A better choice is one of the larger models weighing 1½–2½ pounds, costing $30 to $65, and tolerable for up to 30 pounds—thus serving overnight as well as day jaunts.

Most packs in this size range have a flexible frame or internal stiffener to shape the bag and support the load. Rather than a simple belly band, there may be a *hip belt* (mesh or padded) that transfers weight from shoulders to hips.

Virtually all rucksacks of overnight capability are intended primarily for climbers and ski-mountaineers and thus have attachment points for ropes, ice axes, crampons, and skis. The humble hiker needn't be overawed; the points work just as nicely for strapping on sleeping bag, tent, fishing pole, and watermelon.

OTHER RUCKSACK DETAILS

Nylon has pretty well pushed *cotton* and *cotton canvas* out of the picture. A common nylon for lightweight sacks is 7-ounce (or 7.5) pack cloth, 400 denier yarn, 60×40 thread count (see "Fabrics" in Chapter 9)—very limp stuff with a pillowcase feel. For heavier-duty sacks the preferred nylon is 11-ounce (or 9, 11.5, or 12) cordura, 1,000 denier, 35×40—stiffer, more like cotton canvas. Some sacks, mostly of pack cloth, have cordura bottoms, perhaps double-layer, usually coated for water-repellency. *Leather* rucksacks are still seen on the trail, a quaint picture when combined with lederhosen, but due to the cow shortage are gone from the shops; leather is still used, though, for stress points, such as accessory patches for lashing gear on outside, and sometimes for the sack bottom.

Outside pockets, often omitted from climbers' rucksacks because they snag on rocks, are badly wanted by hikers. Some models have one pocket, others two, three, or four. Zipper closures are favored; straps and buckles are more foolproof but more trouble. *Detachable pockets* give versatility. *Inside pockets,* snagproof and weatherproof, are inconvenient.

The *main bag* may be divided in two vertical compartments to help distribute weight; large models may have a separate, outside-access bottom compartment. Stowing gear is simpler and carrying is more comfortable if there is a *back pad* of urethane foam to buffer the body from hard, sharp things. Most usually the bag is a *top-opener,* closed by zipper or drawstrings; in the latter case a *toggle,* a spring-loaded clamp, is handy for locking the strings. A *top flap* tied with a single strap and buckle or with a pair increases rain protection; an extra sweater or parka, or the sleeping bag, can be carried under the flap. There are two varieties of *panel-opener* rucksacks. A few have a *front-opener* bag, entry via a zipper next to the hiker's back. More common is the *back-opener,* with zippers permitting quick access to the entire interior; risk of zipper failure, a calamity beyond profanity and tears, is reduced

on back-openers that have *cinch straps* to compress the load and remove strain from zippers, as well as serving to carry ice ax, skis, or
tent poles.

Shoulder straps now are almost all padded nylon. Some are adjustable for length at the bottom only or, on fussy models, at the top too.

The *frame,* where it exists, may be an assembly (semirigid or flexible) of tubing, staves, or rods; of aluminum, steel, or fiberglass; forming an H, X, U, Y, or ladder. The frame may be adjustable by means
of mechanical fittings or by means of staves that bend to give a custom
fit. It may be detachable when a totally soft pack is desired; for
example, when stowing inside a packframe-bag.

SOFTPACKS (INTERNAL FRAME)

When in the course of mountaineering events the rucksack grew,
and grew, to hold the groceries and gear of multiday trips while
retaining the close-to-body fit needed for climbing crags and icicles
and swinging turns in powder snow, it outgrew the old name. "Expedition rucksack" was used, but the clientele for that sort of thing is
small—to a manufacturer, depressingly so.

Most commonly the genus is called "softpack," originally appropriate, at least in part, because among the early examples was the Jensen
"monocoque," totally frameless, gaining rigidity through being
loaded in just the right manner. However, the right manner is tricky,
especially stuffing the sleeping-bag compartment, and an improperly
loaded monocoque flops around like a sack of potatoes. The true
believers being depressingly few, most manufacturers moved on.

The designation "internal frame" is gaining favor because the leading designs now are simply overgrown rucksacks with flexible internal
frames of plastic or aluminum or wood or fiberglass, usually in a
parallel or X configuration, of the same sorts found in smaller rucksacks but stronger. *Suspension systems* are more elaborate, of the sorts
found on packframes-bags. One *bag* style is a "gunnysack with shoulder straps," a single-compartment "garbage can." Another is the
"column" with two or more compartments. Materials and special
features are those of rucksacks—and/or packframes-bags. Many have

Representative soft (internal-frame) packs. Left: *Single-compartment "garbage can."* Right: *"Column" design with two compartments, the upper vertically divided, the bottom holding the sleeping bag.*

all-around compression straps to crush the load for compactness; they also serve as lashings for ice axes, tent poles, wands, and the like. Many also have *side compression straps* to narrow the pack profile, for shuffling along those 2-inch ledges.

The demand for the hybrid was once mainly met by imports, notably the Millet from France, but as the dollar plummets the price of foreign gear rockets. American manufacturers are filling the gap handsomely—virtually everyone in the pack business has a "soft" or "internal frame" model, presenting a range of alternatives widely various and wildly ingenious. Capacities extend from 3,000 cubic inches to more than 5,000, weights from about 3 pounds to 4½, prices from $70 to $120.

WHO NEEDS A HYBRID?

The chief disciples of the whatever-you-call-it are climbers and ski-mountaineers. However, among other fans are hikers fond of leaving trails to bull through brush, hop-skip around moraines and talus, and kick steps up and glissade down steep snow. Some models comfortably carry 50 pounds, as much as most people care to carry anytime, anywhere. Unlike packframes-bags that totter high and unstable above the shoulders and have tentacles that reach out and clutch bushes and rocks, the hybrid puts the center of gravity low and snugly against the back, with a "part-of-the-body" feel. Never as the skier leans into a turn does the surly stone threaten to lurch off in another direction.

Even for ordinary trails the genus has virtues. It's versatile, performing well in a broad spectrum of terrains. It serves as a rucksack for day trips from a basecamp. Finally, of interest to hikers who travel to trailheads by airplane or bus or train, it's much more difficult for professional baggage-manglers to destroy.

Perhaps the question should be turned around—who needs anything *except* a hybrid? Well, the story has another side. It's "fussier" than the packframe-bag, demanding more attention as to how gear is stowed. Some models can't cope decently with more than 40 pounds, and none has the capacity of a sturdy packframe-bag to handle 60 or 70 pounds, even 100. And in hot weather the snug fit makes a sweaty back. Finally, the style is rather new, and though abundantly proven for some uses, for others must be tried out a few more years on the trails.

PACKFRAME AND BAG: MINUTE DETAILS OF CONSTRUCTION

Man really is not well designed to walk on his hind legs at all, and placing a heavy weight atop the precariously erect skeleton definitely goes against nature. Yet for a very long time man has been doing so and the history of packing would in itself make a book—the basket or pot carried on the head, the pole balanced on the shoulder by a load at either end, the blanket roll slung over one shoulder and tied on the opposite hip—these are only a few of the ways man has turned himself into a donkey (another poor beast never intended to carry burdens).

Over the centuries and the miles, many a suffering soul has mused on alternatives. Among the designs that evolved in America before

World War II were the "dish rack" and the Ome Daiber "string pack"; most widely acclaimed was the Trapper Nelson, with a wood frame somewhat contoured to the body in the horizontal though not the vertical, a canvas back, and a canvas bag attached to the frame by steel wires connecting eyelet screws in the frame to grommets in the bag. The Trapper, good enough to go to Minya Konka in 1932, then the highest summit attained by Americans, lives on, as do other relics, but mainly in the basements of broken-down sentimentalists.

However, let not the past be so lightly dismissed. The returns of winter underwear and passenger trains and mulching are in sight and with them may come other energy-efficient revivals. The Pack Basket, called "the original backpack," is wickerwork, weighing just over 3 pounds and costing $25; woodcrafter books give instructions for improvising the like by weaving willow shoots and twisting cedar bark. *Make It and Take It,* by Russ Mohney, tells how to build a wooden pack at home, in a few hours for several dollars, as did whole troops of Boy Scouts in the 1930s. For esthetic ecstasy, though, look to the Segen Pack of laminated ash-mahogany, leather, wool felt, and canvas duck—virtually nothing to give aid and comfort to OPEC—and weighing 5¾ pounds. However, being handmade in limited quantities for connoisseurs it currently sells for $165. That may be the future but it's not the past.

Perhaps the 1930s-era Bergan rucksack (actually a packframe) with

a tubular steel frame started the trend to metal, especially when the U.S. Army adaptation flooded American trails in the great age of World War II surplus. Frames of tubular aluminum began to appear, lighter than steel but still not compromising much with the human back, and with a tendency to fall apart when sneezed at, as they frequently were. Then Kelty and other pioneers inaugurated modern times and the continuing quest for the Grail.

A time may come when field-testing by millions of hikers will have sorted out and reduced options. But the same thought was expressed in the first edition of this book in 1972, and packframes and bags still are in flux, and the hiker still may develop a hostility toward manufacturers and their picky-picky tinkering. (Spend a small fortune for a beauty; go forth from the shop and onto the trail in bliss; revisit the shop a year later and find that the design has been improved; become discontented and resentful.) However, he should thank them even when they confuse and frustrate him; they have provided comfort inconceivable to oldtimers bent over under the torture racks they accepted as just punishment for sinful lives.

The following oversimplified and incomplete review of the materials and constructions of contemporary external packframes and bags won't satisfy the deep student. But it may be dangerous to the beginner, who when his mind starts going numb should skip to the next section, on how to choose a packframe and bag.

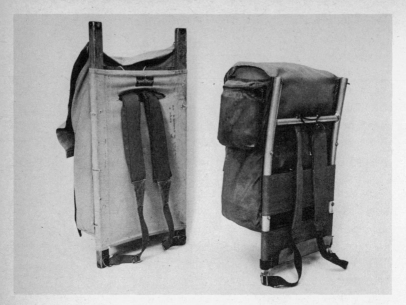

Nostalgia. Left: *The most famous of the old wood-frame packs, the Trapper Nelson.* Right: *An early aluminum-frame pack, Dick Kelty's first model.*

THE EXTERNAL PACKFRAME

The Skeleton

The dominant external frame is the *aluminum S-ladder.* However, other materials compete, and other letters of the alphabet, too.

The usual frame material is high-strength *aluminum alloy tubes,* either "aircraft" quality or the cheaper but adequately sturdy "furniture" grade. Some frames (Kelty, for example) are quite rigid. Others (Jansport, for example) are of thinner tubing with thicker walls, strong but flexing with the body. Both approaches work fine. Experiments with *molded plastic* have resulted in frames (Coleman Peak I, for example, using polypropylene) strong enough but requiring the owner to get used to the sensation of carrying wet spaghetti; others (Alpine Designs' Prospector and Bighorn, for

174

example, using polyvinyl chloride) are somewhat less flexible.

The two most common frame patterns are (1) an *H,* or *"ladder,"* in which the outside members are separate pieces and (2) an *upright or inverted U* formed by bending a single tube; there is also (3) a *figure-8.* To keep weight closer to the body's center of gravity, in the vertical dimension the frame is contoured to the back with either a moderate or an exaggerated bend, a sort of *flattened S* approximating the profile of the upper torso; on some the lower portion sweeps sharply forward to bring weight more directly over the body axis.

Three to five horizontal *crossbars* (in a U design the outside member itself makes one of the crossbars) are curved to fit back contours. They give rigidity yet permit enough flexibility to absorb shocks. Most models can be lengthened at the top with a *frame extension* for very tall loads. Some frames have a *V-truss reinforcement* between the upper sides, particularly good for added strength when the extension is used.

The most frequently used method of joining metal members is *welding* (heliarc, tungsten arc), generally considered the strongest. *Brazed* frames are inexpensive and quite sturdy if carefully made. Several manufacturers use *epoxy* bonding, declaring it stronger than welding, a claim not unanimously accepted. A number of designs dispense with permanent joints in favor of plastic or metal *couplings* (or *bolts* or *screws*), in theory not as rigid as welding but in practice just as satisfactory and offering advantages of adjustability. Indeed, some manufacturers deny that rigidity equals strength; their coupled-together frames flex considerably, resisting stress dynamically. Care in construction matters more than the method; welds can break and couplings slip; of course, the more parts to a frame, the more the cost.

Some frames are *adjustable,* either by using couplings that let the crossbars be moved or by telescoping the outside members; frame length and packbag position can be varied to suit bodies of different dimensions and loads of different weights. Manufacturers whose frames are nonadjustable ordinarily compensate by offering two to four sizes.

Now for something completely different. The S frame accounts for close to 100 percent of sales, meaning that's what the people like—most of them. However, there is a challenger, the *hipwrap (hiploader, hiphugger, wraparound)*, with two padded arms jutting forward from the bottom; when drawn tight by the belt, they tightly hug the hips. Derived from a nineteenth-century patent by Henry Merriam that long languished in obscurity, only recently has the concept been refined (in the Alpenlite, for example). Enthusiasts rave that the hip-wrap is the greatest advance since the Kelty, is the first *true* hip-carry pack. Critics just rave.

Proponents concede that hiphugging makes the ride hot and sweaty and that the pack is so awkward in brush and tippy when teetering over rockslides that it never should leave trails. Still, many say no S frame ever gave them peace, never were they happy until the hip-wrap. Among the convinced are women whose upper torsos are too narrow to cope with ordinary frames, requiring them to support the load on hip bones; men with narrow backs and definite hip platforms; and people with bad backs that won't tolerate an S frame. Finally, some iron men swear there's nothing like it for loads in the 80- and 100-pound class. But be warned: for every hiker who reports joy in a hipwrap, another moans a tale of unmingled woe. A last nitpick: those jutting arms are as awkward in car trunks as they are in jungles; a Saab that easily holds four loaded Keltys can manage only one hipwrap; the roof rack may be a mandatory accessory.

Recalling that not so many years ago the Trapper Nelson gang was sneering at Dick Kelty, contemporary pioneers require at least a nod. To bring the load closer to the body in the manner of the hybrid discussed earlier, a few designs (Cannondale, for example) have a *rigid internal frame,* not so radical an idea but with too limited a trail record to judge. Considerably more interesting is the Bal-Pak, the inspiration of a man whose back was a total wreck; a sort of birdcage arches over the shoulders, carrying half the load in back, half in front. The Modular-Pak breaks into components which serve as tent poles, camp seat or toilet, stretcher, or ladder. In a similar design two packframes can be attached to a wheel (part of the pack-age) as a cart for hauling a deer out of the wilds. Or maybe gold and precious jewels.

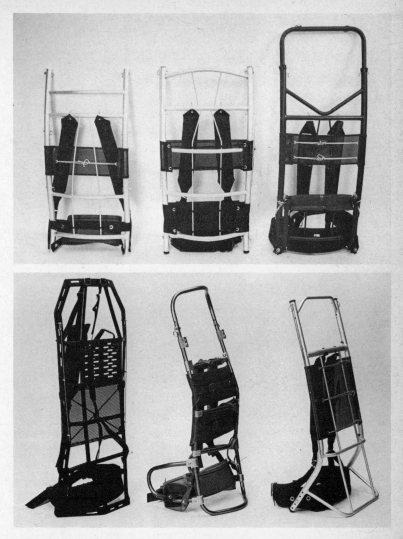

Representative pack frames. Top: *Examples of aluminum S-ladder frames. The one on the right has a V-truss reinforcement and the frame extension is extended.* Bottom: *Some of the newer designs. On the left, a molded plastic frame. In the middle, a hipwrap with arms that hug the hips. On the right, a frame swept sharply forward at the bottom to bring weight close to hips.*

HIP BELT

The key component of the modern pack, the major element of the system suspending the pack skeleton from the body, is the hip belt, hailed as the most revolutionary step in recorded history toward transforming suffering humans into happy asses.

Olden-day packs (Trapper Nelson) were "shoulder carry"; the frame was suspended solely from shoulders, and when these sagged, the whimpering hiker leaned forward to shift weight directly onto the back; in the final extremity he cupped hands under the frame horns and lifted—until his arms went dead.

Dick Kelty, while advancing from old materials and patterns toward something new, didn't immediately renounce the recourse to hands—his first models had lower horns for that specific purpose. He saw the light only when a friend who was trying a pack caught his attention by yelling, "Hey Dick—look—*no hands!*" The friend had stuck the horns in the back pockets of his pants. And so ended the Dark Ages.

The design pioneered by Kelty and Camp Trails and others lets shoulders and back do a decent share of the work but employs the hip belt to place much of the weight on the hips—60–75 percent claim the theoreticians, perhaps 30–50 percent say skeptics; certainly the percentage varies from one model to another and with different adjustments of belt and shoulder straps. The load is carried high, in a vertical line parallel to the body axis; weight is transmitted through the frame to the hip belt, from there to the strong muscles of the hip area, and thence to the sturdy legs. With this "hip-carry" system, strain is lessened on shoulders and back and the hiker walks upright rather than in the old Trapper Nelson crouch.

The original simple belt—two webbing straps about 2 inches wide buckling in front of the waist—is now uncommon. Nearly all hikers demand a *padded hip belt (wraparound* or *full-circle belt)* 4–5 inches wide and extending all around the body. It may or may not be adjustable up and down.

A *quick-release buckle* of one type or another is very convenient at

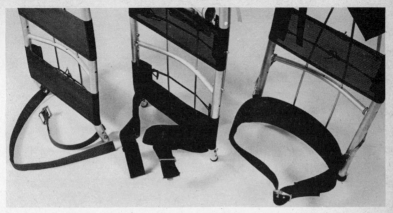

Hip belts. Left: *Simple web belt, now rare.* Center: *Padded belt combined with padded lower backband.* Right: *Padded wraparound belt.*

rest stops, but more than that, is an important safety device. The belt must be completely unbuckled before fording streams, walking logs, or engaging in similar maneuvers that may go wrong and require the pack to be jettisoned in a hurry. Lacking the quick-release, a hiker may not want to fiddle with the belt, decide to take a chance, and if he trips and falls off the log, there he goes, bouncing down the river tied to his stone.

No dogma goes unchallenged. There are burly, broad-shouldered hikers so strong-backed they don't need the hip belt, despise its confinement, and never use it, thus converting modern hip-carrier packs to old-style shoulder-carriers. However, most hikers fully exploit the belt by keeping it tight; if a pack is properly adjusted to put weight on hips, a thumb can easily be slid between shoulder strap and shoulder.

Shoulder Straps

The modern pack hasn't put shoulders on full retirement—they still carry a quarter to half or more of the weight. In portions bearing on the body, the straps are 2–3 inches wide with built-in padding of heavy, dense latex or urethane foam, extending far enough down so the nylon webbing of the lower straps doesn't bite tender underarms.

179

SUNDAY

MONDAY

Two methods, both effective, suspend the pack skeleton from shoulders. The strap tops may be attached to a *shoulder-level crossbar.* There may be two or more sets of attachment points so straps can be moved closer together or farther apart to suit shoulder width. The crossbar may be adjustable up or down. Strap length may be adjusted by a single pair of buckles or two pair.

In the *yoke,* less common, the straps curve over the shoulders, cross in back, and fasten to the frame bottom. Another strap connects

180

shoulder-pad tops to a shoulder-level crossbar. Thus the upper frame is pulled closer to the body. The yoke is said to (1) provide greater stability with less constriction of shoulders and upper torso, and (2) put more weight on shoulders.

Backband

Over the years the pack skeleton has been kept from the body in many ways (upper and lower backband, full-length panel) with many materials (canvas, cords, webbing padded or unpadded). In the method currently dominant, the padded hip belt forms the lower bearing surface and above that is a single backband, usually of nylon mesh, in some models adjustable up or down. Knotted cords or turn-buckles maintain tension in the band, which must be kept taut to prevent crossbars from pressing the flesh.

THE BAG

Nylon has become the standard bag material, either 7-ounce (or thereabouts) *pack cloth* or 11-ounce (or thereabouts) *cordura,* which looks tougher but isn't, though it does have more "body," liked by hikers who hate limp things. Though both fabrics are coated to be water-repellent, any pack dropped in a lake or carried in a Northwest summer rain will let water in; in sopping weather the pack should be protected by an impervious *rain cover,* either an article made for that purpose or a poncho or a sheet of plastic.

A bag may have a *reinforced bottom,* perhaps of leather or heavy-coated nylon. It may have *breathable cloth* next to the hiker's back to reduce sweating. The best bags are *reinforced at all stress points* and are *double-* or *triple-stitched* throughout with synthetic thread, 8–10 stitches per inch, the seams kept away from fabric edges to avoid fraying, and *lock-stitched* (back-stitched, back-tacked, bar-tacked) at ends to prevent unraveling. Leather or nylon *lash points* may be provided for tying gear to the exterior.

The more *zippers* on a bag, the more important that they be rugged and dependable (see "Fabrics" in Chapter 9), with large, easy-to-operate pulls and covered by *rain flaps* to shed water.

Bags have been connected to frames by various devices: bag sleeves that slip over the frame's upper horns; bag snaps that fit on frame-mounted studs; bag bolts that screw into nut plates on the frame. However, almost universal now is the *clevis pin,* a stud that goes through a grommet in the bag, then through a hole in the frame, and is held in place by a split lock ring or key wire. Taping the rings or wires keeps them from falling out, which they tend to do when damaged; the smart hiker has spare sets of pins and rings in his repair kit.

An *expedition* bag extending the *full length of the frame* is preferred by sloppy hikers whose method of "planning" gear and food is to throw stuff in until there seems to be enough. The average backpacker's choice is a bag extending *two thirds of the frame length;* sleeping bag and pad are carried outside, strapped to the frame bottom. (A newer design has an integral bottom compartment for the sleeping bag.) Some frame models permit the two-thirds-length bag to be placed in any of several positions—at the frame top normally, or at the bottom to keep weight low for better balance in ticklish terrain.

The most popular bag is a *top-opener,* with a metal *hold-open frame* to maintain the bag profile or a loose top closed by drawstrings. Over the top goes a *storm flap* tied to the lower bag by straps and buckles or cords and toggles; tent or tarp may be carried under the flap.

A top-opener may be *undivided,* the interior a single large cavity; perhaps one hiker in five favors this style for the general ease of stowing gear, especially bulky or long items. The other four like the neat organization allowed by a *compartmented* bag and don't mind fiddling around to fit in gear of awkward dimensions. The upper compartment is accessible via the open top, the lower via a zipper.

With a top-opener the hiker invariably discovers that any article he wants is at the bottom of the bag; he gropes and mutters and finally dumps the whole mess on the ground. (This can be avoided, however, by organizing contents into large plastic bags or nylon stuff bags, labeled to tell what's in each.) A *panel-opener* (also called a *back-opener,* and also a *front-opener,* indicating a disturbing confusion in some circles) eliminates exasperation, at a price. If there are three to five *horizontally-layered compartments,* each item always is in its assigned spot. However, the cubbyholes may be so small that tent poles have to be lashed outside and the watermelon carried in the arms. If there is a *single compartment* zippered on three sides, never is a frustrating search required—lay the pack down, zip-zip, and everything is in plain view. Of course, if the ground is black muck, laying the pack down is not neat. Moreover, when the bag is overstuffed the zippers jam; should they fail, let passers-by guard their ears; *compression straps* cinching across the back of the bag press the load closer to the body and take strain from zippers, lessening the worry.

Whether top-opener or back-opener, there usually is provision, by a frame extension or add-on crossbar and/or lash points on the bag, for transporting equipment that can't be crammed inside, perhaps a tent or a duffle bag holding food or miscellany. The great advantage of a top-opener is that "overloads" easily can be piled on top, snugged down by the storm flap; with a panel-opener the extra gear may have to be tied and draped all over the outside.

Outside *pockets,* ordinarily zippered, range from none to nine, possibly including a map pocket in the storm flap. Extra pockets may be purchased and sewed to the bag or, in designs with proper attachment points, clipped on.

STUFF BAG

With the most-favored pack-bag style, extending two thirds the length of the frame, the sleeping bag and perhaps sleeping pad normally are lashed to the bottom of the frame. These being light in comparison with dense food and stoves and cameras, the method helps keep weight high on the body.

Particularly in wet climates and in brush or rough terrain, the sleeping bag should be stowed in a stuff bag. The best for all purposes is *waterproof nylon,* with a drawstring closure and a weather flap to cover the opening; weight, about 5 ounces. A laminated *polyethylene* stuff bag, 1 to 5¼ ounces, is less practical because of its tendency to snag and tear but serves well inside the pack bag, where

Packbags for very bulky loads. Left: *Full-length "expedition" bag, two compartments, the lower for the sleeping bag, the upper undivided, top-opening. More gear can be piled on top, held by the top flap.* Right: *Two-thirds-length bag, undivided, with six outside pockets. More gear can be piled on top by use of the extension frame (hidden in this photo). Still more can be lashed to the exterior attachment points.*

one may also use light nylon stuff bags, about 1–1½ ounces, or *poly bags* in various sizes weighing a fraction of an ounce. A *compressor* stuff bag has an outer cinching device to facilitate squeezing to tiny size.

The stuff bag is attached to the packframe by two (not one) straps with buckles, 36–40 inches long (or longer if tarp, poncho, or whatever also is to be carried here), wrapped *around* the two lower horizontal frame bars and *outside* the two vertical center bars. Elastic shock cords are not recommended; they may catch on brush or rocks and pull away from the pack, possibly letting the stuff bag escape and certainly throwing the hiker off balance.

Representative two-thirds-length packbags. Top left: *Divided bag, main compartment top-opening with hold-open frame, lower compartment zippered; five outside pockets; space for sleeping bag below the bag.* Top right: *Undivided bag, access via both top and zippered panel.* Bottom: *Panel-opening bags, upper and lower zippered compartments, with compression straps.*

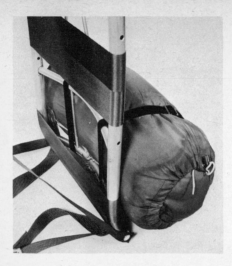

Attachment of sleeping-bag stuff bag to frame with two straps.

CHOOSING A PACKFRAME AND BAG

The waters now thoroughly muddied, time for an important announcement: despite the array of options, it's hard to go far wrong in choosing a packframe and bag from the stock of a reputable outfitter. There is not, for each person, one and only one pack exactly right with all others hopelessly wrong.

The years of inventing and field-testing and tinkering have established a standard, upheld by all the principal manufacturers whatever variant paths they have taken toward the Grail, that is very high indeed. Some trail veterans become fussy about straps and pads and zippers and toggles, and even novices are often fascinated by intricacies of compartment design and stitching. However, the ordinary hiker can be perfectly happy with any of the excellent models on the market.

What is the most back-easing *frame style*? Who knows? Bodies are infinitely varied and so are opinions. A person with an "average" body (whatever that is) probably mates as well with one standard design as another. Those with deviant bodies (short torsos, narrow shoulders, thinly covered bones) may wish to experiment with the intricate models; they do well to seek the counsel of experienced hikers of similar build or a backpacking shop clerk who seems to know what he or she is talking about. (Note the "she": having a different skeletal structure than men, women may require a different frame design and can be led astray buying a pack solely on the advice of men.)

More critical than style is *frame size*, and here it must be stressed that a person's height is less relevant than the length of his or her torso. As discussed below, ideally the novice should spend an hour or two in a shop, marching up and down the aisles wearing various packs—loaded, or nothing is learned. If a shop with rental service is handy, much more instructive is taking several packs out on the trail before purchase. Adjustable models should be tested with crossbars, backbands, and shoulder straps in a number of positions. Nonadjustable models usually come in two to four sizes; more than one should be tried.

Every *bag size* on the market is adequate for a weekend, or for a week if outfit and commissary are planned precisely. However, a lot of bags are too skimpy for 10-day trips in rough and stormy wilder-

A family on the trail for an overnight or longer hike. Father, son, and daughter carry various representative packframe-bags in sizes large to small. Mother hauls the baby, her gear on the other backs.

nesses which demand considerable bad-weather and emergency gear. The little tiny bags that look so chic in the shop may be dandy for travels in benign meadowlands but are infernal nuisances in a trackless alder bottom, where the gear lashed and draped all over the outside tangles constantly with bushes.

A pack is useless in itself, providing neither shelter, calories, nor entertainment, so *weight* is a consideration. However, packs all weigh about the same, between 3 and 5 pounds, 4 the average. Those on the low side (the range drops to 2 pounds) require extra careful handling; those on the high side (the range rises to 6 pounds) may be sturdy or accessory-cluttered beyond any normal requirement.

Doubtless a majority of novices select the first pack largely on the basis of *price*. At any shop of sound reputation the rule is you pretty much get what you pay for. Due to economies of scale a best-selling pack costs less than a slow mover of equal value; generally, though, price reflects (1) quality of materials and care of manufacture, factors which determine durability, and (2) the number of special conveniences, each of which adds expense. The novice must ask: "How much durability and convenience do I really need? And how much can I afford?" The hiker whose rambles are limited to trails in Appalachian forests or High Sierra meadows needs less pack than the masochist plunging into British Columbia jungles or slogging Yukon glaciers.

FOR THE DESERVING POOR (UNDER $50)

With all due respect to your friendly neighborhood Handy Dandy Super-Thrifty Discount Drugs and Surplus, packs sold there must be viewed with suspicion. Simply to look at the $5 "Scout-type" pack sends shooting pains up and down the spine. One approaches a $10 "cruiser-style" pack in fear and trembling. "Backpack paralysis" is not a joke but a recognized medical problem, also called "rucksack palsy," particularly common among growing boys and girls saddled with cheap and cruel packs. However, crippling is unlikely on short trips. Never forget, through all the Dark Ages, packs no better were carried by generations of hikers and few are actually in traction. On the bottom rung of the price ladder, though, a youth (or parent) would do better to buy Mohney's book and make a pack in the basement workshop.

A $20–$40 "overnight" rucksack, discussed earlier, bridges the transition from day hikes to weekend experiments.

Not so prominently as in the early 1970s, but still occasionally, a mass-merchandiser advertises Asian imports which on quick scan appear identical to packs costing much more. Why spend a bundle, wonders the novice, when here is a $40 Kelty? No reason at all if one plans merely a few lightly loaded (under 30 pounds) hikes a summer and gives tender treatment and carries a repair kit of wire and cord.

FOR THE THRIFTY WORKING CLASS ($50–$90)

Once upon a time the strata of pack society were distinct and widely separated. Way down there was the Trapper Nelson. Way up there was the Kelty. Lonesome in the middle, lacking many niceties of the latter but a quantum leap above the former was the REI Cruiser, considered good enough in 1963 for Jim Whittaker to carry to the summit of Everest, still the highest mountain climbed by Americans.

However, with passing years has come a leveling—upwards. Costs of material, energy, and labor have so swollen the irreducible expense of constructing any pack whatsoever as to pretty well squeeze out "economy" models. Let not another factor be overlooked: the further the Trapper recedes in ancient history, the higher the expectations of hikers rise, and fewer are content with much less than the best.

Sum it up as inflation—of everything. Even the REI Cruiser, which began life in the 1950s around $20, enters the 1980s (in a fancier incarnation, to be sure) at $50–$70, depending on frame size and bag style. Among other large suppliers, Camp Ways starts its line under $50 and goes up to $75; Eastern Mountain Sports begins at $55; Camp Trails, in the $70 range; Coleman, with the Peak I, $75; and Alpenlite, with the Pac Eze, nudging above $80.

But then, Kelty lives here too—the Mountaineer frame combined with various bags sells from $83 to $89. No longer is there a gap between the classes, which now merge indistinguishably.

Before climbing the imaginary step to the next class, mention must be made of a unique pack for special purposes, the Camp Trails Freighter, an unadorned frame (no bag), heavy-duty, reinforced with V-truss, with many lash points, designed for heavy, odd-shaped loads, such as outboard motor, half a moose, crate of watermelons.

FOR THE GREAT MIDDLE CLASS ($90 AND UP)

The $90 to $110 range covers the majority of packframe-bag sales, and if that dazes a Rip Van Winkle awaking from dreams of the 1950s, in terms of constant dollars the beautiful—and economically mass-produced—packs of today often cost less than the old homelies of yesteryear. In fact, many a Rip, after treatment for future shock, aspires still higher, to the regal models in the $150 range and above, and finds them bargains.

Scores of manufacturers are active and their entries run in the hundreds. Every year they improve old models and invent new designs. Kelty, of course, is synonymous with quality; indeed, "kelty" has entered the language as denoting *any* modern packframe-bag, and in some foreign nations young American tourists with long hair and little cash are called (with a scowl) "kelties." While honor is due the pioneer, justice requires acknowledgment of the host of other manufacturers offering superb packs. Some of the names a hiker is most likely to run across in this range: A-16, Alpenlite, Alpine Designs,

Camp Trails, Eastern Mountain Sports, Eddie Bauer, Gerry, Himalayan, Hine/Snowbridge, Holubar, Jansport, Kelty (Massif frame combined with any of several bags), Mountain Equipment, North Face, REI, Stephenson's Warmlite, Sunbird, Synergy Works, Trailwise, Universal Field, and Wilderness Experience. But there are others. And more every year.

It's folly to wrangle over which are best, that being a matter of personal opinion, even if dressed up as an "objective rating" by a consumers' organization. A week or two of examination by a half-dozen experts is no substitute for being hauled a million miles by thousands of assorted hikers, average, un-average, and weird. A fair rule is that if a model has been around a few years, it has met the test of the trails with at least passing marks. If brand-new, it may still be worthy, though it may have to wait awhile for wide approval.

Perhaps a majority of hikers, if they continue backpacking long enough, eventually buy the very best pack they can afford, feeling that over the long run—which with careful choice can be a lifetime—the price of contentment will be cheap. Having made a choice, they may become fanatic loyalists, exalting their mate above every competitor. Or they may go through life flirting with each pretty face.

FOR SMALL ADULTS—AND FOR CHILDREN

Hikers shorter than 5 feet or so—or somewhat taller with unusual torsos—may need to try other models than the standard.

The Kelty S-T-R-E-T-C-H packs have adjustable, telescoping frames excellent for people who change size with the years; the 4-C, for example, fits those between 4 and 5 feet tall. Weight is less than 2½ pounds, cost about $45. The Jansport Mini-Rover, for even smaller folk, weighs 1¾ pounds, costs about $30; three height adjustments let the pack grow with the owner. Comparable is the Camp Trails Compact I, about 2 pounds, $30; a pin-spacer kit allows two additional shoulder-strap adjustments. The small packs usually lack hip belts, because little kids usually lack hips.

No packframe-bag is small enough for a child under a certain age (rather, below a certain height). Nevertheless, any child being raised as a backpacker, either because the parents think it's good for him or because they can't afford baby-sitters, should be introduced to load-carrying almost as soon as he ceases being a load to be carried. Besides, at this age the kid often demands a pack, especially if an elder sibling has one; too late the young fool learns it's not a toy. The first expedient may be a rucksack from the parents' free and simple past; straps can be shortened to keep the bag from dragging. If such is not available, there are tiny rucksacks, weighing less than ½ pound, costing less than $10, that hold a sweater and a teddy bear and a box of animal crackers.

FOR CARRYING CHILDREN

Any failure or misuse of any product for children triggers lawsuits and congressional investigations, and manufacturers thus tend to be scared out of the field by insurance premiums and notoriety. Unfortunately, therefore, the choice of child carriers is restricted—and varies from year to year as this or that model is yanked from the market in fright. However, several excellent offerings currently are available.

Best for the early days is a "soft" baby carrier. An example is the Snugli, a frameless "sack with straps" ingeniously adaptable for slinging in front (so the babe can nurse or wave its hands in Mommy's face, or so Mommy can carry a rucksack on her back) or in back (so babe can tangle Mommy's hair, or so Mommy can take pictures of the flowers). The corduroy fabric is machine-washable; tucks and darts permit expansion to accommodate growth. Weight is 1¼ pounds, price about $45.

When the child becomes a real lump, 20 pounds or so, it's time to switch to a carrier with a lightweight aluminum frame. An example is the Gerry Kiddie Pack. The tot rides on the adult's back, facing forward so as not to feel lonesome. Space under the seat holds baby-type gear or even a sleeping bag. The frame sits on the ground as a stable stand. Weight is under 2 pounds, price about $25.

At the awkward age when the child is a crushing burden (30 wiggling, squirming pounds weigh more than 60 that ride quietly), yet toddles too slowly for the family to cover many miles, recourse may be made to a regular pack, left empty and with the Gerry lashed on. An alternative is the Antelope, a standard packframe-with-carrier, priced about $60, that accommodates the child and some gear; when not needed for human cargo, a standard bag, $25, can be attached.

FITTING AND USING THE PACKFRAME-BAG

A person buying a pack unaided by an experienced clerk or friend should proceed as follows: Load about 20 pounds in the bag to prevent it from "floating." Don the pack. If the suspension is from the crossbar, adjust shoulder straps so the crossbar is level with the shoulder tops. Fasten the hip belt around the upper, curved part of the hip bone. While doing this, hunch shoulders; upon unhunching, pack weight should have settled on the hips. The pack is a good fit if, with hip belt in proper position, shoulder straps run almost horizontal from crossbar over the shoulders. If they angle sharply downward, the frame is too short; if sharply upward, too long. (Ignore a minor angle.) If trying all sizes and adjustments of one model fails, try another. Hikers with "average" backs may quickly find a perfect fit. Others may seriously consider switching to suitcases.

With a yoke suspension the fit is proper when, with hip belt in place, there is no space under the straps where they cross the shoulders. Fitting a hipwrap frame is more complex than an S, requiring consideration not only of the vertical distances but the width between hip bars.

Once on the trail, experiment with adjustable components (shoulder straps, backbands, hip belt) to find the most comfortable fit.

Any packframe, no matter how sturdy, can be broken; never drop a loaded pack, especially on rocks—always lower it gently. Keep the pack away from fire or excessive heat. In camp, remove all food to disinterest animals, both mouse-type nibblers and bear-type slashers.

Carry a repair kit of spare clevis pins and locking wires (or whatever is suited to the particular packframe-bag) and nylon cord for emergency lashings in the rare case of the frame failing at a joint or the bag ripping.

In loading the bag, locate heavy items close to the back and up high

—a process simplified by compartments. Keep metal objects away from the back; they may rub against the frame and wear holes in the bag. In wet climates place all gear in waterproof nylon or poly bags so that if water finds an entry it doesn't soak the entire contents; be especially sure to put wet clothing in poly bags before stowing inside.

The past lives. In 1979 Trudy and Jack Turner carry groceries to their home deep in Canadian wildwoods using home-made wooden packs of two different styles, both ancient. And cheap.

11:

MANY a backpacker with still a few miles in his legs remembers how poignant the sunsets of yesteryear were—not as symbols of the death of day, but as reminders that soon the hour would come to leave the campfire and begin the night-long ordeal. To be sure, there were rumors of better equipment owned by the immensely wealthy, but the ordinary hiker carried a rectangular wool or kapok sleeping bag that weighed a large part of a ton and never kept out the chill of a summer night in alpine meadows. At that he felt luckier than pals who couldn't afford a bag and wrapped up in blankets. Boy Scout troops of the 1930s often ended by morning as a circle of bodies tightly coiled around a fire.

The World War II surplus bonanza introduced a whole generation of low-income Americans to the down sleeping bag, formerly the raiment of princes and magnates and climbers, and to the revelation that night need not be miserable.

Reactionary veterans scorn what has happened since. They feel today's youth is robbed of the full wilderness experience, that man ought to shiver at night for the good of his soul. But as has been said, "The past is a foreign country: they do things differently there." The backpacker now accepts as inalienable his right to sleep warm, and with modern bags there's no reason he shouldn't, most of the time, if he chooses right.

There, again, is the rub. The sleeping bag is a garment worn by a hiker roughly a third of his trail life and must be bought with care. But a single shop may stock a dozen or more styles and the offerings of American outfitters run in the hundreds. The beginner, having wrestled with boots, then a pack, now must face a third agonizing decision. Candidly, though, it's not as complicated as this chapter may suggest.

First, for any average person planning ordinary spring-to-fall backpacking, many different bags of various designs and prices will serve perfectly well. Were a beginner to walk in a shop blindfolded and grab a bag at random, the odds are it would do the job.

Second, many bags can be ruled out simply on the basis of weight.

The person of average size and metabolism should sleep warm, in typical trail conditions, in a bag weighing less than 5 pounds and perhaps as little as 3. Bags of more than 5 pounds are designed for car-camping or high mountaineering (or winter) and should be ignored.

Third, it is not necessary to wipe out the family fortune for a night's sleep. There are luxury bags offering lavish refinements in every detail but also economy bags that never would win blue ribbons, yet provide comfort enough at reasonable prices.

Fourth, beware of strangers bearing gifts. Mass-merchandisers sometimes advertise bags at astonishing prices. The bargains may or may not be genuine; the beginner, unless guided by an experienced friend or unless the retailer has a good reputation, has no way of knowing.

So much for preface. Time now to dig into the guts of the bag. As in previous chapters, the novice may wish to skip the following section on intimate details and proceed directly to the section on how to select a bag. No hard feelings.

ANATOMY OF THE SLEEPING BAG

A sleeping bag is an article of clothing that retains body-generated heat by trapping innumerable tiny pockets of dead air. Not the components of the bag themselves but rather the air (a poor conductor and thus a good insulator) provides a barrier between the hot body and the cold, cold world.

The warmth of a bag is determined by several factors: (1) the kind and amount of insulating material—down or polyester; (2) the structure—the shape of the bag and the manner in which insulating material is compartmented; (3) the bag closure—by zippers and drawstrings; and (4) to a lesser extent, covers and liners.

INSULATING MATERIAL (FILLER)

Many a material has been used in the past as sleeping-bag filler, and as in the case of wool and kapok, abandoned. Very likely new materials will be introduced in future, perhaps better than any now known. Of those currently common, polyester and down are overwhelmingly dominant.

Polyester

Polyester, a synthetic fiber, has long been a sleeping-bag filler but only in the early 1970s, with introduction of a second-generation form, began gaining the popularity that by the late 1970s saw it oust down from three decades of leadership.

A number of virtues are claimed for the new champion: (1) Unlike down, which, once soaking wet, doesn't dry completely for days, the fiber absorbs less than 1 percent of water by weight. Crawl into a wet bag at night and by morning it will be dry from body heat alone. (2) Unlike down, which clumps up, flattens out, and loses much loft in humid conditions and 80 percent when saturated, even if drenched the fiber loses only about 5 percent of its loft. Wring out a sopping bag, shake it vigorously, snuggle in and be warm. (3) Unlike down, which flattens to zero loft under the sleeper, the fiber resists compression and gives a certain amount of bottom insulation. (4) Unlike down, the fiber is nonallergenic, can be washed regularly and easily to get rid of dust, and thus is the forced choice of people who sneeze at feathers and dust.

It would be very wrong to suppose that all those claims are swallowed by feather merchants and their fans. Wet is wet, they say, and whether down or poly, *cold*—"warm when wet" is hogwash. In humid-steamy forests (Eastern America in summer), poly may indeed hold up, while down collapses. But in steady rain (the year around in coastal mountains of Northwest America) the bag —any bag—jolly well had better be kept dry, easily done with simple precautions.

Even boosters admit that the new poly has only 70–75 percent the insulation of down. Down loyalists turn the mathematics around, saying goose down with a fill power of 550 cubic inches has 70 percent more insulation value than poly. Depending on whose statistics are accepted, for equal warmth a poly bag must be 1 or 2 pounds heavier than a down bag.

Boosters further concede poly isn't so nicely compressible, requires more effort to cram in a stuff bag, and always takes twice the space in the pack.

What—aside from faster drying and relentless advertising—has poly got? Price. Popularity has grown every passing year as the goose has jumped higher and higher, practicing to fly over the moon. However, sensational bargains should not be expected. Filler cost is merely one part of total bag cost; a zipper costs the same, wherever, and so does a yard of nylon. Poly bags for warm weather can be rudimentary and cheap; those for the cold must be complex.

Further, first cost and final cost are different things. Down has proven abundantly that it can last for years and years. Poly hasn't been around long enough for fair comparison, but reports tell of delofting and separation, and though these may result from improper care based on the common belief "poly can take it," the opinion grows that down is tougher and the best buy. Some observers say poly loses half its original loft in 2 to 3 years.

As a last note on cost, let the source of poly be kept in mind—the price tag is riding the same leaping camel as gasoline.

Through the 1970s the Down-Polyester War shared the battlefield with a Polyester Civil War. The new poly was marketed in two different versions. Polarguard (Celanese) was cut in fibers 100 or more inches long and resin-coated to stay in stable position. Hollofil II (originally called Dacron Fiberfill II; DuPont) and Kodofil (Eastman), basically identical, were (and still are) cut in 2-inch fibers with no bonding agent applied but held in position by other means, such as a backing of Remay, a cobweblike material that tangles with the fibers.

DuPont and Celanese—and to a lesser extent, and later on, Eastman—skirmished back and forth over the pages of five-color magazine ads and in the offices of purchasing agents of bag manufacturers. After some years of experiment, manufacturers reached a consensus on the proper places for the competitors. Polarguard, in stable batts (sheets of matted fiber) that could be edge-stabilized rather than stitched through (see below), was found to give better loft and thus most warmth for weight; used for cold-weather bags, with features appropriate for the needs, it dominated the higher price range. Hollofil II and Kodofil were used for bags that lacked frills and thus were in a lower price range; the light ones were meant for comfort in mild climates, the heavier ones to be carried short distances or not at all.

Then, in 1979, to the consternation of backpackers who thought their sport was really big business, Celanese threw in the batt, discontinued Polarguard. Makers of bags and garments instantly began scurrying about to adapt Hollofil/Kodofil to Polarguard's former domain, experimenting with such recourses as laminating the poly to eliminate the weight and loft restriction of the Remay backing, thereby simulating the free-floating batts that characterized Polarguard. However, the obituary proved a little bit premature, because Polarguard some-how remains alive. The 1980s begin, therefore, in uncertainty.

Goose Down

Down, the fluff growing next to the skin of waterfowl, traps air more efficiently than any other readily available lightweight sub-stance, yet allows body moisture to breathe out; compacts in a small bundle for carrying, yet is extremely resilient, quickly expanding when released; and withstands thousands of compression-and-expan-sion cycles before getting too bent and broken to rise to the occasion.

Two chief objections are made. First is price. However, the gap between down and polyester will narrow if (1) the world petroleum price continues climbing and (2) new trade agreements with the People's Republic of China, source of something between 60 and 85 percent of the world's down, let America receive a share at a lower price, and directly rather than circuitously, as in the past, through Hong Kong and Germany. Second, even if carefully protected from storms, down accumulates moisture from the body and the air, and over a trail week or so collapses; this can largely be avoided by keeping the sleeping bag inside a breathable cover, and entirely pre-vented by draping it in the sun every day or two. (In Arctic conditions, down fails to breathe out body moisture and gets wet; a vapor barrier, discussed below, is the solution.)

Eiderdown, gathered from Arctic nests, mainly in Iceland, of the wild eider duck, is reputed to be the finest of downs. Few hikers will ever have a chance to test the claim; the total world supply is perhaps 100 pounds a year and the price was $100 a pound in the early 1970s, after which nobody bothered keeping track.

The reigning champion is the goose, eaten (along with duck) by most of the world the way America eats chicken and turkey, though not Kentucky-fried. There are geese and geese. The best down is from a large, mature domestic fowl raised in a cold climate, the plucking done in early winter when the down is thickest and sturdiest. How-ever, with demand going up at the rate of 50 percent a year during the 1970s, merchants went beyond such traditional sources as Germany, Poland, and Mennonite communities in Canada and began combing the planet for geese of any kind, from anywhere. A scrawny Taiwan goose disrobed in summer has little to brag about. Further, geese are raised for eating, the down a by-product, and a tender youngster tastes better than a tough old bird; consequently, few live to full prime-down maturity.

Since many suppliers are now refusing to sell their best down by itself, rather mixing it with otherwise unsalable down, the overall quality is declining; the fill power of loft (see below) of today's typical top-grade down is about a quarter less than that of past decades.

To confuse the issue, what *is* "down"? The Federal Trade Commission requires a "down" product to contain at least 80 percent down; articles manufactured in states where laws are not stricter (as some are) than the federal regulation may contain "goose down" that is up to 16 percent goose feathers, 2 percent chicken, turkey, and pigeon feathers, and 2 percent "miscellaneous" (floor sweepings).

The merchants who buy raw mixed feathers and down from traders launder, separate, blend, and grade the down. They sell a number of grades for a variety of commercial purposes. Each merchant swears his top grade is the supreme and gives it a fancy but meaningless trade name. In fact, merchants argue about what makes a good down. Despite evidence that color is irrelevant, a few stubbornly insist white is better than gray. Some point with pride to a low feather content (all down has 8–20 percent feathers and miscellaneous, since hand-separation of down from tiny feathers would be prohibitively expensive); others brag about feathers, stressing that a certain proportion is essential for strength and resiliency.

The consumer's life would be easier if every down bag carried a hang tag stating its insulating characteristics. The insulating value of down is determined to about 60 percent by *fill power,* or *loft,* the ability to fluff up and trap air; and to about 40 percent by *recovery power,* the ability to spring out to full expansion after being crushed. Loft is measured in a cylinder to determine how many cubic inches of space an ounce of down can fill; the present industry norm for a good down is 550 cubic inches. Recovery power is measured by another simple procedure. Why are the results so rarely given by sleeping-bag hang

tags? Because fill power and recovery power vary with humidity, cleanliness, and other factors, and no uniform measuring standards have been adopted. Many a manufacturer is reluctant to tag his bags with their "honest loft," which may look bad by comparison with a competitor's "dishonest loft." Until uniform standards are adopted and enforced, figures given for loft will be useful in comparing the bags of any one supplier but possibly misleading in comparing bags of different suppliers.

The subject is altogether too arcane for a layman. The average hiker does well to forsake his attempt to pursue consumerism to the last percentile of perfection in favor of patronizing trusted outfitters who use the best materials they can obtain and whose standards far exceed those set by the most rigorous federal regulation or state law. Beware of Super-Thrifty Drugs and War Surplus. But feel fairly safe at a backpacking shop.

Duck Down

Everything said above about geese applies also to ducks. Only under a microscope, with difficulty, can duck down be distinguished from goose down. In Canada a distinction is usually not made and both are mixed in "waterfowl down"; eventually this may become the rule everywhere.

If a goose and a duck were raised side by side to the same age, the goose down would be superior to that of the duck, mainly because the goose, and thus its plumes, would be larger. However, a good duck is better than a bad goose. The quality difference in their downs as marketed is often minimal, or even in favor of the duck.

The top-grade duck down in most bags has a loft in the range of 480–520 cubic inches (but is available to 550), overlapping the 500–550 cubic inches of top-grade goose down. Weights of filler and construction details being equal, a duck bag may be ever so slightly less warm than a goose bag; but because snobs are driving up the goose price faster, the duck bag costs less.

Polyester and Down

Combination bags (often advertised as "fiber-down"), originally devised to conserve down, have other virtues that have earned them prominence, in some shops dominance.

The bag is filled on the sky side with down for the better loftiness, on the ground side with poly for the better resistance to flattening under body weight. Result: warmer on top than an all-poly bag, warmer on bottom than an all-down bag. But the sleeper must remember to keep bottom on bottom and top on top.

Chicken Feathers and Whatnot

Other materials may be encountered in sleeping bags.

Mixtures of down and feathers approach the warmth of pure down at lower cost; most of the "down" bags of World War II were such. When comparing prices, a hiker must keep his mathematics straight. A "60-40" bag is 60 percent down, 40 percent feathers; a "50-50" bag is half and half. But since "pure down" legally can be as little as 80 percent down, a 60-40 may actually be 48 percent down; a 50-50, 40 percent.

Approach with caution bags advertised as "duck down" or just plain "down" and at ridiculous prices, as low as $20. The filler may truly be down—but stripped from scraggly goslings and ducklings in a torrid jungle and having as much loft as wilted lettuce. It may be

—despite the strictures of law—an outright fraud. During the Korean War the U.S. Army invented the Tan-O-Quil-Qm process to increase the curl, and thus the loft, of chicken feathers. The Army decided the end product was junk but rumors abound of pushcart entrepreneurs lurking at trailheads.

A polyurethane open-cell foam has the air-trapping capacity of down, retains full loft when wet, and doesn't go flat under the body, but is heavier than down for equal warmth, quite incompressible, extremely bulky to carry, soaks up and wicks water like a sponge, and doesn't cuddle a sleeper. Few bags made of it are around, or ever have been.

The "old poly," the only poly there was until 1971, is much less expensive than the new and continues to be an excellent choice where not much insulation is needed and/or weight is no concern, as when car-camping in a summer forest. Parents or youth leaders outfitting a bunch of kids to go backpacking also may feel a few extra pounds and shivers are justified by the savings. Better to carry a bag of Hollofil 808 or any other "old poly" than a wool blanket. Or not go. However, the hiker should know what's being offered: "synthetic fill" or "poly down" mean old polyester; the new is always pridefully identified by trade name.

Thinsulate (see Chapter 9, "Clothing") has been tried for bags, but tests to date are negative: the material breaks down under stress, and it's so stiff that the bags can't be stuffed.

Your neighborhood Handy-Dandy Super-Surplus Bargain Basement may tout "acetate" or "acrylic" bags for under $20. Whatever these cheap synthetics may actually be, they are not warm or durable.

In the annals of infamy is a $4 bag, filled with golly knows what, sold as "good for up to 2 weeks" and "disposable—don't pack it back." There has even been a "7-day disposable bag" priced at 99 cents. Heaven preserve us.

STRUCTURE OF THE BAG

The insulation value of a bag is determined partly by the kind and amount of filler and partly by various aspects of the structure. In order

WOW! LOOK!
SLEEPING BAG SALE
BIG SPECIAL
$5.⁰⁰ 2 FOR ONLY $9.⁰⁰
GENUINE 100% RECLAIMED
KLEENEX FILLER

of importance as affecting warmth are (1) the shape of the bag; (2) the method employed to stabilize the filler; and (3) the construction of the inner and outer shells (the fabrics which hold the filler).

Shape

Other things being equal, the smaller the bag the warmer, since there are fewer interior air spaces to be heated and more of the insulation is near the body rather than off in distant corners. The configuration of the upper opening, where the sleeper extends some portion of his face or head out of the bag, also is significant; the brain receives 20 percent of the body's blood supply and thus the head area can radiate a great deal of heat.

The warmest design, and the choice of nearly all backpackers, is the *mummy* bag, contoured to the body and closed at the top by a drawstring that completely shuts off breezeways, leaving exposed, when desired, merely the sleeper's nose and mouth. Most mummy bags are roomier than was once customary and are called *streamlined* or *modified mummy,* pretty well eliminating nightmares of ancient Egypt.

Severe claustrophobics prefer a *barrel* bag, which, rather than tapering from head to foot, bulges outward at the midsection to let elbows and knees maneuver. The design adds weight as well as comfort. Generally barrel bags are square-cut at the top with drawstring closure for sealing off the outer chill.

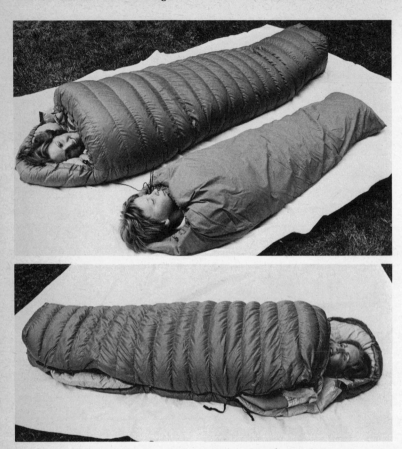

Representative mummy bags. Top: *example of a three-season bag.* Center: *Child's bag.* Bottom: *Example of a four-season bag with all the frills—which, however, are only appreciated from an inside perspective.*

Roomiest and heaviest—and rarely seen on the trail—are *rectangular* bags, usually with no top closure, thus allowing heat to escape and breezes to enter; at low elevations and in warm climates this is, of course, an advantage. A *tapered* rectangular bag maintains the ease of ventilation and saves weight at the foot.

As a rough generalization, in bags of comparable filler and baffling (see below), barrel bags are about 10° colder than mummy bags and somewhat heavier; rectangular bags are about 20° colder and considerably heavier.

Compartments (Baffling)—Down-Filled Bag

If down were merely stuffed between an outer and inner shell it would soon lump up in certain spots, leaving others unprotected. Therefore some compartment system is required to hold the down in place. The aim of a designer is to get the most loft for the least weight of filler and compartmenting fabric; another consideration, especially in economy bags, is to do so at least cost. Compromises are necessary on several counts and are evidenced by all backpacker bags.

The simplest and cheapest construction is *sewn-through (stitch-*

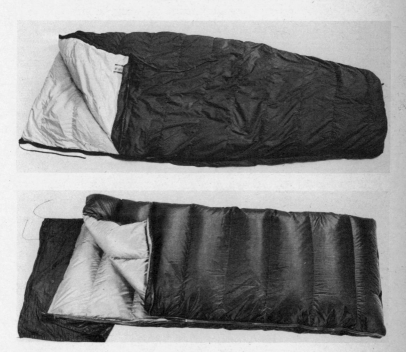

Top: *Representative barrel bag.* Bottom: *Representative rectangular bag.*

through), where inner and outer shells are stitched directly together. The stitching lines offer no insulation and are "cold spots." This method is employed on down bags intended to be placed within outer bags for extreme cold.

Most down bags are built with panels (baffles) sewn between inner and outer shells. Almost always the compartments run around the bag *(circumferential,* or the variant *"chevron cut")* instead of in a line from top to bottom *(longitudinal),* in which pattern the filler tends to collect at the foot.

The panels commonly are of a nylon tricot or nylon mesh which is light, inexpensive, easy-breathing, and gives maximum compressibility. A few manufacturers prefer nylon cloth, a bit heavier and more costly but preventing movements of down between compartments.

A step up from sewn-through construction and eliminating cold spots is the *box,* in which the panels form right-angle compartments.

Generally considered the most efficient is the *slant tube (slant box, slant wall, parallelogram),* providing maximum loft for minimum panel weight, and in the judgment of a majority of experts, the greatest warmth per pound of total bag weight. When released, the parallelogram walls straighten into rectangles, thus letting the down loft better than in ordinary boxes. Though construction expense is the same as with the box, more baffle material is required, adding a bit to weight and cost.

The *overlapping tube (diaphragm tube, V-tube)* method holds the down very closely in place but somewhat restricts loft, thus giving slightly less insulation than the slant tube for equal amounts of filler. Also, construction expense is greater and the extra paneling increases weight and cost. (In the quest for perfect down control it is possible to "over-panel.")

A *laminated* bag has two sewn-through layers stitched together in an overlapping fashion to eliminate cold spots. Because of the weight of the additional fabric, few down backpacker bags are of this design.

Bags often have a *channel block (cross block baffle),* a continuous baffle down the side of the bag opposite the zipper that prevents down from migrating around the circumference—and for that reason disliked by many hikers. They point out that down beneath the body is com-

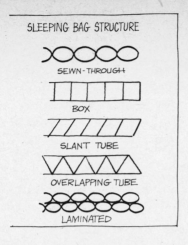

SLEEPING BAG STRUCTURE

SEWN-THROUGH

BOX

SLANT TUBE

OVERLAPPING TUBE

LAMINATED

pressed virtually to zero thickness (thus the need for a sleeping pad, discussed below); before going to bed in cold weather they "chase" down from the underside of the bag to the upperside where it can do some good. However, a block is standard on those bags—most, nowadays—that gain maximum insulation from a given amount of down by putting 60 percent on the sky side and 40 percent on the ground side.

Batting Stabilization—Polyester-Filled Bag

Polyester comes to the sleeping bag manufacturer not in sacks of loose fluff but in rolls of batting. The batts don't require compartmenting but must be stabilized to prevent shifting.

Because of the ease of construction, the least expensive bags are *sewn-through* (see above), adequate for mild climates. Warmer (and heavier) is the *sewn-through with a cover* that adds insulation and covers the cold spots.

Bags in a middle range of cost and warmth are *laminated (double-quilted, double-offset quilt, double-offset baffle, shingle)*. Two separate batts are sewn-through but with seams staggered so that thin spots on one batt overlap thick spots on the other.

At the top of the poly line is the *edge-stabilized sandwich,* with a third batt sandwiched between the other two on the sky side, which thus

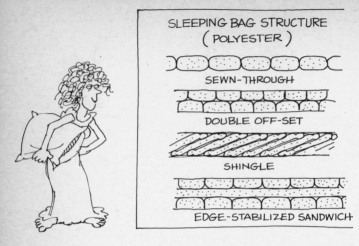

SLEEPING BAG STRUCTURE
(POLYESTER)

SEWN-THROUGH

DOUBLE OFF-SET

SHINGLE

EDGE-STABILIZED SANDWICH

is one third thicker than the ground side. This batt is free-floating,
sewn to the shell around the edges only, permitting maximum loft.

The Shell—Outer and Inner

Nearly all backpacker bags have *outer shells* of nylon—strong, easy-
breathing, wind-resistant, and effective at keeping filler from escaping. Cotton, cheaper and less vulnerable to campfire sparks, is heavier
for the same strength and mainly used for car-camping bags. The
nylon usually is one or another high-count taffeta. Ripstop, very "in"
a few years ago, now is quite "out" for bags. Down bags designed for
the most warmth at least weight may have a heavy, strong taffeta on
the ground side, where the hard wear comes, and a light taffeta or
nylsilk on the sky side in order not to flatten the down, if ever so little,
under the weight of the shell. (For fabric definitions see Chapter 9.)

Some *inner shells* are taffeta, but hikers who hate slippery sleeping
prefer trinyl, a cotton-nylon-polyester blend with the feel of cotton,
giving between-the-sheets-like comfort.

Pages of logic and rhetoric are devoted by catalogs to debating the
optimum way to cut the shells. Many bags have a *differential cut (concentric cut),* which is to say, the inner shell is smaller than the outer. The
theoretical advantages are that the filler is permitted to loft more

freely and that sleepers (especially those who thrash around a lot with knees and elbows) cannot so easily press the inner shell against the outer and create cold spots. Proponents claim such bags are warmer for equivalent amounts of filler.

Some manufacturers disagree and use a *space-filler cut,* with inner and outer shells the same circumference. Their theory is that the inner shell folds around the sleeper and fills air pockets. Proponents claim such bags are not only less expensive but have less inside air to heat and thus are warmer. They also say that in any event the concentric cut doesn't prevent cold spots as claimed.

Innocent bystanders suspect it doesn't make any difference.

The body gives off not only heat but water vapor; while retaining the former, the bag must freely breathe out the latter. Beginners used to ask for a waterproof sleeping bag and were told by clerks that if one existed it would sweat a sleeper like a sauna; skeptics then sometimes snuck off and ruined bags by applying waterproofing. Now, however, the dream has become reality—an outer shell of *Gore-Tex.* (See Chapter 9.)

OPENING AND CLOSING THE BAG: ZIPPER AND DRAWSTRINGS

Insulating material and structure have much to do with the warmth of the bag; the method by which it is closed (to freezing blasts) and opened (to cooling zephyrs) also affects warmth, and the overall comfort and convenience as well.

Incidentally, so much moisture is exhaled in the breath that even on the coldest nights a sleeper should try to keep his nose outside the bag to avoid dampening the interior. In extreme cold he may wish to protect the nose from freezing by breathing through a sweater.

As noted above, the head of the bag is a particularly critical area and thus may be treated first, followed by zippers.

Head of the Bag

Rectangular bags ordinarily are wide open at the top, though some have a drawstring.

Mummy and barrel bags usually have a drawstring closure to shut the airway. There may be a drawstring at the shoulders plus an extended *hood* which can be left flat in warm weather or drawn tight around the face with another drawstring. Or there may be a single drawstring around the top to form a hood.

For easy opening, to avoid a trapped feeling, a hiker does well to use a *toggle*, a spring-loaded clamp, on the drawstrings, or a *cord-block*.

Some manufacturers offer a down hood, or *collar*, which can be either sewn to the top of any bag or attached by Velcro ("sticky") tape.

Zippers

Very light bags dispense with a zipper altogether (the more zipper, the more weight) and the sleeper wriggles and slithers in from the top.

Most bags have a *side* zipper, on either side *(left-opening* or *right-opening)*. Choice mainly matters when two bags are to be zipped together, in which case one of each is required.

Mummy bags often have *half-length* zippers some 36 to 40 inches long, extending about halfway down from the top; as a general rule the less zipper, the less of a cold spot and thus the warmer the bag.

Other mummies and barrels and most rectangulars have a *full-length*

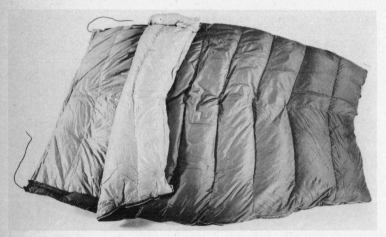

Two barrel bags zipped together to make a double.

(70-inch or so) zipper. Some have a zipper running the *full length and across the foot* for complete temperature control in warm weather, or *full-length zippers on both sides.*

Hikers who travel mainly in warm climates prefer a lot of zipper to avoid night-long stewing in their own juices. Cold-country hikers generally want much less zipper: when a full-length zipper fails (which occasionally happens even with the best) the sleeper is faced with either a shivering night or a massive hand-sewing job by flashlight; when a short zipper fails the comparatively small opening can be adequately closed with several safety pins or by clutching the fabric with the hands.

Two bags with full-length zippers can be joined—if the zippers are compatible—to make a double bag. Many couples like to have this option, either for the theoretical warmth of snuggling or simply for a meaningful relationship. Another advantage is that a small child can be accommodated, saving the weight of an extra bag. However, some couples (old marrieds) declare that in cold windy weather so much heat is lost through the top that a double bag is like no bag at all, and that sleeping with a squirming, kicking infant is no sleep at all.

Bags (barrels only) of different fillers can be combined for versatility (again, if the zippers are compatible). For example, if a couple has one bag with 2 pounds of down, another with 3 pounds, the two can be joined with the 2-pounder on top for warm nights, the 3-pounder for cold ones. Similarly, a polyester and a down bag can be combined, the former on the bottom, since polyester compresses less and gives better ground insulation, and the down on top for its better air insulation.

The best zippers are *nylon,* which, unlike metal, doesn't conduct heat, freeze, or rip the shell fabric when snagged, and of the *tooth* design—"good for 20,000 zips"—rather than the cheaper, lighter, riskier *coil.* The highest-quality bags have "oversize" or "heavy-duty" zippers for greater dependability.

As with all special features a *two-way (two-slide)* zipper adds expense but is convenient in allowing the bag to be opened from either top or bottom; in warm weather, the feet may thus be ventilated without chilling the shoulders.

213

Since the zipper is a line of zero insulation, in the best down bags it is covered by a *down-filled tube (draft tube)* to prevent heat loss. (Incidentally, when buying two bags not the same model that are intended to be joined, make sure the insulating tubes overlap; otherwise the zipper will be uncovered, a full-length cold spot.)

Covers and Liners

A separate sleeping bag *cover* of cotton or nylon may be slipped over the bag to protect it from wear, to keep it clean when cooking and eating while stormbound in a tent, and for extra warmth. The similar *bivouac cover* of nylon, waterproof on bottom, breathable on top, is not to be confused with the Gore-Tex bivy sack (see below). Covers of this sort are used mainly by climbers and winter hikers; few backpackers find the added protection worth the weight.

A sleeping bag *case* of ripstop nylon with a coated bottom, built-in foam pad, and drawstring hood is designed for extreme cold, such as sleeping on snow, and is of little interest to the average hiker.

Many hikers insert a light *liner* of nylon, cotton flannel, or cotton/polyester to keep the inner shell of the bag clean or because they prefer to sleep within snuggly cotton rather than slippery nylon. A liner adds a bit of extra warmth; during the night it also twists into interesting tangles.

In Arctic conditions where down fails to breathe out moisture from the body, an impervious liner can be inserted as a *vapor barrier* (see Chapter 9). Though a person may feel he's sleeping in a swamp, it's a warm swamp, and doesn't escape the barrier to deloft the down. Advocates declare it's not really like a swamp at all, merely moist, and anyhow, swamps are nice, that's where we all came from.

Sleeping bags are usually carried in *stuff bags* (Chapter 10). However, between hikes they should be kept in larger *storage bags* that let the filler fluff.

Gore-Tex Bivy Sack

A Gore-Tex bivy sack *(bivouac cover* or *bag; burrow)* is intermediate between a sleeping-bag cover and a tent, excluding rain, wind, and bugs and adding some 10° of warmth. Fitting the body snugly, the sack

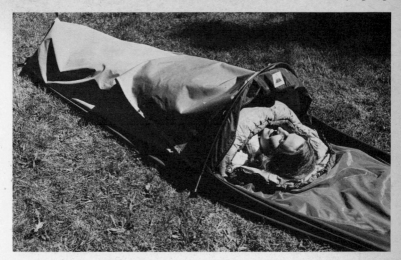

Example of a Gore-Tex bivy sack, here used only for warmth and to keep the dew off the sleeping bag. When needed, the bug netting can be zipped in place over the sleeper's head, and also the head of the "roof."

exploits the Gore-Tex principle as clothing does (Chapter 9) and avoids the problems tents have (Chapter 12).

In some models the floor is coated nylon for durability (but some inner wetness) and only the "roof" is Gore-Tex laminate; in others the laminate is all around. Designs range from a simple envelope weighing 1 pound and costing $50 to structures with guylines or fiberglass wands to support a hood for headroom, weighing about 1½ pounds, costing from $80 to $100. All have bug netting, and there's a blessing.

Make no mistake—the sack is not a tent. One could save a person's life in a cold storm, but after a couple of days inside he might not care. However, a lone hiker can dispense with tent or tarp; when morning comes and claustrophobia compels, he can crawl out in the storm and run for it.

SELECTING A SLEEPING BAG

Time for plain and simple talk.

There is no single sleeping bag ideal for everyone in the whole wide world. Choice of this intimate garment depends on very personal needs.

Most obvious is the matter of *body length/bag length*. Bags come in various lengths, and obviously the bag should be long enough to contain the entire body, keeping in mind that a 6-foot bag is insufficient for a 6-foot sleeper; the body is longer when lying flat; also, extra inches are essential to let toes flex and neck stretch. However, for reasons of warmth, weight, and expense a person should buy the smallest bag into which he fits comfortably. A complicating factor is that some suppliers list the inside length of their bags, others the outside; at any shop, therefore, one must ask which system is used and what bag lengths are recommended for various body lengths. (When in doubt, better to choose a too-long bag than suffer cramped knees and neck. However, most beginners buy a bag longer than they need.)

Body girth/bag girth matters. The old mummies turned with the sleeper along with his underwear. The new mummies and all other designs are cut generously enough for the sleeper to roll over inside without rolling the whole bag, generally thought the most comfortable arrangement. Ease in keeping top on top and bottom on bottom is very important in the increasingly popular designs with polyester below and down above, or 60 percent of the down above and 40 percent below. A reliable test: if within a zipped-up bag you can just manage to take off your socks, you'll be able to roll while sleeping, and the girth is just right.

Make this test in the shop, as well as the test for length. If the management objects, go to another shop. A person shouldn't be expected to spend $100, or $200, or $50 for a dress or jacket—or bag —without trying it on for size. Further, if planning to zip two bags together, do so in the shop to make absolutely sure the zippers are compatible.

By these methods, proper bag dimensions can be determined rather easily. Not so simple are the three central and intertwined considerations of weight, cost, and warmth.

(*Note:* Here and hereafter, the weights and prices given are for "regular"-size bags for the average-size adult body. Weights and prices are lower and higher for "short" and "long" sizes.)

As a generalization about *weight,* down bags range from about 3 pounds to 6, those on the lower end for mild temperatures, on the upper end for extreme cold. The most popular choice is roughly 4 pounds, suitable for most hikers in most areas. In polyester bags the range is from about 3½ to 6½ pounds, with 5 pounds perhaps the most popular. The beginner who sticks near the midrange won't go too far wrong. (Don't confuse *weight of bag* with *weight of filler,* discussed below.)

If a bag is to be carried long distances, weight matters a lot and the hiker may wish to sacrifice warmth for the sake of a light load. On the other hand, if the bag is for short backpacks, an extra pound or two is insignificant.

Paralleling weight is *cost,* the sum of many factors—method and care of construction, type of filler, and niceties of zipper and all. Down bags of most interest to the average backpacker range from about $100 to $175; polyester bags from about $25 to $100; down top and poly bottom, around $120.

If a hiker has all the money in the world, he'll never look at a bag's price until satisfied with its warmth and weight and conveniences. On the other hand, a thin wallet may influence him to carry an extra pound or shiver a little to save $50. Still, he should buy the best bag he can afford; with proper care a quality bag can outlast a series of make-do substitutes and be more economical in the long run—and more comfortable in the short.

It's when a hiker investigates *warmth* that he finds himself plunging through thick mists, staggering from sinkhole to quicksand, deafened by creatures of the mercantile jungle screeching conflicting opinions. The explorer must plot his route with careful attention to two considerations—how much warmth is required, and how much a bag provides.

First, *how warm a bag does the hiker need?* If most trips are planned for summer and/or low elevations, the choice should be a light-weight, inexpensive bag, perhaps rectangular. Adequate ventilation to avoid sweltering is important, meaning a full-length, possibly two-way zipper. If many trips will be in high mountains and/or winter, a

heavier and costlier bag is essential, of mummy or barrel shape and with minimum and/or heavy-duty zipper.

Two other factors influence choice. Hikers who sleep in tents don't need as much bag as those who sleep under tarps. In still air the interior of a closed tent (or bivy sack) is about 10° warmer than the surroundings; in a wind the differential is greater (see the wind-chill chart in Chapter 6). Individual metabolisms vary enormously in their abilities to produce heat. Generally a beginning backpacker already knows if he/she is a cold person or a warm person; a cold sleeper may shiver on a tropic night in a bag designed for the South Pole, while a warm sleeper wrapped in an old horse blanket may snore up a storm on an icecap. (Incidentally, a cold sleeper can raise his thermostat setting by eating a supper high in fats, which during night-long digestion generate a great deal of heat.)

Second, *how warm is a bag*? Here is the arena of claims and counterclaims, bickering, opinion, nonsense, and little objective data. Testing programs under laboratory conditions suggest that not type or quality of down, not method of construction, not amount of loft, not care of workmanship, and certainly not retail price are clear indicators of thermal efficiency, which seems to be determined by a complex and obscure relationship among shell, baffles, and filler.

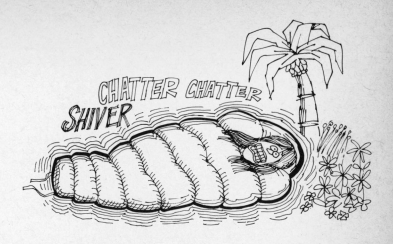

Perhaps in coming years, industry-wide standards will evolve, cooling the arguments. Ultimately every bag may have a hang tag stating a federally approved rating of thermal efficiency; a purchaser will then know exactly what he's buying. (Dream on, dream on.)

While hoping for a better future, how to cope with a muddled present? Some suppliers give a *warmth rating (minimum temperature rating or comfort rating),* saying a bag is warm (or comfortable) down to 32° or 0° or whatever. Such figures must, of course, be treated with caution, since no scientist has studied sleeping with the thoroughness devoted to more athletic bedtime activities. None has measured the difference in cold toleration between fatties and skinnies. Moreover, such ratings assume a dry bag, brand-new, untouched by wind, in a tent, with a ground pad, and therefore are very approximate. Still, when provided, they at least permit comparison among bags offered by any one supplier.

Most manufacturers and retailers stress the bag *loft* as the best indicator of warmth. Before going on, a distinction must be noted. As previously discussed, *down loft* is measured in a cylinder, yielding a figure for the number of cubic inches an ounce of down will fill when fluffed. *Bag loft* is measured in conditions of standard temperature and humidity by spreading out a bag, closed and fully fluffed, no weight inside or on top, and counting the inches from bottom to top. This is the *total loft.* However, because the bottom half of a bag is squashed more (with down) or less (with polyester) flat by the weight of the sleeper, many suppliers give only the *top loft,* which is to say, the loft of the upper half. (Some shops don't make clear whether they're speaking of total or top loft; bad cess to them.)

The problem is that the U.S. Bureau of Standards has not approved any set of rules for measuring bag loft, and methods vary from one manufacturer and retailer to another, leaving much room for maneuvering, misrepresentation, and misunderstanding. Nevertheless, loft figures are excellent for comparing bags in any single shop, though not necessarily from one shop to the next.

Assuming a manufacturer has not goofed in his design and prevented full fluffing, the amount of loft is determined mainly by the *amount of filler.* Down mummy bags in the "regular" size, meant for "average" conditions, contain from 2 to 3 pounds of down, which provide a top loft of between 2½ and 5 inches. (A barrel bag requires more down for the same loft, and a rectangular more still.) For summer trips in high mountains where night temperatures frequently drop to freezing, most hikers are content with 2½ pounds of down and a top loft of 3 (true) inches. For mild climates or warm sleepers, 1½ pounds and 2 inches may be satisfactory. Partly it depends on how often a person is willing to shiver a bit.

(A related question often debated is whether to sleep fully clothed or seminude. Some prefer the former for the supposed extra warmth and the ease of going to bed and getting up. Others say they sleep warmer near-naked and place clothes underneath the bag to pad hard spots or insulate cold spots.)

Polyester mummy bags in the regular size have from 1½ to 4 pounds of filler, a top loft of 1½ to 3½ inches. Most hikers find that a bag decent enough for high mountains in summer has about 3 pounds of filler and a top loft of 2¾ inches. Again, less suffices for warmer climates.

Now, how does the hiker decide between down and polyester? There's no dodging—earlier pages previously skipped now must be read.

In conclusion, many shops make a very useful distinction among their bags on the basis of how many seasons they can handle decently. A *three-season* bag makes no pretense of coping with a North Dakota gazebo in January but promises to handle alpine meadows once the blizzards quit. A *one-season* or *summer* or *recreational* bag is forthrightly modest. The only backpackers who should consider a *four-season* or *winter* or *expedition* bag are those who mush around in snow a lot—or whose inner furnaces burn so low that summer is something they read about and never feel. Let it be noted that the same folks who buy boots so heavy that they walk like Frankenstein's monster buy bags intended to be cozy submerged in liquid hydrogen—and then go camping in the tropics and melt right into the jungle floor. *The most common blunder of novices is buying too much bag*—too much warmth, too much weight, too much money. On the trail as in the budget, one should observe the rule of the ancient Greeks: in nothing too much.

Following paragraphs describe representative bags. The key word is "representative"—these are a very few points on a continuum of hundreds of bags. In a particular shop the hiker may find nothing exactly matching details given here; certainly he will observe innumerable variations and a wide range of prices, reflecting convenience features as well as basic quality. However, the examples suggest the range.

Note: The "comfort ratings" used here are for comparisons among the described bags and may have little to do with real people in the real world.

VISITING THE PAST—UNDER $40

Were a Boy Scout of the 1930s to read this chapter, he'd be struck dumb. Then the hills would come alive with the sound of his hysterical laughter and taunting cries of "Sissies! Sissies!" If all a hiker of today can afford is a bag of "old" polyester, such as Dacron Hollofil 808 (perhaps advertised as "synthetic fill" or "poly down"), costing maybe $20, he's still better off than those poor little blue Scouts—few of whom actually shivered themselves to pieces.

Better, and a very decent choice for a beginner on a slim budget, or anyone in summer in elevations or ranges of benign climate, is a rectangular bag weighing 4¾ pounds, filled with 2½ pounds Kodofil or Hollofil II, sewn-through batting with cover, top loft 1¾ inches, comfort rating 40°F (only a little shivering), about $25.

A step up is a barrel bag weighing 4¼ pounds, filled with 2½ pounds Kodofil or Hollofil II, sewn-through batting with cover, top loft 2 inches, comfort rating 35°F, about $35.

GETTING THROUGH TODAY, NEAT BUT NOT GAUDY—UNDER $100

The best-selling bags, good for three seasons on virtually any trail in the temperate zone below altitudes of 2½ miles, are in this category.

On the low end of the scale is a modified mummy weighing 3¼ pounds, filled with 1⅞ pounds Kodofil or Hollofill II, laminated, top loft 3 inches, comfort rating 15°F, about $65.

Up a bit in cost, weight, and warmth is a modified mummy weighing 4½ pounds, filled with 2⅞ pounds Kodofil or Hollofil II, laminated, top loft 3½ inches, comfort rating 5°F, about $80.

Now down bags begin sneaking through cracks in the price wall. A barrel weighing just 3½ pounds, filled with 1⅝ pounds of a mixture of 60 percent duck down and 40 percent feathers, slant tube, top loft 2½–2¾ inches, has a comfort rating of 30°F (shivery when the frost is on the pumpkin), costs about $90.

Nudging the top boundary of this group, warmest and heaviest, is a modified mummy weighing a tad over 5 pounds, filled with 3⅝ pounds Kodofil or Hollofil II, laminated, top loft 3½–4 inches, comfort rating –5°F, about $95.

INVESTING IN THE FUTURE—UNDER $175

The family preparing to go hiking with five kids and two dogs isn't worrying about next year—next week is where the trail is at. The once-in-a-while backpacker, too, gains all the durability wanted in the lower price class. However, the person who goes tramping often, year after year, finds the best buys upstairs, long life combined with warmth and lightness.

The uppermost aspiration of unmingled polyester is a modified mummy weighing 6 pounds, filled with 4⅝ pounds Kodofil or Hollofil II, laminated with edge-stabilized sandwich, top loft 4½–5 inches, comfort rating –25°, about $110. A sure cure for cases of congenital goose pimples—but at the cost of extra weight.

Now, transitional in price, enter the polyester/down combinations. A modified mummy weighing about 3½ pounds, with 1 pound poly on the bottom, laminated, and ¾ pound goose down on top, slant tube, top loft 2½–3 inches, comfort rating 10°F, costs about $110. Another, similar: 4¼ pounds, with 1¼ pounds poly and 1⅛ pounds goose down, top loft 3½–4 inches, comfort rating –5°F, about $120.

Ushering in all-down bags is a modified mummy weighing only 3¼ pounds, with 1½ pounds goose down, slant tube, top loft 2½–3 inches, comfort rating 10°F, about $130.

Combining high loft, low weight, and many niceties is a modified mummy weighing 4 pounds, with 2 pounds goose down, slant tube, top loft 4–4½ inches, comfort rating –20°F, about $160.

And now the miracle, a Gore-Tex rain-repeller. A modified mummy weighing 4½ pounds, with 1½ pounds polyester on the bottom, laminated, and 1¼ pounds goose down on top, slant tube, and the Gore-Tex cover as water barrier and wind shell, top loft 3½–4 inches, comfort rating –10°F, costs about $160.

SHOOTING THE MOON

Having attained escape velocity, there's no limit to how high a bag can go. The $400 barrier has been broken—can $1,000 be far behind? Few hikers can breathe the rarefied air of the economic stratosphere, and fewer still have any earthly use for spaceman raiment. Ah, but the bags are lovely to look at, delightful to hold, and heaven at night. Moreover, in the long run they frequently are tremendous bargains.

A fine choice for icecap rovers is a modified mummy with much delightful gingerbread, weighing 5¾ pounds, with 3 pounds goose down, slant tube, top loft 5½ inches, comfort rating –30°F, about $225. The person who doesn't sleep warm in this is dead.

Way up here the comparisons among bags are tricky. The price may be sky-high for one or more of four reasons: (1) More down is used, as well as such other costly ingredients as Gore-Tex. (2) More special features have been added, achieving more warmth for the same weight and adding comfort and convenience but ballooning a basic $150 bag to $250. (3) Manufacture is done with tender loving care in home workshops by meticulous craftsmen oblivious to cost control. (4) The bag is a ripoff.

The bag gourmet can have as much fun shopping in the catalogs, and in the tiny ads in backpacker/climber magazines, as checking out Ferraris and Bugattis. And if he avoids Reason No. 4, he may get himself a real keen sleeping machine.

SPECIAL SLEEPING BAGS

Double bags, mummy or rectangular, may appeal to couples certain they will always want to sleep together; for equivalent weights such bags are warmer than two singles united; of course, they lack the separate-bed option.

An *overbag* can be used over a regular bag for extra warmth or alone in warm weather. An example weighs 2½ pounds, is filled with ½ pound polyester, costs about $50.

Another way to go is with a *liner bag* weighing 1½ pounds, costing $40.

SLEEPING BAGS FOR CHILDREN

One reason many married couples buy sleeping bags that can be zipped into a double is to make room for little kids. The weight of an extra bag is saved and the kid (or kids) can snuggle between Mommy and Daddy—which is perhaps the only place they will sleep in the strange environment of the wilderness.

Family togetherness is, however, a disaster if the kids kick and squirm all night. In any event, beyond a certain size the child needs a separate sack.

Long-time hikers with a basementful of old gear often take a worn-out bag, chop off the bottom, patch as needed, and thereby make a child's bag with no cash outlay. Others use an insulated parka—though not without precautions against wetting.

When a bag must be purchased, the same rules given above apply. Children, though, being smaller and generally having better circulation, don't need bags with so much insulation or weight (or expense) as adults to gain equivalent warmth.

Bags for infants are available for parents who can't stand company. Examples are a Sportline model selling for about $30 and a Frostline kit for $17. Both are polyester-filled, about 3 feet long, and weigh 1 pound.

A common strategy is to buy a bag for the child to grow into, saving the expense of a new sack every year, but requiring the tyke to warm up vast amounts of space before he can be warm. The alternative is a bag that grows. One style can be rolled up and tied off to match leg length. Another, sold by kit firms, is an add-on barrel; each year or so a new baffle is bought and sewn on the head end.

Important note: down bags should be used for children only after they are potty-trained; repeated cleaning destroys the loft (see below). Polyester is best for bed-wetters of any age.

CARING FOR THE SLEEPING BAG

There is no formula for predicting the life span of a sleeping bag. Every-night use for months on end, as during an expedition, may finish it off. If slept in only a few weekends a summer, it may last years. However, more important than the amount of use is the manner. Proper care can greatly extend a bag's life and carelessness can kill it while still new.

The nylon shell of the typical backpacker sleeping bag is strong but very thin and must be protected from wear and especially snagging. Therefore—and also to keep the bag dry—a layer should be placed between bag and earth, such as tent floor, sleeping pad, or ground sheet, and the bag should be carried in a stuff bag. The hiker's repair kit should include a roll of ripstop tape for patching holes through which filler might escape.

Nylon shells must be scrupulously guarded against fire; even a tiny spark instantly melts a hole in the fabric—and could kindle a smolder in the filler. Using an unprotected bag as a seat cushion for campfire seminars usually leads in the course of an evening to several holes per cushion, despite constant cries of "Spark! Spark!"

Even more perilous is steaming out the residue of a rainstorm. All fillers require some time to dry, but down takes forever and during the long process spark holes are inevitable. As patience becomes exhausted one moves closer to the flames; the fabric is scorched and disintegrates. All the more reason not to let the bag get wet in the first place.

Bags—down especially, but also polyester—should not be stored in the stuff bag between trips. The more time the filler spends tightly compacted, the more it bends and loses resiliency and loft and warmth. Instead, the bag should be loosely rolled and kept in a special storage bag or, better, hung on a wall or draped over a line in the basement or a hanger in the closet.

By the same token, a bag should be thoroughly fluffed before being slept in. The rule is, as soon as camp is reached and the tent or tarp rigged, the bag is unrolled, shaken vigorously, and placed under the shelter to finish attaining full loft.

Any bag, but down especially, should be air-dried after each trip to avoid mildew and rot and to prevent the filler from matting. Indeed, on multi-day hikes the bag should be aired every day or two, weather permitting, to dry body moisture breathed into the filler at night.

HOW TO CLEAN?

Ideally, a sleeping bag should be kept clean, not only for reasons of hygiene and social acceptability but to prevent the shell from rotting or being nibbled by small creatures (in the mountains or in the basement) which lust after salt and oil. Further, some people are allergic to the dust that collects on filler.

With polyester bags there is no problem; they must never be dry-cleaned (the filler dissolves) but can safely be washed in tepid water with a mild soap. A front-loading ("tumble") machine ad-

justed to the gentle or delicate setting can be used, the bag unzipped to prevent it from tying itself in knots. Hand-washing is
safer and not all that difficult. *Never* put a poly bag in a drier—the
filler melts. In any event, poly dries very quickly, in an hour or
less, in the open air.

Down is something else. Experts agree that more down bags are
ruined by improper cleaning than all other causes combined, including long hard use. Because of the perils, suspicious conservatives
declare absolutely: "Never clean a down bag! If it gets too dirty for
fastidious tastes, buy a new one."

However, sanitation is not the real issue. Body oils absorbed by
down attract dirt which mats the down and in time destroys its resiliency. Dirty down loses loft, and thus warmth, and if dirty long
enough, loses its power ever to be lofty again.

Nevertheless, there is merit in the argument of the conservatives.
The hiker should not be a fanatic. With average use, one cleaning a
year is sufficient to maintain loft and protect the down. The more the
cleanings, the greater the danger of quickly killing the bag; and the
question is open as to how many cleanings, however careful, a bag can
tolerate before the down turns to string.

Each of the two usual cleaning methods has advantages—and hazards.

Dry-Clean the Down—but Afterward Breathe with Care

Safest for the bag and simplest for the bag owner is dry cleaning, the method employed by manufacturers and retailers. However, these people know precisely what they're doing. Does the average hiker? Not often. Because cleaning solvents are toxic and have killed sleepers in the night, the U.S. Bureau of Standards warns against dry cleaning as altogether too risky.

Partisans say there is no danger if a mild petroleum-based compound (such as Stoddard Solvent) is used and the bag completely air-dried afterward—for at least a week—until the solvent odor is gone. Though they admit the solvent lessens the water-repellency of the nylon shell and attacks the down's natural oils, already largely removed by processors, they think the harm done by one cleaning a year is acceptable.

But the chlorinated hydrocarbon (perchlorethylene) used by most dry cleaners turns down into string and remains lethal to living creatures even when the odor is barely noticeable.

Cautious hikers unwilling to trust their local dry cleaner say: Better dirty than dead.

Wash the Down—but Gently, Sir!

Most experts recommend that the hiker clean his bag by hand-washing, unquestionably safe for the hiker and safe for the bag *if done right.* At any of a number of points, though, one false step and the bag is wrecked. Following are precise instructions:

Use any of several brands of down soap (Fluffy, Loft). If such a product cannot be found, any *mild* soap (Ivory) may be substituted, but not detergent.

Dissolve the soap in 10–12 gallons of warm (never hot) water in a bathtub or a large top-loading washing machine. (But *do not* use the wash cycle of the machine.)

Press the bag into the soapy water, starting at one end and keeping the other end dry (to allow air to escape more readily) until most of the bag is submerged. Squeeze out remaining air so the bag will stay submerged. Let the bag soak 1–2 hours (if longer, the fabric colors start to run), turning it *gently* a couple of times. (Once the bag is sopping wet it must *never* be roughly handled or abruptly lifted—the weight of the saturated down will instantly tear out the baffles and for all practical purposes the bag is a total loss.)

After the soaking period, scrub off surface dirt with a sponge or soft brush. Drain water from the tub or machine and press as much as possible from the bag by hand or perhaps foot. Refill the tub or machine with fresh warm water and gently knead the bag to work out the soap solution. Drain again, rinse again, and repeat until the water is clear and free of soap, residues of which will clump the down. Again remove all possible water by hand-pressing. Lift out the bag—carefully, both hands underneath.

The safest and most economical method of drying, and one that gives excellent results, is air-drying. Gently *drape* the bag along a line *(don't hang it)* in a warm, dry place. After a day turn it inside out. As the down dries it begins to expand. Gently pat and shake the bag occasionally to aid the fluffing. Complete drying may take 3–5 days. Another argument for taking pains to keep the bag clean.

If short of time and willing to gamble, use a large commercial drier set on "Air" (no heat); so many cycles are required, possibly a dozen or more, that the cost is considerable, but if departure for a trail is imminent, worth it. Many bags have been ruined in home driers, whose heaters invariably burn the nylon.

Some experts recommend what they claim are safe procedures for washing a bag in an automatic machine. In practice, few hikers are ever successful. Better hand-wash than be sorry. Or buy a polyester bag.

BETWEEN BAG AND GROUND:
SLEEPING PAD, AIR MATTRESS, GROUND SHEET

The bag is only one of the three parts of the "sleeping system." Another, the tent or tarp, is the subject of Chapter 12. The third is what goes between bag and ground.

The old-style backpacker sought to live off the land. In high meadows he luxuriated in one of the grandest of earth's mattresses, a clump of heather. In forests, when ground was wet or snowy, he cut branches from living coniferous trees to build a sumptuous bough bed.

Farewell, pioneer! There is not enough heather in the remaining wilderness of America, not enough greenery of trees, for these scarce resources to be utilized for *sleeping.* There is barely enough for *looking.* A friend of the Earth must carry a complete sleeping system and not improvise a missing part by attacking the scenery with ax or knife or saw.

THIS IS
A "NO NO"

FOR INSULATION ONLY—THE SLEEPING PAD

Recognizing the flaw of the sleeping bag—that bottom insulation flattens under body weight and loses value—manufacturers no longer think of it as an article to be used alone. In assigning comfort or temperature ratings, they assume a sleeping pad as not an optional accessory but an essential component of a complete system.

The most popular pads are *closed-cell foam,* in which neither air nor water moves through the cells. A number of materials are used: PVC (polyvinyl chloride) compounded with nitrile rubber, marketed as Ensolite (mostly type ML) and Presst-O-Cel, etc.; polyethylene, marketed as Volarafoam, Ethafoam, Minicell L-200, Blue Foam, etc.; EVA (ethylene-vinyl-acetate), marketed as Evazote, Regalite, Unipack, Blue (or Orange or Gray) Mountain Foam, etc. No consolidated information is available comparing insulation values; colors and weights and textures and durabilities vary within a rather narrow range; all seem satisfactory for ordinary purposes.

Pads come in various thicknesses: ⅜ inch is standard for three-season use; winter campers lean toward ½ inch; hikers whose bags are polyester on the bottom may find ¼ inch enough. The pads are cut

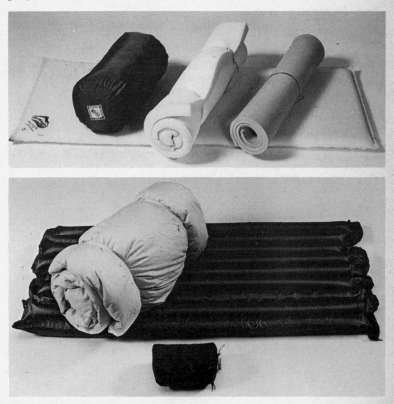

Top: *Sleeping bag in stuff bag, 1 ½-inch-thick sleeping pad of open-cell foam, and ⅜-inch-thick pad of closed-cell foam—displayed on a Therm-A-Rest mattress.* Bottom: *Nine-tube airlift mattress, inflated and in carrying bag.*

in many lengths, many widths. Some are laminations of closed-cell and open-cell foam (see below).

Two common representatives are: Ensolite (type ML), ⅜ inch, 28 by 56 inches, weighing ⅞ pound, costing about $10; Blue Foam polyethylene, ⅜ inch, 24 by 48 inches, 6 ounces, $5. These sizes are adequate for the shoulder-to-hips area where most body weight rests; they weigh little and roll into small diameters.

Some hikers prefer a *urethane* (*polyether* is similar) pad 1½ inches thick, giving not only insulation but cushioning. The most popular 24- by 48-inch size weighs 1¼ pounds and costs about $4.

Urethane is an open-cell foam, much softer and more resilient than closed-cell foams, which eventually fatigue and stay compressed. However, because of the softness about three times the thickness of closed-cell foam is required for equivalent insulation; a major effort is required to roll 1½-inch urethane into a diameter less than enormous. Also, open-cell foam is a sponge, wicks water from damp ground into the bag, and when wet, is as cold as a water bed; in damp terrain it must thus be used in conjunction with a ground sheet. But then, body moisture may condense on the ground sheet and be absorbed by the foam. Adding a coated-nylon cover eliminates the problem but adds weight, probably justifiable only in winter.

FOR CUSHIONING MAINLY—THE AIR MATTRESS

An air mattress gives more cushioning than a urethane pad, and being deflatable, makes less bulky baggage. However, despite also giving wetness protection, when used alone its insulation value is minor; convection currents in the air cells efficiently carry heat from bag to ground.

Another disadvantage of some air mattresses is the evening-and-morning time needed to inflate and deflate. Another is the aggravating habit of letting the sleeper down in the night, either from a tiny puncture invisible to the naked eye, a valve failure, innate crankiness, or practical jokes by surly companions.

Full-length mattresses are splendid for weekends but too heavy (3

pounds or more) for extended backpacks. Long-distance walkers whose thinly covered or old bones demand pampering are generally content with a size reaching from shoulders to hips. A "shorty" *rubberized* or *vinyl-coated nylon* mattress weighs about ½ pound and costs about $15.

Cheaper are *all-vinyl* mattresses—more to be warned against than used. Vinyl punctures at a frown; however, one can carry a kit of cement and patches and while away many an hour in camp searching for and repairing holes.

The best mattress for backpacking (next to the Therm-A-Rest, below) is the *airlift,* vinyl tubes in pockets of ripstop nylon; the six to nine air tubes, 2 inches in diameter, are independent. Inflation at night is easy, about two puffs a tube, and deflation in the morning quick. Even if one or two tubes develop leaks, the sleeper is still in business. Patching is simple and replacement tubes cheap. The "shorty" weighs ¾ or 1¼ pounds, costs about $20.

If a mattress is used for comfort, an Ensolite pad may still be wanted for insulation between mattress and bag. An alternative recommended by snow-camping veterans is to sleep seminude and put trousers, shirt, and sweater between mattress and sleeping bag; they swear the method gives all necessary insulation.

A few hikers appreciate an air or polyester *pillow* weighing 5 or 6

233

ounces, costing about $3. Others improvise a pillow from the stuff bag filled with extra clothing or a boot wrapped in a sweater.

FOR BOTH INSULATION AND CUSHIONING

Cushioning *and* insulation can be obtained from an ordinary air mattress by slowly, patiently inserting down. As little as 2 ounces suffice for a cozy-warm sleep even on snow. The drawback, major, is that a pump thereafter must be used to inflate the mattress to keep the down dry. Even so it may find a way to get wet.

Far superior is the ingenious *Therm-A-Rest mattress,* consisting of a pad of open-cell foam within an airtight skin of waterproof nylon, extremely durable and leak-resistant.

Upon arriving in camp, open the valve and the mattress self-inflates as the foam sucks up air and within a few minutes attains a thickness of 1½ inches. (More time is required in extreme cold; however, the moisture in human breath does no harm and a few quick puffs suffice to inflate.) Close the valve to trap air in the foam and go to bed. The cushioning is superb, and since the interior air can't circulate well through the foam, so is the insulation.

In the morning, open the valve while getting final winks, and body weight presses out much of the air. Finish the job by rolling up the mattress to a diameter of 4–6 inches, close the valve to prevent self-inflation on the trail, and away you go.

The regular-size Therm-A-Rest is 19 by 47 inches, weighs 1½ pounds, costs about $30.

FOR MOISTURE PROTECTION—THE GROUND SHEET

For any sleeping bag—no matter what the filler—to get damp or soaked in the course of a trip is always a minor or major catastrophe, to be avoided by every available manner and means.

Neither pad nor mattress can be trusted to keep the bag absolutely separated from wet ground; during the night a shifty sleeper slops over the edges. The tarp-camper therefore must carry a ground sheet. (The tent-camper, with a floored tent, needs no sheet to keep his bag dry but may want one to prevent abrasion of the expensive floor.)

A 7- by 8-foot sheet of 3-mil polyethylene, large enough for two or three sleepers, weighs a pound or so, sells for so little as to be "disposable"—and that's the problem, the poly plague whitening the backcountry. Coated ripstop nylon is costlier but so durable as to be a better buy over several years than all those poly sheets that punctured or cracked, letting the bag get wet, and never quite burned up in the campfire, just melted on the rocks, nasty messes. (PACK IT OUT.)

12

TENTS AND TARPS

LOOK back several decades, deep in the memories of veterans still pounding trails despite trick knees and backs, arthritic hips, broken arches, inflamed tendons, sour stomachs, and other scars from the era of nailed boots, wooden packboards, wool sleeping bags, and half-stewed prunes and charcoal-crunchy oatmeal.

In the mind's eye, see a band of these pioneers sack out in a mountain meadow under a clear sky. What is between them and the stars? Nothing but the thin envelope of earth's atmosphere and millions of miles of space. See them fall asleep, and soon begin to shiver, and periodically, wakened by the cold, rolling over to find a closer approach to fetal warmth, glance up to make sure the stars remain bright. And when the stars turn watery, then vanish? Shivers lessen with the great tarp of clouds hung over the meadow, reducing heat loss by radiation. But sleep grows expectant, broken by frequent semiconscious glimpses upward, hoping for stars to sparkle through. Then, "pit!" Instantly alert, though still asleep, waiting for the "pat!" With "pit-a-pat, pit-a-pat" comes full consciousness. Then, "SPLAT!," and sadly they crawl from bags, gather gear in arms, stumble across the meadow to the forest edge, and snuggle up to trees, hoping it's not a three-day blow that will saturate the whole blessed world.

Why are these pioneers naked to the sky? Are they idiots?

In the mind's eye, see—on the same night in the same meadow—a second band of hikers smugly bedded down in tents. They sleep sounder than the others, partly because they are wealthy enough to own tents and rich people always sleep better, and partly because they are much wearier from having hauled pounds of heavy fabric to the highlands. They are not wakened by the "pit," the "pat," or even the "pit-a-pat." But they stir with the "SPLAT" because the blob of rain is not stopped by the tent, only broken into a fine spray. After an hour of "SPLAT-SPLAT-SPLAT" they are awake and damp and miserably aware that if it's a genuine three-day blow, they will despite their wealth get as wet as the poor boys cuddling the trees.

The choice for backpackers then was between (1) carrying a heavy tent (assuming one could afford it) and thus reducing the miles-per-day traveled, punishing a back already suffering under the weight of other primitive gear, and gaining in exchange meager protection, and (2) carrying no tent or tarp at all, trusting to good weather, interwoven branches of trees, overhanging rocks, the trail cabins and lean-tos then numerous and uncrowded, and accepting the inevitability of now and then being blasted right out of the wilderness in a retreat-from-Moscow stagger.

A few gimpy old troglodytes preserve the no-tent-or-tarp tradition, saying modern gear feeds the base lust to "conquer nature," that man is better for the humility of vulnerability.

In shelter as in so much else, World War II was the boundary between old and new. With V-J Day the backcountry of North America blossomed in a glory of orange-and-blue 7- by 11-foot life-raft sails of the miracle fabric, nylon, light and strong, coated to be waterproof, and given away by surplus stores for a dollar or two. Pioneers rigged them as tarps or converted them to tents, confessing that their motive for trusting to luck in the past had been not asceticism so much as poverty.

Since then, in what some hail as the millennium and others as a warning of impending judgment, hikers of moderate means and load-carrying capacity have grown confident that they can always build a snuggly wilderness home secure against any but the most fanatic attacks. The expectation is excessive in some climates, some elevations, some seasons. In general, though, it is true the backpacker of today can gain protection beyond the dreams of his grandparents.

Is this decadent, depraved, sinful? Perhaps. However, just as nobody really wants another Depression (also now said to have been ennobling), no hiker really wants to get soaked or frozen or bug-bitten to frothing hysterics.

Purism remains an option. The difference is, discomfort used to be compulsory. Now there's a choice.

CHOOSING A SHELTER

There still are hikers who cast off chains of comfort for the liberation of risk, and not all are doddering anachronisms; some are matured flower children who know they have not truly escaped the city as long as they haul with them its high-energy high-chemical high-price technology. The pendulum swings. The ball bounces. Bands of youths are even out in the wilds seeking totems, just as in the time of Hiawatha.

However, most beginners would as soon defer that initiation until they've learned to cope with blisters and black flies. They don't want to actually conquer nature but would like to avoid conquest of themselves, and to avoid being routed and put to the sword, are willing to tolerate bits of the city. Ordinarily, then, selection of shelter is one of the Big Four basic decisions. Two preliminary questions:

First, after battering by boots, pummeling by pack, stunning by sleeping bag, *how much money is left*? If next to none, a sheet of polyethylene costing a dollar or two fends off enough of nature's nastiness to get through most nights. A single-wall tent copes with more, and in economy models at a cost of as little as $30. A double-wall tent—well, the bargain basement is around $75, the luxury level $200, $400, and out of sight. Yet such a trail home can last years— years of rapturous nights. Knowing this, a beginner may want to rent tents—several styles—from a backpacking shop to learn for himself what's what before investing any sum, large or small.

Second, *what is the shelter for*?

Rain, of course, but how much, how often? A hiker who never will encounter more than summer drizzles (ocean beaches) and an occasional afternoon thundershower (High Sierra) is silly to spend the money and pack the weight to defend against ceaseless downpours (Cascades and Olympics).

Blizzards and monsoons? For those a person should look beyond the "three-season tents" emphasized in these pages to the "four-season" models.

Winds? Aside from Arctic gales there are several species. Some drive rain and fog—or dust—through any manner of tarp rig, and then shred the tarp and blow the bits to the next county. Even mild breezes are cooling; partly due to this, partly to the conservation of body heat, a tent interior is about 10° warmer than the outside; in a strong wind, due to the wind-chill factor (Chapter 6), the differential is much more.

Sleeping under stars is one of the grandest experiences in backpacking. It may also be one of the coldest because the body-and-bag unit, together with all the rest of the world, radiates heat to the sky. On overcast nights the clouds usually reflect heat back to earth, but on clear nights it goes straight to outer space; especially in the thin air of high meadows the ground cools, and so do uncovered sleepers. The starry nights are chilly. They may also be wet when next-to-ground air is cooled below the dew point and beads of dew or crystals of frost form on the sleeping bag. A shelter, whether tent, tarp, or tree, greatly reduces radiation heat loss and gives a warmer (and drier) sleep.

In hot open country it is quite possible to get too much sun; a tent or tarp may well be wanted for a shady retreat.

In popular camps many hikers grow sensitive to being stared at by neighbors; a tarp offers a partial screen but only a tent gives complete privacy, particularly appreciated by—for example—unliberated females and males who don't enjoy undressing in public. (However, beware of night activities in a candlelit tent that may draw crowds out of the bushes to watch what in the 1920s was called a "shadow show" and extensively legislated against; in some jurisdictions such performances are still felonies.)

Finally, in some places at some seasons the major menace is not moisture or cold or voyeurs but bugs, both those with wings and the creepy-crawlies. A tarp puts no obstruction in the paths of insects or small beasts; a floored tent with netting bars just about anything that lacks sharp teeth and claws.

Other questions arise:

How many people are there? A tarp of proper dimensions can cover any number from a loner to a platoon. Virtually all tents are designed for two adults, the most common combination on American trails, but readily accommodate a child or two. Big families have a problem. Another problem.

How much weight can the hiker carry, and how much does he want to? Shelter weights range from 0 pounds for the martyr-saint to the pound or so of a poly tarp, to two-person tents of 3½-8 pounds, to circus tents up to 10 or 12 pounds. As a rule of thumb, *shelter weight should be no more than 3–4 pounds per person.* Most backpacker tents are under the limit when occupied by the maximum potential population. If the shelter is carried only short distances, a few extra pounds are a minor concern; on long jaunts every ounce matters and less protection may be accepted.

INTRODUCTION TO TENTS

To return briefly from technology to sociology, it is truly said that the past is a foreign country; backpackers of the 1980s resemble their

ancestors of the 1940s about as much as scarlet tanagers do pterodac-
tyls. Nowhere are the contrasts more evident than in camp. Those
cold-blooded old reptiles felt that feathers (tents) were for sissies; the
gaudy-plumaged wildlander of today considers tarp-sleepers barely a
figleaf from stark naked. Betraying saurian prejudices, the first edition
of this manual discussed tents only after extravagantly praising tarps.
However, public opinion has prevailed and here tarps have been
shuffled off to chapter's end. Perhaps in another decade they'll have
gone the way of the Trapper Nelson and tricouni and dehydrated
spinach.

The typical beginner wants a tent, whether he needs it or not, and
his decision is not necessarily an affront to reason and nature—or even
the budget. Recent years have brought new materials and sophistica-
tion that almost convert a reptile. Moreover, due to economies of
semi–mass production, some of the marvels cost little more than a tarp
and even the most expensive cost comparatively less than the trail
hovels of decades past.

In no part of the trail outfit has creativity so run amok—such tent
architects as Bill Moss are spoken of in the same breath as Buckmin-
ster Fuller. But the humble hiker innocent of esthetics needn't be
intimidated; with or without a refined eye, amid the wide variety he'll
find any number of very decent choices for his purposes.

Keeping the purposes clearly in mind is the key. Most backpackers

do best with a "three-season tent," lighter and less elaborate and cheaper than the "winter" or "expedition" tents. Beyond that lies not quite chaos but certainly confusion, as is apparent in following sections that try to sort out models in simple, logical categories. First, though, some remarks are in order about matters common to tents in general.

MATERIALS

Cotton has disappeared from tenting except for car-camping and canoeing and the like; *nylon* is the usual material nowadays. Typically the floor is an abrasion-resistant *high-count taffeta,* coated for water-repellency with polyurethane, polymer, or vinyl; the walls are uncoated *ripstop* or *nylsilk,* lighter than taffeta; and the rainfly is a coated ripstop. (For definitions of fabrics, see Chapter 9.)

Dacron, heavier and costlier, is used by a few manufacturers. It has less stretch and better resists ultraviolet radiation, which in a few years of frequent exposure can cut nylon's strength in half.

Discussions of *Gore-Tex* and *aluminized nylon/mylar laminate* are deferred to "Single-Wall Tents," below.

Many states have laws requiring tents and tarps to be *flame-retardant.* However, some materials (Gore-Tex, polyethylene) can't be treated and thus some tents can't be sold in some states. And some can be sold —but not as tents. Gore-Tex bivy sacks, for example, must often be advertised and catalogued as sleeping-bag covers, and poly tarps as ground sheets.

A tent lacking *bug netting* is really a mere tarp. *Mosquito* mesh is exclusive enough for most places but *no-see-um,* though costing more, preserves the peace from all but microscopic marauders.

COLOR

When the French poilus charged to the Battle of the Frontiers in 1914, full of *cran* and élan, they got their red pantaloons and blue jackets shot off and belatedly understood why the Germans wore uniforms of field-gray, the British of khaki (the Hindi word for "dusty"), and Robin Hood of forest-green.

During the 1960s, backpackers, formerly blending into the land-scape like Leatherstocking, similarly began charging to wild frontiers in hues meant to catch the eyes of sharpshooters (with cameras). Disclaiming exhibitionism, though, they argued that vivid colors make a lost hiker easier to find, that in wet climates an orange or red tent gives a warm feeling, that in hot climates a blue seems to blunt the fury of the sun.

Maybe so. However, just as a city's honking horns rack nerves and murder sleep, so does *color pollution* disrupt wilderness. Grass is meant to be green and snow white, not orange and red and yellow polka dots. From miles away the modern tent leaps out, grabbing the reluctant eye of a hiker who otherwise might enjoy the illusion of owning the whole valley. To enlarge a shrinking world, we go slower. To enwilden a crowd-madding world, we hide.

Further, neon tents advertise—stand on a peak and spot the colors, zero in with binoculars, and the joint is cased to the satisfaction of any backcountry burglar.

Though manufacturers have been slow to respond, demand is growing for *earth tones*. Such as forest-green, khaki, field-gray.

CARE

Immediately upon buying a tent, the hiker should set it up at home. Several purposes are served. He learns *how* to set it up, better here than on a stormy night in the wilds. He confirms that the vendor has included all the promised parts. Finally, he takes the first and essential step in tent maintenance: using a compound sold by a backpacking shop, he paints and seals the seams, a process to be repeated annually. (But note: nylon can be waterproofed only under factory conditions; once the tent fabric loses repellency, all attempts to treat with spray-on or paint-on compounds are fruitless.)

Fire is the chief threat to tents (and tarps). If sparks from blazing logs are blowing toward the shelter, either the fire should be damped or the shelter moved. To repair sparkholes, rips, and punctures, part of the tent kit should be repair tape. Cloth tape 2 inches wide with adhesive backing is recommended for polyethylene, coated nylon, and other nonporous materials; 2-inch ripstop tape is standard for ripstop nylon.

Generally speaking, a tent is not meant to be cooked in. Moisture from steaming pots adds enormously to interior wetness, commonly to an extent that cannot be alleviated by cross-ventilation or breathing out through the fabric. More dangerous, with many stoves there is the chance of a flare-up that might instantly melt a huge hole in the roof. Cooking is best done outside the tent, or at least in the vestibule, if any. Expeditioners may have to take the risk frequently, but backpackers rarely. (Nevertheless, there are wildland veterans who always cook in tents when wind frustrates the stove or bugs devil the chef, not to mention when the weather is plain lousy miserable. But they do so carefully—*very carefully.*)

To protect the tent floor from gumming by pitch and abrasion by rocks, it is wise always to place a lightweight poly sheet underneath.

A tent should never be washed but may be sponged off occasionally; better, really, to let it acquire a dignified grime and character.

However, gritty dirt tracked or blown inside should be scrupulously swept out to avoid sandpapering the fabric. Fastidious hikers carry a small whiskbroom for the purpose—and a sponge to mop up puddles.

Moisture inevitably accumulates in a tent during a trip, if not from blown-in rain or tracked-in water, then from exhalations of human bodies. Though nylon doesn't mildew, other fabrics in zippers and

elsewhere may. Thus, before a tent is folded for extended storage it should be erected in the yard in sunny weather, or in the basement or spare bedroom, and thoroughly air-dried. (And swept clean.)

DOUBLE-WALL TENTS

Whatever else a tent does, most owners demand above all that it keep out rain. Not so difficult with modern chemistry's better things for better living. However, when tent pores are so tight that the rain can't pound in, how does body moisture breathe out? Since a human exhales a pint of water a night, in a sealed tent the interior is damp by morning, a swamp by the end of a three-day blow.

This was the dilemma of the single-wall tent wrestled with by designers from the era of Whymper's scrambles in the Alps. Periodically a miracle fabric was invented, claimed to bar exterior moisture and release the inner, and mountaineers cried "Hallelujah!" Then, in a year or so, rejoicing subsided to mumbling and soon no more was heard.

Later in this chapter a new miracle and an old heresy are discussed, as well as single-wall tents of nonmiracle and purely orthodox materials and design. However, currently accepted universally (almost) as the sole remedy for prolonged rain, and excellent for every other purpose, is the double-wall tent. The inner, or main, tent has walls of lightweight, breathable fabric that let body moisture exhale freely,

and a floor—extending several inches up the wall—of tough, water-proof cloth. The door is zippered (in economy models, perhaps merely tied) and backed with bug netting. To minimize the condensation that occurs in any tent (nothing's perfect), there are one or more ventilator windows with storm flaps and bug netting. The outer tent, or rainfly, *separate* in most models, in others attached to the inner tent *(integral fly),* is a lightweight, strong, waterproof cloth. When the only protection desired is against fog, wind, radiation heat loss, voyeurs, flying bugs and creeping beasties, the rainfly needn't be rigged. For hard rain it is rigged, at some distance from the inner tent to allow airflow space: farther away in warm weather, when sun protection may also be wanted; closer in cold weather, when warmth too is thus provided. In balmy weather the fly alone may be rigged, as a tarp, to keep the moon from shining in eyes, the morning sun from baking the bag.

So is defined the basic standard tent carried by nearly every back-packer. But so diverse are they in actuality that one is reminded of the zoologist who finished writing a definition of a dog, looked out the window, and saw the neighborhood pack romping—a St. Bernard, a Mexican hairless, a borzoi, a dachshund, a dingo. After reflecting on what an odd neighborhood he lived in, the zoologist wondered, "How do they all know they're the same thing?" Not by looking, that's clear.

An obvious way to categorize tents is by *size.* About 95 percent of all those currently sold are for two or three persons. If advertised as "two person," space suffices for two adults, perhaps with some gear left outside in giant poly bags or under a poly tarp. If "two-three-person," two adults are comfortable (most gear inside); three can squeeze in (gear outside); mother and father and one or even two small children fit nicely. If "three-person," the capacity is three adults and gear or two parents and two middle-sized kids. Tents in this range are discussed in the following two sections, larger (circus) tents in a third.

Another way to sort things out is by *method of support:* (1) the free-standing tent, a canopy hung from a self-supporting frame of stressed poles; (2) the tent supported by poles anchored to the ground by pegs.

Another is *shape:* (1) geodesic dome; (2) tunnel; (3) A-frame; (4) weirdos that fall through cracks and will not be further discussed here despite the temptation—Gerry Windjammer (two-man teepee), Springbar No. 40 (free-standing box), and Upland Standard Fastent (release this—cautiously—from the stuff bag and—POP!—it leaps up to become a free-standing tent).

Rudimentary calculations show that tent categories are limited in number only by the patience of the categorizer. In these pages precision is leavened with Heisenberg's Principle to better portray the real world. Though there are A-frames that are free-standing and tunnels that require pegging, most free-standing tents are domes and tunnels, and most guyed-and-pegged tents are A-frames, and therefore all two-three-person tents are dumped in two bins. But remember, there are mongrels.

FREE-STANDING TENTS (TWO-THREE-PERSON)

In the 1970s the free-standing tent emerged from decades of eccentricity and obscurity. And lo, in several summers the meadows were in full geodesic bloom and the revered A-frame had slipped to second place. Whether this is a wise evolution, or a topic for an addendum to Charles Mackay's classic of the nineteenth century, *Extraordinary Popular Delusions and the Madness of Crowds,* is debatable. However, the tarp having been demoted, consistency dictates priority for the free-stander. At least for this edition.

A major reason for the popularity is a roomier interior than the old A-frame—half again more cubic inches for equal floor area. Lying down is not the mandatory position for most of the people most of the time, everyone can sit up, much pleasanter for lacing boots and drinking soup and playing hearts.

Aerodynamic performance is very different. Winds that smack flat walls of an A-frame, setting them flapping and cracking, flow quietly around the curved walls. (The other side of the story is that even moderate winds push the wall in, perhaps not threatening tent stability but crowding the soup drinkers. Further, blustery, shifting winds that don't bother semirigid poles of the A-frame start the flexible poles dancing. Finally, a free-stander of the dome style may be a scene of stark terror in high winds, occupants sitting in a circle and mumbling prayers all the long night while momentarily expecting a gust to wedge under the floor, tip the dome over, and roll it like a basketball across the tundra, over the cliff. Or carry it flying off to Oz.) In anything but still air the free-stander must be guyed and pegged—and can never be so tightly pinned to earth as the A-frame.

The walls are less given to collapsing under the weight of falling snow. (But the roof is more given to sagging, letting snow pile and rain puddle.)

The setting up is faster (although some A-framers deny it, say it actually is slower.) Fit pole sections together, slip them through sleeves or collars, clip rainfly to tent frame (no separate rigging lines), move in the furniture, and go to bed. If the site proves too sunny or bumpy, no need to de-rig, simply pick up the erected tent and move it. When leaving, shake it clean. In calm weather, no guylines to tighten, no pegs to trip over.

Shifting unquestionably to the debit side, free-standers cost more than A-frames, and due to more poles, weigh 1–2 pounds more.

The most serious objection to free-standers is that they may not stand at all, due to broken *poles* or *wands,* usually four to six in number, in some designs slipping into sleeves, in others totally exterior, the configurations myriad. Manufacturers continue to experiment with materials: solid fiberglass; hollow, wrapped fiberglass; fiberglass with aluminum ferrules; and all-aluminum. Other sports are exploited—the fiberglass comes mainly from fishing rods, the aluminum from arrow shafts. Whatever the material, great care must be taken while erecting the tent to engage pole sections firmly before bending—fail to do so and they may snap. A mandatory precaution is always to carry one extra section.

Dome

The style of free-stander that has captured the crowd is the *dome* or *geodesic tent,* in smaller sizes called the *wedge.* Some are in the "expedition" class, with special features discussed below under A-frames. In those meant for the average backpacker, details vary considerably but all models are excellent in forests and meadows, though sometimes uncomfortable—or dangerous—in highlands of strong winds.

One example is a two-person wedge, total weight with rainfly, poles, pegs, cord, and carrying sack, 5½ pounds, price about $135.

Representative two-three-person, three-season domes weigh from 7 to 8½ pounds complete, cost from $200 to $300. Winter tents weigh and cost more.

Tunnel

Also called *half-cylinder* or *barn-shaped,* a tunnel is exceptionally long, giving plenty of room for gear, and combines the headroom of a dome with a lower and more wind-stable profile. Most tunnels are

Example of a free-standing tent, dome design. Inset: *With rainfly rigged.*

Example of a small dome, or wedge. Inset: *With rainfly rigged.*

not completely free-standing but require some guying. Other than climbers and winter mountaineers, enthusiasts typically are hikers fond of tundras and moraines and gales.

No single example is truly representative. There are two-person models weighing around 6 pounds, costing from $200 to $325; three-person models of 7–8 pounds, $225 to $275; and a hybrid between tunnel and A-frame, 10 pounds, $225. Most are in the "expedition" class.

Free-Standing A-Frame

Some folks prefer mongrels to purebreds. A number of models have the old A shape but an external frame of sleeved poles, combining stability with headroom.

Among current offerings are two-person tents weighing 6 pounds, complete with integral fly and all other usual paraphernalia, costing

Example of a free-standing tent, tunnel design, with rainfly rigged.

about $190, and economy models that weigh more, up to 7 pounds, but are as little as $90.

A-FRAME TENTS (TWO-THREE PERSONS)

From the days of Whymper to the middle 1970s, when a hiker said "tent" he meant "A-frame." A century of experimentation with materials, shapes, and special features went into the design; countless person-nights on every continent in every season, from summer forests of North America to icy ledges near the summit of Mount Everest, provided a rigorous field test. Conservatives who believe true progress is deliberate bewail the folly of abruptly and blithely casting all this away to run madly after the free-stander. They nod with sage approval to see that many beginners show proper respect by choosing A-frames because "That's how a tent is supposed to look."

251

Example of a free-standing, A-frame design. As with many free-standers, some pegging is desirable if not essential. Inset: *With rainfly rigged.*

Characteristics of the A-frame called disadvantages by opponents are considered advantages by friends: headroom is scant. (The low profile better resists hurricanes.) Wind doesn't flow smoothly around the flat walls. (They may flap but they don't push.) Guylines and pegs cannot be dispensed with even in absolutely still air, must always be there, time-consuming to rig, tangling the feet. (The A-frame is never seen sailing over the valley.)

Some virtues are unmingled and uncontested: there's less to go catastrophically wrong which would leave hikers untented in the wild night. Because the poles (usually telescoping aluminum with fail-safe connector of shock cord inside) don't have to bend, they are unlikely to break—though carrying one spare section is nevertheless advisable. Rain sheds neatly. High winds bring noise but not peril. Finally, among double-wall tents the lightest loads, the lowest prices, will always be those of A-frames.

Example of the traditional A-frame tent, poled, pegged, and guyed. Inset:
With rainfly rigged.

Details, Variations, and Elaborations

The century of experimentation neglected no portion of the A-
frame, developed niceties from top to bottom and end to end. Lightweight, low-cost models embody the fewest special features,
"expedition" designs the most. Certain of the following details are
also found on free-standers.

Weight is saved on some designs by having a single vertical pole
at each end, or A-frame poles at the door and a vertical pole at the
rear. Another has an A-frame at the door end, no poles at all at the
rear.

Side pullouts, tie loops attached to the centerpoint of the walls and
anchored to the ground, eliminate center sagging and maximize interior space.

A neater and more expensive way to achieve the same end is to
construct the tent with a *catenary cut,* in which the fabric is cut on a
curve in such a way that it pulls taut when rigged, eliminating flapping

253

Example of the traditional A-frame, this design saving weight by only one pair of poles. Inset: *With rainfly rigged.*

and sagging, and again enlarging the interior. The catenary cut (though still usually supplemented by pullouts) is characteristic of the best tents, substantially increasing stability in storms.

On some designs the rainfly extends out from the door far enough to form a *vestibule* for extra wind and rain protection, storing gear, and cooking. On others a vestibule is an integral part of the inner tent. In either case the result may be a "2½-person tent."

A few models have an *integral fly,* permanently connected to the inner tent, with advantages of quick rigging, there being only one set of pegs to drive, and disadvantages of nondetachability; this style must be dried with special care before storage.

Some tents have a drawstring-closed *tunnel entrance* instead of a zippered doorway—or perhaps a tunnel at one end, zipper door at the other. Since even nylon zippers can freeze or blow apart, the tunnel provides a fail-safe entry for high, cold mountaineering; for summer backpacking, though, it merely adds weight and expense.

A *frost liner,* a detachable inner wall of light cotton, collects ice crystals that otherwise would form directly on the tent wall and be shaken loose by wind to create an interior snowstorm; also, when the crystals melt, the cotton soaks up the moisture. The liner is valuable for temperatures below 20°F but not for most backpacking.

Because cooking in the tent is often necessary in high-altitude and winter mountaineering, some tents have a zippered *cook hole* in the floor so spilled soup will run into the ground or snow rather than onto sleeping bags. The zipper can be a leak point and thus is not desirable for a three-season tent.

Among other features on the more elaborate (expedition) tents are pockets on inner walls for storing small bits of gear; loops at peaks for stringing a clothesline; on the outside, snow/sod flaps for added stability in wind.

For guylines, a *shock cord* of rubber stringers sheathed in nylon or cotton stretches in wind gusts, then returns to original length and tautness. Shock cord should *not* be used to guy an inner tent because it allows flapping that strains the fabric; better in such case to let the pole be bent. However, shock cord should always be used with a rainfly, which balloons in the wind, and being of a coated fabric, may rip unless strain is transferred to the cord.

A *tent-cord tightener* is a device of nylon or aluminum that does the job of the traditional taut-line hitch, which probably only a handful of backpackers know how to tie or care to learn. With one of these gadgets on each tent (or tarp) line, ground pegs can be placed approximately and the proper tension in lines obtained by adjusting tighteners rather than repeatedly relocating pegs.

Examples

A dying breed? More likely, just lying low, waiting for the free-standers to blow away. The A-frame continues to be represented by more models, demonstrating the faith of the manufacturers, even if more free-standers are sold at the moment.

A survey of current catalogs found two-person A-frames of "normal" design, with all basic three-season features (rainfly, bug netting,

ARE YOU SURE THIS IS WHAT THEY CALL "THE *FAMILY* TENT"?

floor) for as little as $75 (weight, complete, 6 pounds) and $85 (6 pounds). Most examples were above that in price—from $115 to $140—and about the same weight (5¾ to 7¼ pounds). Models with A-frame poles only at the front end ("low-ender") and light materials throughout, and no zipper, were $115 (5¾ pounds) and $135 (4¾ pounds).

What would be "over-tenting" for most hikers is just right for the four-season, winter, expedition folks. Weights range from 5½ to 8 pounds, prices from $150 to $250; at the top of the line, the tents meant for wintering at the South Pole, the numbers soar beyond.

CIRCUS TENTS

The two-three-person tent is the most versatile size, accommodating twosomes (the vast majority of the trail population) and also parents with a small child or two. Should the party be larger, a second tent serves.

However, parents with more than the ecologically permissible 2.1 children may find that at a certain age and size they won't lie inert all night the way sardines are supposed to, yet aren't quite ready to go off to a separate tent to face the lions and tigers and bears. The "family" or "stand-up" tent with plenty of wiggling room is particularly appreciated then, as well as during days of rain when each squirming kid must be kept from bloody war by being assigned an

WELL, I THINK ITS A GOOD EXAMPLE OF OVER-TENTING!

inviolable territory. In another sort of ménage, companionable adults may not wish to pair off but stay in a group—for bridge tournaments, recitals by recorder quartets. In either case, though the weight of a circus tent (and the price) may seem formidable, the individual share is often less than with a multiplicity of two-person tents.

Demand being relatively small, choice is rather restricted. Climbers descending from Arctic climes to go hiking with the family often use their "expedition headquarters" tent, such as the Mount Logan (Mount McKinley), with a centerpole, more than 7 feet high at the peak, suitable for four adults and gear or any number of children, weighing 12 pounds complete with rainfly and costing about $360. Other examples are two models by North Face, the Oval Intention (dome, three-four adults) at 9 pounds, $315, and the Morning Glory (central A-frame with end poles, four-five), 13½ pounds, $395. The Jansport Trail Dome holds four–six people, weighs 13 pounds, and costs about $310.

Few indeed are three-season circus tents. Among them: Eureka Timberline (free-standing A-frame, just under 6 feet high, four adults), 10¼ pounds, $160. Gerry Camponaire II (A-frame, just under 6 feet high, three-four), 9½ pounds, $200. Gerry Fortnight (A-frame, just under 6 feet, four-six), 11¼ pounds, $220. Sierra Designs Three-Man (tripod-supported with hexagonal floor, 6 feet high, three-four), 8 pounds, $235.

The final word is a tent that brings hikers from miles around to goggle in awed admiration, the Bill Moss Trillium, a free-stander with three carrels, each as large as a two-person tent and each with separate entrance, a six-person palace weighing merely 13 pounds, costing not quite $400.

SINGLE-WALL TENTS: MIRACLES AND HERESIES

So dominant nowadays is the double-wall tent that within the great central majority of hikers it's hardly possible to get up a debate. However, from the sides come dissenting voices. On the left are those who say of Gore-Tex, "I have seen the future and it works." On the right, energetically defending his naked truth, is Jack Stephenson.

GORE-TEX

Gore-Tex is judged to have won its case for clothing (Chapter 9), staked a solid claim in sleeping bags (Chapter 11), and provided a new and superb weather-beater in the *bivy sack* (Chapter 11), usually advertised as a sleeping-bag cover but really a tiny one-person tent. For larger tents, however, the jury is still out, arguing. In some fervent opinion Gore-Tex delivers from every evil, save only erupting volcanoes and falling stars. Others consider it excellent for most three-season uses but questionable in extreme cold and extreme humidity. Skeptics feel that in tents the miracle has reached the level of its incompetence—but few are ready to write off a new material still being improved, designs still evolving.

Advantages—potential, at least—are great. The tent with a single wall of Gore-Tex laminate is more windproof and warmer than a double-wall tent. Absence of a rainfly means less weight, quicker rigging, better wind-spillage, no flapping, and greater freedom of design.

The problem derives from the nature of the stuff. What makes it work is body heat pushing water vapor out through the fabric—but much of the time bodies in tents are inside sleeping bags, keeping their heat to themselves. Moreover, in warm weather and high humidity (as, say, summer in the Appalachians or on an ocean beach) there is no "push" because wet air inside can't be forced into wet air outside. And in freezing weather the pores clog with frost, and breathing then ceases, and the pint of water per person per night swamps the tent floor. To help the "push," tent laminates are lighter than those in clothing, sometimes tending toward flimsiness, and the interior is kept small, making for cramped quarters.

Two other complaints: Gore-Tex laminates cannot be made fire-retardant and so their use for tents is illegal in many states; the material costs like the dickens.

Nevertheless, the hiker wishing to join the jury can find a few offerings, though he may have to become a smuggler and scofflaw. The Early Winters Light Dimension, a free-standing, streamlined tunnel with more space than an A-frame, rigs in a minute, weighs a meager 3¾ pounds, yet holds two adults, costs about $220. From the same firm is the Winterlight, similar but for four seasons, 4½ pounds, $255; and the Earth Station, a four-person geodesic dome, 9¾ pounds, $385. From Marmot Mountain Works comes the Taku, a free-standing semi-tunnel for two persons, four seasons, 6 pounds, $295.

Example of a Gore-Tex single-wall tent, kept chummily small, almost of bivy-sack size, in order for the "heat pump" to work.

259

STEPHENSON

Jack Stephenson says that Gore-Tex either doesn't work or isn't needed and that the double-wall tent is based on ignorance of physics. Attempting to summarize his arguments here would be unjust even if they were fully understood; the reader is referred to his catalog. Objections to his tents are as vigorous as his are to others, a common criticism being the danger of drowning in sweat. However, defenders scoff at that and declare the heresy works, especially in cold weather. The simplicity and lightness certainly are spectacular.

Stephenson's substitute for breathable walls is "differential-height vents" at the tent ends, at ground level and peak level. Body heat pushes warm, wet air out the high vents, replaced by cold, dry air sucked in the bottom vents. As an essential complement, the people sleep in bags with *vapor barriers* (see Chapter 9), which in Stephenson-made bags are built-in; though body heat stays inside the bags, so does body moisture.

The single wall is ripstop nylon/mylar laminate, waterproof and very light and strong, aluminized to reflect radiant energy and thus be cool in the sun, warm under stars. The aerodynamic tunnel (half-cylinder) splits every wind. There is no spiderweb of guys; setting up (only three pegs) takes less than 5 minutes. The Silver 2X (two adults) weighs merely 2½ pounds, costs about $200; the Gold 3X, 3½ pounds, $250.

SINGLE-WALL TENTS: POOR BUT HONEST

A hiker may travel such country at such times as to be fairly sure the worst he might encounter are brief thundershowers, clouds of whining mosquitoes, or a heaven of stars draining heat from the earth.

Or a hiker may be willing to settle for less than a suite at the Ritz, ask only modest amenities.

Or a hiker may somehow have evaded the prosperity that seems nigh universal among the beautiful people of today's trails.

For any of these reasons he may content himself with a single-wall tent of one kind or another.

Example of an A-frame tent with a single waterproof wall, no rainfly. Ventilation is essential to minimize interior condensation.

VENTILATION

A tent with not only the floor but the single wall coated to be waterproof must rely on ventilation to minimize sweating. Typically, both ends can be opened wide to let the winds blow through, bugs filtered out by panels of netting. When there are breezes they usually prevent condensation on wall interiors; when not, not; calm nights are drippy. The ends have storm flaps; if closed only briefly, then opened when the squall passes, no harm is done; if kept shut during a three-day blow, the occupants may have to get buckets and bail for their lives.

One two-person example is a very light A-frame with single vertical poles front and back, weighing just 3¼ pounds, costing just $35. Others range up to 4¼ pounds and $70.

NETTING (BUG TENT)

In hot country the worst enemy may be bugs. Coping magnificently is the two-person Eureka Mojave, with a fabric floor but A-frame walls entirely of netting. However, a fly is supplied for rain or as a sunshade. Weight complete with fly, 6 pounds, $75.

TUBE TENT (INSTANT TENT)

A lone hiker, especially if poor, finds much to admire in the tube tent of .003-inch polyethylene 9 feet long, 3–5 feet wide at the base when rigged; 1¼ pounds, $7. Three grommets at each end permit easy rigging with nylon cord, which in heavy weather can be threaded through the grommets to draw the ends tight—though not for long without severe condensation. Capacity is one adult plus pack. A two-person tube weighs 2 pounds, costs $8.

Tubes are so cheap and light and quick, protect so well against rain and (ends drawn tight) wind, that they often are recommended for emergency kits, potential lifesavers in sudden storms.

TARPS

Three species of hikers habitually sleep under tarps. One is the creaky old crock whose 7- by 11-foot war-surplus life-raft sail is enshrined in memory with his Model A and who always has felt tents are for (1) winter, (2) nights in the summit crater of Mount Rainier, and (3) girls. The second is neither creaky nor old but has been on the trails long enough to comprehend that tent-campers are retreaters-to-the-womb, that tarp-campers, livers-with-nature, intimately know not only wind and bugs but also sights of moonlit clouds and shooting stars and dawn, scents of pine needles and flowers and grasses and prowling skunks, sounds of little feet scurrying in the darkness over sleeping bags and faces. They experience more of everything except claustrophobia, and in retrospect their wilderness nights are as memorable as their days. The third tarper is the beginning backpacker who compares weights and prices and decides (shrewd chap) that tents are for rich donkeys.

These are the free spirits, a select band, smaller and more select by the year, who ask protection only against downward rain, heat loss and dew accumulation through radiation, and hot sun. The creepy-crawlies they accept, perhaps becoming inordinately fond of beetles,

One-man polyethylene tube tent. In emergencies the corners need not be pegged, the weight of the hiker and gear preventing wind from blowing the shelter away. String a line between two supports, and the "instant tent" is erected.

and the buzzing wings they foil with a "habitat" of no-see-um netting (Chapter 15). Mild breezes they welcome, and the gentle mists they may carry, bathing the brow. And as part of the bargain they accept the occasional Armageddon when forces of evil rage in the night, chewing up tarps and spitting them out, sending naked-to-the-sky refugees fleeing through the tempest, whimpering.

VARIETIES OF TARP

Hardware stores sell very thin (.002-inch, or "2 mil") and cheap transparent polyethylene ("poly") tarps intended for such purposes as painters' drop cloths. A 9- by 12-foot size, large enough for two or three adult sleepers and their gear, weighs about 1 pound and costs perhaps $2. (Backpacking shops stock "emergency shelter" tarps a bit more expensive but essentially the same.) The material is waterproof until punctured or ripped or abraded—which happens very easily. Hikers often carry two or three of these tarps, perhaps one for shelter, another, doubled, for a ground sheet, another for covering gear left outside the tarp or at the rain-unprotected edges. Unfortunately, due

to the cheapness and fragility, hikers also leave these tarps all over the landscape.

Backpacking shops generally begin their tarp line with various sizes of poly sheets .004-inch ("4 mil") thick, a translucent white to reflect sunlight (which transparent tarps do not, a serious flaw in blistered country where shade is badly wanted), with no grommets. Visqueen is a common trade name. The 9- by 12-foot size weighs 2 pounds, costs about $6. The 12- by 12-foot size, accommodating four adults or a married couple and several children, weighs 3 pounds, costs about $8. Such tarps are heavier than drop cloths but far more resistant to tearing and puncturing.

Available from a few shops is polyethylene reinforced with crossed nylon threads; such "tearproof" tarps weigh and cost more but cannot be ripped or shredded, though they can be punctured. A Griffolyn reinforced poly tarp in the 8- by 12-foot size weighs 2¾ pounds, costs $13.

Much tougher and less likely to rip in a wind or be punctured by sharp sticks, and very abrasion-resistant, are tarps of polymer-coated 3.1-ounce nylon in blue or yellow or other colors. These tarps last for years with proper care, compared to a summer or two (or one wild storm) for poly tarps; the coated nylon also weighs less. Equipped with eight grommets the 9- by 11-foot size (for three sleepers and gear) weighs 2 pounds and sells for about $38. A variation is a tarp

(green, orange) of 2.2-ounce ripstop nylon. The 9- by 10-foot size is 2 pounds, $28; the 12- by 10-foot, 2¾ pounds, $35.

Some shops offer more elaborate "multi-tie" nylon tarps with 8 to 16 grommets on edges and 5 reinforced pull-out tie loops on the surface for incredible versatility in rigging. A 9- by 11-foot tarp of 3.1-ounce nylon weighs 2¼ pounds, costs $45; in 2.2-ounce ripstop, 2 pounds, $35.

The wonder of the age, fit company for his Trillium, is the fabulous Bill Moss Parawing, a hyperbolic paraboloid. The 12-footer is $45; the 19-footer, $90.

GROMMETS AND SUBSTITUTES

The simplest way to attach rigging lines to a poly tarp is to bunch up the corners and tightly wrap them with a number of turns of cord. This method allows only four attachment points—the corners—which may not be enough to hold the tarp even reasonably close to the ground in a wind or to prevent it from sagging under the weight of rain.

A better technique is to push a rock, pine cone, or wad of paper against the tarp to form a protuberance around which a rigging line is then wrapped. In this manner a line can be attached at any point along the edge or in the middle.

The Vis-Clamp, a metal ring and a rubber ball, complicated to describe but easy to use, does the same job, working like a garter. The Versa Tie employs a disc rather than a ball.

Tarp-campers do well to carry a roll of 2-inch cloth tape with adhesive backing to reinforce tarps where they show signs of pulling apart and to repair rips and holes.

Polyethylene tarp (4-mil, translucent) rigged as shed roof, adequate protection against gentle rains, radiation heat loss, and glaring sun.

RIGGING A TARP

A tarp can be spread belatedly as a blanket when the party has gone to bed without erecting a shelter and doesn't feel like getting up to cope in any more elaborate way with showers. In the course of a full night, however, exhaled body moisture condenses on the inside of the "blanket" and thoroughly dampens sleeping bags.

Nylon tarp with built-in grommets, quickly and easily rigged as A-tent by use of two aluminum poles and eight lightweight pegs.

Accompanying photos show the two most common tarp rigs—the *shed roof* and the *A-frame*.

Two trees conveniently spaced, or a tree and a boulder, can support the tarp. Where nothing suitable of the sort can be found, the *bipod* comes to the rescue. The tarper first scouts around for four sturdy poles, perhaps washed up on the beach by waves or swept down to the cirque by avalanches; a length of about 5–7 feet serves. Construction proceeds in the following sequence: (1) one end of the ridgeline cord (see below) is tied to a heavy boulder or log or a peg (see below); (2) one pair of poles is stood upright, crossing, and the cord is wrapped around their junction to lash them into a bipod; (3) the cord is stretched out taut a dozen feet or so and lashed to the second pair of crossed poles, the second bipod; (4) the cord is drawn out taut and tied to a second boulder or log or peg; (5) the tarp is rigged over the ridgeline as an A-tent; (6) rocks, logs, sticks, or pegs anchor ground edges.

Tarping in any of the above manners involves searching for a perfect match-up of tarp-supporting trees and sleeping-smooth ground and/or scrounging for boulders and logs and poles. To avoid

the trouble—and possible disturbance of the landscape—some tarpers carry two aluminum poles and eight pegs, a package weighing maybe 2 pounds total; with these and sufficient cord they can homestead just about anywhere.

The tarp kit includes two varieties of *nylon cord.* Best for the ridge-line is a 50-foot length of ¼-inch, 1,100 pound test—an amazingly heavy load is placed on the line when the tarp is running rivers of rain and billowing in the wind. For anchoring corners and edges the ⅛-inch, 520-pound test, suffices; tarpers carry a substantial coil and cut pieces as needed for guylines, pack repairs, bootlaces, and dog leashes.

The best *poles* for tarping are telescoping or collapsing aluminum. An example is a ⅝-inch pole in take-apart sections connected by *shock cord*—elastic that runs through the sections, keeping them together. Three that form a pole 3½ feet long weigh 6½ ounces, cost $3.75. That length is a bare minimum; better to add a fourth section for an extra 13 inches. Another example is a pole that extends to 6 feet, telescopes to half that, weighs 1 pound, costs $5. *Note:* The insides of nesting poles must be kept clean to prevent jamming; especially at the ocean, where salt air rapidly corrodes aluminum, they should be wiped frequently and thoroughly.

The eight *pegs* or *stakes* cost little, in sum weigh ½ pound or less. A number of types are available:

Curved aluminum pegs nest to save space in the pack and hold well in everything except rocky ground. The 6½-inch length, ¾ ounce, usually does the job. The 8½-incher is better in beach sand.

Twisted, tinned steel wire ("skewer stake") drives into rocky ground, such as moraines, that resists other stakes. Length is 7 inches, weight less than ½ ounce. There are also aluminum skewers.

Cast-aluminum stakes are very strong and never deform; they are a bit heavier—1½ ounces for the 6½-incher—and cost a bit more.

Stakes of high-impact plastic ("power pegs") penetrate readily and hold well even in forest duff and beach sand. They make larger holes than others, objectionable in tender meadows. Weight is 1½ ounces for the 9-inch length.

13

TIME was when novice hikers planning wildland kitchens were inspired by a popular genre of American art, the calendar painting. There, all in florid color, they saw a band of hardy woodsmen gathered around a wall tent and massive stone fireplace, wearing pistols and Bowie knives, surrounded by double-bitted ax, chopping block, crosscut saw, rifles, fishing poles, cast-iron frying pans, iron kettle, monster coffeepot, sides of bacon and sacks of flour and salt and beans, table and chairs hewn from logs, laundry lines strung between trees, antelope suspended from a pole tripod, smokehouse full of trout, faithful Indian guide skinning out a bear—and the herd of horses or fleet of canoes that carried the ton of gear and supplies.

Led astray by such portraits of a largely imaginary past, many a person once sought to duplicate, to the limit of his carrying capacity, the ideal frontier kitchen. However, that old ideal is as long extinct as passenger pigeons darkening the sky and bison blanketing the prairies. The new ideal, that of the modern ethical hiker, is a kitchen kept as simple as possible to avoid damage to fragile ecosystems. And his back as well.

After the anguish of selecting boots, pack, sleeping bag, and tent, the beginner can relax when assembling his kitchen. The few, light, inexpensive elements are: (1) a fire; (2) cooking pots; (3) eating tools;

and (4) miscellaneous accessories. A number of handy gadgets are available for gracious living, but the novice does well to start with nothing but the basics and add frills very gradually, if at all.

FIRE—WITHOUT STOVE

WOOD FIRE

As explained in Chapter 4, the backpacker is by necessity growing accustomed to camps and kitchens lacking that old symbol of the

Cooking with a wood fire, using a lightweight metal grate. On driftwood-littered beaches, wood fires will long be possible in good conscience, unlike many other provinces of American trail country.

wilderness home, the wood fire. It's sad to see grand traditions recede into ancient history, but the world changes and only sometimes for the better. Still, a wood fire is not yet everywhere morally a sin or legally a crime. To cook with wood several bits of equipment should be carried.

Matches, of course, a main supply in a poly bag, an emergency supply in a waterproof packet or box of foil, plastic, or metal. The ordinary city match is acceptable but inferior to matches that are waterproof, windproof, or both. Gadgeteers may be intrigued by a "metal match" or "flint stick" that, when struck or scraped, emits a shower of high-temperature sparks. Less fun but much better is a butane lighter.

Hikers depending on wood fire in wet country should carry a *fire starter,* such as Fire Ribbon (a jelly that squeezes from a tube), candles, or solid hydrocarbon "fuel tablets" (Heatabs).

The easiest way to cook on a wood fire is with a metal *grate* or grill. Weight should be not much more than ½ pound and preferably less, the width narrow enough to slip easily into a pack (carried in a nylon or poly bag to avoid sooting the interior), and legs omitted as worthless. Few outdoor shops stock designs that can be recommended. The best is a rectangle of three stainless-steel tubes 15 inches long and 5 inches wide; weight, 3½ ounces; cost, about $5. Cake racks from the kitchenware section of a variety store are excellent grates, weighing and costing next to nothing.

Recommended in some jurisdictions is a *fire pan;* one example is a cake pan 8½ by 12½ inches at the bottom, with sides 2½ inches high, flaring to 10 by 14 inches at the top. Though the pan does not eliminate soil sterilization and charcoaling, it confines the fire to a modest size and simplifies the subsequent scattering of ashes. Where established fire rings are officially condoned a pan serves no purpose, but in virgin-seeming sites it helps achieve "no trace" camping.

SOLID CHEMICAL FUELS

The fuel tablets mentioned above as fire starters, and also "canned heat" (Sterno—jellied alcohol), can be used for rudimentary cooking. The simplest method is to ignite them between two rocks arranged to support a pot or cup. Folding canned-heat stoves give wind protection and easy pot support; a more elaborate cooker set includes a windscreen and a 1-pint pot.

These fuels generate relatively little heat and can rarely be made to boil water. However, they often serve well enough for a person dining alone, wanting only to warm a can of stew, fry an egg, or get water hot enough to dissolve cocoa.

STOVES

In choosing from among the dozens of stoves on the market, the backpacker must ignore the heavy models designed for car-camping, canoe-camping, and other trips where weight doesn't matter, and focus on those of around 1–2 pounds. He must then decide which fuel he prefers: gasoline, kerosene, butane, propane, or alcohol.

GAS STOVES

With the exception of one design, noted below, gas stoves don't burn automobile fuels, which contain lead—or, if unleaded, other additives—that clog the mechanisms. The proper fuel is pure naphtha, better known as "white gas," sold under such brand names as Pressure Appliance Fuel, Blazo, and Coleman Fuel. Unlike the white gas that used to be sold in bulk by gas stations, these products are filtered clean and stabilized with additives to stay good for three years in a sealed can or six months after being opened.

The flash point—the ignition temperature—of white gas is –40°F.

Cooking on a stove, no fuss, no muss. When the party leaves, no sign of its stay will remain except temporarily flattened grass.

It is thus the easiest of backpacker fuels to light—and requires the most care to avoid catastrophe. A well-aimed Molotov cocktail can disable a Tiger tank; a mishandled gas stove can wipe out a tent.

To outdoorsmen of old, "primus" was a synonym for "gas stove." However, due to corporate rearrangements there is no longer a Primus gas stove; there is still a Primus butane stove, but the former Primus gas models are now made by Optimus, as is the Svea. No matter—they're dependable as ever, performance-proven by hundreds of thousands of hikers. Moreover, replacement parts are readily available at large backpacking shops, some of which offer a top-to-bottom repair service, over the counter or by mail.

For decades the most popular model has been the Svea 123R, with a built-in windscreen and a cover that inverts to serve as a small pot; weight is 1⅛ pounds, cost about $30. Next in popularity has been the lower and more stable Optimus 8R, which stows neatly in a steel box (the Optimus 99 is identical, except that the box is aluminum); weight is 1½ pounds, cost about $33. Larger and heavier, giving more heat and equipped with a pump for faster starting and greater dependability in cold weather, is the Optimus 111B, weighing 3½ pounds, costing about $65. Reliable and sturdy, handed down from father to son, the 111B is ideal for hikers who normally cook in groups of six to eight; the blowtorchlike flame does the job of two smaller stoves.

Challenging the old leaders are new stoves with a new sort of automatic pump; no priming is required except at and below freezing temperatures, when Fire Ribbon is used. The Coleman Peak 1 Mini-Stove is noted for a fine-tuned burner control that permits both fast boiling and slow simmering; weight is 2 pounds, cost about $30. The similar Optimus 323 Purist I is 1½ pounds, $45.

Phoebus models, with standard pumps, are famed for really blasting out the heat. Expeditioners and winter campers love them. The 625 weighs 2½ pounds, costs about $40. Sad to report, Phoebus is getting out of the business; stoves and replacement parts will gradually vanish from the scene.

The unique MSR stove is an intricate machine in four or so parts: a gas-carrying bottle that doubles as stove tank; a pump that screws into the bottle and is connected to the burner by a "pipeline"; an aluminum-foil windscreen; a built-in sparker to eliminate matches. Also unusual, in the GK multi-fuel version it burns white gas, automotive gas, aviation gas, kerosene, diesel oil, stove oil, Stoddard solvent, and what-have-you-got. It boils 1 quart of water in 5 minutes and is a marvelous conversation piece. Weight, 1¾ pounds, cost about $65.

Few other stoves are widely distributed. Requiring nervous mention is the "Taiwan Svea," a crude copy selling for as little as $10 in hardware stores and drugstores. Made of pot metal. No replacement parts, no repair service. Some nasty habits—such as now and then blowing up.

Popular gas stoves. Clockwise from left: *Optimus 111B, Optimus 8R, Coleman Peak 1, Svea 123R with stovelid/pot and pot lifter.*

Mini-Pump, Fuel Carriers, and Accessories

A contributor to their simplicity and popularity, most Optimus (including Svea) stoves don't have pumps and in ordinary conditions work just fine without them. However, many a hiker in extremely cold and windy climes has wished he could complicate matters with a pump and get the blamed thing burning. Optimus has responded to prayers blown on mountain gales by supplying a mini-pump, weighing

2 ounces, costing about $6, that can be used with any of the pump-lacking models—though not while they are encased in windscreens or other walls. The need for priming (see below) is not eliminated, but operable tank pressure is more readily attained.

The fuel for gas stoves (and kerosene as well) must be transported in a leakproof metal container—not glass, which breaks, and not poly bottles, which are leakproof for other liquids but not fuel.

The favorite is an aluminum *fuel bottle* with screw cap and rubber gasket, very sturdy and fitting easily in an outer pack pocket—the best place to carry fuel, since some fumes inevitably escape any container, and if within the pack, permeate food and clothing. A most desirable accessory to avoid spillage is a *vented pouring spout.* The plain-finish .6-liter bottle weighs 4 ounces and sells for about $4.50; the liter size weighs 5 ounces and costs a bit more. Anodized bottles are corrosion-resistant but should not be used to carry alcohol, booze, or acidic fruit juices; these tend to dissolve the lacquer, for example turning a white wine to a red.

A tin-coated *fuel flask* with vented pouring spout is flat for easy

Stove accessories: *aluminum fuel bottle, vented pouring spout for the bottle, Optimus Mini-Pump, eyedropper, and plastic funnel.*

storage but must be handled with care to avoid crushing. Just as with a "tin can," when the plating is eroded through or cracked, the underlying iron rusts. The ½-liter size weighs 4 ounces, costs about $7.50; the ¾-liter and liter sizes weigh and cost more.

When the camper uses carriers lacking pour spouts, a small *funnel* of nylon, polyethylene, or aluminum, preferably with a filter (of value in any event to keep garbage from the fuel tank) is essential to avoid spillage.

An *eyedropper* is handy for starting a gas stove, as described below.

Using a Gas Stove (Some Remarks Applicable to Other Stoves)

Before the camper fires up any gas or kerosene stove, the tank should be filled—but not to more than 75 percent of capacity; with a too-full tank the fuel lacks proper room to build vapor pressure for optimum operation. Also, when a gas stove gets hot, the expanding fuel shoots from the burner in a frightening flame and leaks from the cap and ignites, making a generally hectic kitchen. In the case of kerosene, a too-full tank prevents bleeding air to the outside to lower the flame.

The next step in preparing to fire is to clean the fire hole. Most gas stoves have a *built-in self-cleaner,* a rack-and-pinion device; turn the knob and tiny bits of soot or whatever are pushed out through the nipple. When a stove malfunctions, the hiker's typical reaction is to disassemble the self-cleaner, usually a mistake because a failure to reassemble it correctly results in fuel leaking out around the burner rim. Any shop that sells stoves can give simple over-the-telephone instructions for getting the teeth in the proper grooves.

Some models are equipped instead with a *separate cleaning wire.* This should be plunged two or three times into the gas vent in the burner head to ensure free passage for the vaporized fuel. The wire pushes tiny trash out of the way; however, interior pressure may push large trash back to the vent once operation commences. When a stove grows impossibly cranky it is usually because of such chunks; the cleaning wire avails naught and the only recourse is complete disassembly and cleanup.

To start a stove equipped with a *built-in standard pump,* three or five strokes are given to pump air pressure in the tank. Apply match and away she goes.

A stove with a *built-in automatic pump* (Coleman Peak 1, Optimus 323 Purist I) is safe when used correctly but very unforgiving to the careless. The manufacturer's instructions must be followed precisely and religiously; failure to do so can lead to all sorts of trouble, including a terrifying fireball.

Similarly demanding is the *mini-pump,* which in the hands of a sloppy operator can turn a Jekyll of a stove into a Hyde of a bomb. Hikers in ordinary spring-summer-fall conditions never need it and shouldn't bother. Climbers and cross-country skiers and others who travel much at high altitudes or in the cold (25°F and below) may well find it indispensable—but must take pains to learn safe usage. The proper procedure is as follows: attach mini-pump to stove; pump no more than two–three strokes (at 0° and below, several more may be needed); let enough gas drip down to fill the priming cup; close the control valve to halt fuel flow; continue with normal start-up as described below. If during cooking the stove starts to sputter, and the tank is known not to be nearing empty, give the pump two–three strokes. *Do not over-pump*—better a late supper than an explosion.

A *no-pump stove* (Svea), used without mini-pump, operates on self-pressurization from heat, similar to a gasoline blowtorch. The first step in start-up is to preheat the vaporizing tube located between the tank and the burner head. One method is to extract gas from the tank or fuel bottle with an eyedropper, fill the small depression at the base of the vaporizing tube, and (with the control valve in closed position for safety) ignite. (Alcohol is much cleaner, since it leaves no soot.) When the outside gas (or alcohol) has nearly burned off, open the control valve; with the gas in the vaporizing tube now heated to the vaporization point, the stove—maybe—roars into life. If not (as perhaps in cold wind), try again. The goal is to get the stove as hot as possible before opening the control valve *without* starting a conflagration that scares the wits out of everyone in camp and perhaps overventilates tents.

In windy weather the cooling makes initial pressure generation

difficult and gusts blow out the flame, requiring the stove to be shielded by rocks or logs or aluminum foil. However, the shield must not be so effective as to risk the stove overheating and blowing the safety valve. A stove must never be buried in dirt or tightly walled by rocks and logs; a Svea must never be used with windscreen inside a Sigg Cooker.

In very cold weather the tank may need insulation to maintain pressure. Wrapping in an old sock may do the job—again, with care not to overinsulate and overheat. On snow the insulating is best done by setting the stove on a piece of Ensolite.

For several reasons the flame should be regulated by the control valve to somewhat less than maximum output:

First, flame pouring out around the sides of the cooking pot wastes heat and fuel.

Second, overheating can blow the safety valve. Usually the valve prevents the tank from exploding like a bomb, but the scene is only a little less dramatic when a valve lets go, releasing vapor which instantly ignites in a three-foot stream of fire. When this happens the proper action is to kick the stove off into the weeds or run like hell.

Third, the major cause of stove malfunction is a scorched wick. The cotton wick draws up fuel from the tank into the vaporizing tube, where, on contact with hot metal, vaporization occurs. If a stove operating wide open and very hot abruptly runs out of fuel, the now-dry wick is scorched and loses wicking capacity. The relit stove sputters and stutters.

Gas stoves—and stoves in general—are simple contrivances but tricky, and only practice makes perfect. The beginner should try his under ideal conditions, such as in the yard at home, before depending on it in a dark and stormy wilderness night.

Any stove should be kept clean, and the fuel free of impurities. When the stove is left unused for extended periods, the fuel should be drained from the tank to prevent accumulation of clogging lacquers.

In case of malfunction and attempted field repairs, never fiddle with the pressure-release cap on any stove. This safety device is precisely set at the factory to ensure that above a certain pressure the cap will vent the excess. A cap with problems must be replaced.

A gas stove—and the gas—must at all times be treated with caution. Never fill the tank near an open flame. Never refill a hot stove—let it cool first. (That's why the tank should be filled before starting a meal, to avoid having to stop in the middle, letting half-cooked food cool. Further, in cold winds only a near-full tank can maintain operating pressure.) Never operate any stove in a tightly sealed area, whether tent or snow cave; fumes may cause sickness, and oxygen starvation and carbon-monoxide poisoning can be fatal. When a stove is used in a tent, be supercareful, keeping in mind that house and home and all wordly goods might vanish in one great flare; since the start-up holds the most potential for drama, conduct the operation outside the tent—if wind allows.

It has been observed that novice backpackers, having digested all the above, increasingly decide to buy any other kind of stove but a gas burner.

KEROSENE STOVES

Kerosene has approximately the same BTU rating as white gas. With a flash point (ignition temperature) of 110°F, compared to −40° for white gas, it's a bit harder to nourish to healthy flame, but by the same token, it is far less likely to explode, making for greater peace of mind. (Incidentally, kerosene stoves will also operate on stove or diesel oil should kerosene be unavailable.)

The most popular model is the Optimus 00, with roarer burner, weighing 1¾ pounds, costing about $38. Similar but smaller is the Optimus 96. Similar but larger is the Optimus 48, with silent burner. The Optimus 45, the same as the 48 except for having a roarer burner, weighs 2½ pounds, costs about $40.

A kerosene stove is started by putting a bit of Fire Ribbon or Sterno

Popular kerosene stoves. Left: *Optimus 48.* Right: *Optimus 00. Burner plates available for both.* Front: *Fire Ribbon for priming.*

in the cup at the base of the vaporizer and igniting. Once the vaporizer is hot, pressure is hand-pumped in the tank and the kerosene begins to burn.

Kerosene stoves generally do not have control valves. More flame is obtained by pumping; less, by opening the air screw on the tank. A safety valve is unnecessary, since kerosene does not build up dangerous pressure.

Though white gas can be used in kerosene stoves equipped with roarer burners, the practice is extremely dangerous. With no control valve and no safety valve, pressure builds up and up, the fire gets hotter and hotter. If the leaping flame frightens a camper and he opens the air screw wide to vent pressure, gas vapors may spew out and there goes the neighborhood.

BUTANE STOVES

Butane stoves outsell all others. The fuel is a liquefied petroleum gas contained under pressure in a thin metal cartridge; when vented to atmospheric pressure by the control valve, it instantly vaporizes—apply a lighted match and the stove is going. Butane stoves are quick and easy to start, dependable, virtually free of tricks, "tent safe," and the fuel is conveniently carried and used with no fuss, no mess. Unlike most gas stoves, which when turned to a low flame tend to be blown out by every zephyr, they can readily be adjusted down to simmer or sauté or to fry a decent egg or pancake. Though the stuttering roar of the typical gas or kerosene stove is considered homey by oldtimers, the new hiker calls it noise pollution and appreciates the silent butane flame for not drowning out the birds.

The advantages are so great that backpackers gladly have accepted —and solved—problems that in the early 1960s, when butane stoves were introduced in America, led gasmen to say they were a passing fad. Problems and solutions: (1) Butane freezes solid at 15°F and *at sea level* doesn't freely vaporize below 32°F, and thus the stove operates poorly in the cold of winter and strong winds. (Insulate the tank bottom from snow or cold ground by setting it on a sleeping pad or the like. Perhaps wrap the tank with an old sock. In freezing conditions—*but not on warm days*—shield the tank with aluminum foil to reflect back heat. By such means the stove can be run beautifully down to 20°F or less at sea level. Before mealtime, though, it may be well to warm the cartridge inside a jacket, next to the body. Or sleep with it for the sake of a fast breakfast. Now—attention, mountaineers: because the butane is pressurized at sea level, the higher the elevation the greater the pressure differential between cartridge interior and exterior, the hotter the flame, the lower the vaporization temperature —at 10,000 feet, as low as 12°.) (2) There are those dang cartridges to carry around. (For a gas or kerosene stove there is the dang fuel bottle to carry around.) (3) Fumes leak from an opened cartridge and have a retchy perfume smell. (Tape the orifice. Carry opened cartridges in poly bags, in outside-pack packets. Fuel bottles also leak. Gas and kerosene stink too.) (4) "Disposable" cartridges garbage up the backcountry. (PACK IT OUT.) (5) Even an "empty" cartridge, not to mention a full one, contains enough energy to wipe out a machine-gun nest. (Do not be stupid—do not change cartridges by a campfire or another stove in operation or any other open flame.) (6) Since butane emits less heat than gas or kerosene, cooking time is substantially longer; also, as pressure drops in the cartridge, the heat output drops—the last supper may be lukewarm. (This is true at and near sea level, but the higher butane cartridges climb, the hotter they burn, as hot as any other fuel, and that's why the stoves are used on Himalayan expeditions.) (7) In the absence of a set of scales one never knows how much fuel remains in a cartridge. (Some things you just got to learn to live with.)

Shops that service stoves say butane models are rarely brought in for repairs. Virtually the only problems are cartridges that leak because the top recess has been dented by rough handling (don't buy or use a cartridge so dented) and cartridges that somehow have lost the rubber seal from the orifice, permitting fuel to blow out around the burner rim (don't lose the rubber seal, don't use a cartridge lacking one).

The pioneer model on the American market and still the overwhelming favorite is the French-made Gaz S-200-S Bleuet, bulky and tall, requiring care to position it on an absolutely flat surface. Without cartridge the stove weighs 1 pound, costs about $12; the optional windscreen is ¼ pound and $2. Gaz C-200 cartridges, good for 3 hours, weigh 10 ounces full (5 ounces empty), cost about $1.50. A compact version, the Gaz Globetrotter, equipped with two pots, weighs 1 pound, costs $20. It uses a half-size cartridge, the Gaz GT, which weighs 6 ounces full, costs about $1.25, no bargain.

The Gaz is a *vapor-feed* stove; the butane goes directly from cartridge to burner, meaning that for efficient performance the entire cartridge must be kept warm. Other vapor-feed models are available here and there, using either a Gaz cartridge or a Ranger, Optimus, or other. Many of the stoves are excellent and cherished by owners, but none—not even such name brands as the Mini-Modul Optimus and Primus Ranger—has received anything like the attention of the Gaz; distribution is limited and models come and go on the market with few to know or care. Pity.

In a *liquid-feed* stove the butane flows from cartridge to a vaporizing chamber; since the chamber is the only part that must be kept warm for steady operation, there is little loss of efficiency in windy or cold weather; however, during start-up these stoves have a disconcerting tendency to flare. One example of the liquid-feed design is the Op-

Popular butane stoves, with cartridges in place. Left: *The big favorite, the Gaz S-200-S Bleuet (vapor feed).* Right: *Example of a liquid-feed stove, the EFI Mini-Stove, marketed under many brand names.*

timus 731 Mousetrap. Another is the E.F.I. stove, marketed under that name and many house labels. Both are low, compact, and stable. The American-made cartridge used by most liquid-feed models has the advantage that it can be removed from the stove with no loss of fuel, and replaced later.

PROPANE STOVES

Propane, also a liquefied petroleum gas, is much superior to butane in cold weather, since it vaporizes down to −50°F. However, it is kept under a pressure of about 124 psi (at 70°F) and thus must be contained in a fairly heavy steel cylinder—on a multi-day hike the empties grow weighty indeed. Though worthy of consideration by expeditioners, current models are unsuitable for ordinary backpacking.

ALCOHOL STOVES

Alcohol has about half the BTU rating of white gas and kerosene but is nontoxic and nonexplosive and appeals to nervous hikers who don't mind spending a lot of time cooking.

A major problem with alcohol stoves is finding one. A few backpacking shops carry a very simple, foolproof, light (4 ounces), inexpensive (about $4) model.

WHICH STOVE TO BUY?

Most factors involved in choosing a stove have been discussed above. Obviously both stove and fuel should weigh as little as possible. Stove prices, ranging from $12 to $65 or more, need to be eyed. Fuels vary in cost from very cheap kerosene to expensive butane, but amounts used are so tiny that even with the dearest fuel the average hiker's outlay for cooking during an entire summer would run about the same as a package of freeze-dried porkchops. Ease and convenience are considerations, and safety, but here personal preference enters in: the person who wants to blowtorch a snowbank into instant buckets of tea may not be the same one who wants to simmer subtle sauces for his spinach; the climber who loves excitement may be more willing to take risks than the birdwatcher. Such tastes mainly determine whether a hiker chooses gas, kerosene, butane, propane, or alcohol—or any particular model.

For what it's worth, when the Gaz Bleuet arrived in America, novice hikers immediately began buying nothing else, while old crocks clung to the gas or kerosene that added so much drama to their wilderness experience. Nowadays, however, butane is favored for summer use by tyros and ancients alike; among the butane models, Gaz is far and away the leader. Folks who frequent cold and windy areas and winter still lean toward drama.

Fuel availability is an important consideration. White gas is becoming hard to find in America, and outside the United States it scarcely exists. Kerosene, sold everywhere in America, is also the universal fuel of underdeveloped nations and thus is an excellent choice in Mexico and South America. Around the world in developed nations, and especially in Europe, the Gaz cartridge is ubiquitous, sold at every grocery store and hostel and campground, easier to obtain than kerosene. (Outside the United States a refillable Gaz cartridge—banned by American law—is sold for less than a dollar, empties turned in for the refund.) Other butane cartridges are very spottily distributed.

Of minor consequence on short hikes but very important on long, multi-day trips are *fuel consumption* and *heat output.* The accompanying table compares these and other attributes of the most popular stoves.

In theory a supper for three persons, at low-to-medium elevations, in reasonably calm weather, can be cooked—if quite simple and carefully scheduled—in about the time required to bring 3 quarts of water to boil, *each quart separately.* That is, first a pot of soup, then a main course, then the water for cocoa-coffee-tea-Postum. Thus, to use the Svea as example, burning time for supper might be as little as 20 minutes, perhaps half that for breakfast. One ⅓-pint filling of a Svea with a burning time of 1 hour therefore might cook (on the average) two suppers and two breakfasts, and 1 pint of gas approximately suffice for a three-man 6-day trip.

Similarly, a Gaz cartridge with a burning time of 3 hours but a lower heat output might cook three suppers and three breakfasts so that two cartridges would serve the same trip.

That's the theory; the practice is something else. First, many soups and main courses must be not merely brought to a boil but boiled for 10–20 minutes, especially at higher elevations. Second, some gas is inevitably spilled, some heat inevitably wasted. A good rule of thumb is to double the theoretical figure, and for that three-man 6-day trip with a Svea to carry 1 quart of gas, and 2 quarts if the meals are elaborate.

Beginners on short trips can eliminate worries about uncooked food by always carrying plenty of gas or kerosene or butane; in the process they gain some notion of how much fuel is about right for their purposes.

Statistics in the table may be used (with due caution that they are approximate) in calculating the amount of fuel for extended trips.

POTS AND PANS AND ALL

A beginner can improvise a cooking kit from Number Ten cans, coffee cans, and kitchenware picked up at thrift shops for nickels and dimes. Indeed, sentimental veterans insist food doesn't taste right unless cooked in a Ten Can. However, pots stocked by backpacking shops have many advantages, such as bails or handles, tight-fitting lids, ease of cleaning, and the compactness of nesting sets; they are also light and not really expensive, though admittedly more so than a coffee can.

The backpacker should avoid the heavier pots intended for car-camping. Beyond that, his choice depends on how many people will be in the cooking group; a lone person needs nothing more than a small kettle and a cup, while a group of four or more may require several pots in various sizes. Outdoor shops offer a number of styles in a number of brands; the following examples suggest the alternatives.

The *Sigg Tourist Cooker* includes a Svea stove, aluminum pots of 2½- and 3½-pint capacity, a lid which can serve as a fry pan (and makes a good double-boiler, used with any pot underneath, for fondues), a stove base and windscreen. Total weight, 2¼ pounds; cost, about $50. By itself the set suffices for three people—or more by adding another pot or two.

A set of *nesting billies* (three aluminum pots with capacities of 1, 2, and 3 quarts, individual lids that double as plates or fry pans, the inner pot large enough to hold and thus carry a Svea stove) weighs 1¾ pounds, costs about $15, and serves four to five people. The large pot can be left home for two-man groups; a lone person may want only the small pot.

Incidentally, lids keep out stray ashes and flying bugs and speed cooking. They can be improvised for Ten cans and coffee cans from

STOVES RECOMMENDED FOR BACKPACKING

These are currently the most popular among the many models available.
Note: No two stoves of the same model operate with exactly the same efficiency; the operation figures are those of tested samples and may be somewhat different in other samples. No wind and a moderate temperature are assumed.

Fuel	Stove Model	Capacity of Tank or Cartridge (pints)	Approximate High-Flame Burning Time of One Tank Filling or One Cartridge (hours)	Approximate Time to Boil 1 Quart Water (minutes at sea level)	Weight *without fuel **weight of full cartridge (pounds)	Approximate Cost *without fuel **cost of one cartridge
	Svea 123	1/3	1	6–8	1 1/8*	$30*
	Optimus 8R and 99	1/3	3/4	7–9	1 3/4–1 1/2*	$33–$36*
White Gas	Optimus 111B	1	2 1/2	3–5	3 1/2*	$65*
	Coleman Peak 1	2/3	1	3–4	2*	$30*

Type	Stove					
	Phoebus 625	1	2½	3–5	2½*	$40*
Kerosene	Optimus 00	1	2½	4–6	1¾*	$38*
	Optimus 45	1¾	4	5–7	2½*	$40*
	Gaz S-200-S and	¾	3	10–12	1*	$12*
	Gaz C-200 cartridge				⅝***	$1.50**
Butane	E.F.I. and	⅜	3	10–12	½*	$20*
	cartridge				⅝***	$1.50**
Alcohol	Simple burner	¼	½	11–12	¼*	$4*

aluminum foil but never fit tight and blow off in the wind.

Nesting kettles heavier and more expensive than billies, in sizes from 1 to 5 quarts, are less good for extended backpacks, where weight is important.

Cook sets and *kits* come in a variety of combinations of pots and eating utensils, at various weights and prices, serving a solitary Scout, a family, or a whole Scout troop.

Though most pots have bails and many lid-fry pans have handles, a desirable accessory to avoid burned fingers and dinner spilled on the ground is a *pot gripper.* The best is a spring-loaded steel model that

Top: *Sigg Tourist Cooker, on left disassembled; on right assembled for carrying, stove and all.* Bottom: *Nesting billies, disassembled on left, assembled for carrying on right.*

gives a strong hold on loaded pots; weight, 2 ounces; cost, about $1. Some hikers prefer a pair of *pliers* which can also be used to work on the stove, open jammed fuel bottles, and extract teeth.

A *stirring spoon* with a long handle is useful; wooden ones don't melt or get hand-burning-hot if left in the soup.

Hikers who do a lot of frying, as of fish, hot cakes, and omelettes, often become disenchanted with lids of nesting pots or pieces of aluminum foil and carry an honest-to-gosh *fry pan.* Some declare it's impossible to fry properly except with steel; a pan 8¾ inches in diameter, weighing 12 ounces, costs about $6; a light steel spatula completes the unit. Others like an easy-to-clean Teflon-coated aluminum pan, 9½ inches in diameter, weighing 15 ounces complete with the nylon spatula that must be used with Teflon (wood is also suitable); cost $5. Fanatic frycooks, including parents and Scoutmasters who love to show off by making hot cakes for the whole crowd, favor a *griddle* of thick aluminum, 10 by 16½ inches, 1¼ pounds, $10.

Hikers needn't deny themselves biscuits, coffee cakes flavored with fresh huckleberries, or hot brownies. Though aluminum foil can be crimped into shape for the purpose, much neater is the Optimus *Mini-Oven,* usable on a wood fire and most stoves, weighing 1 pound, costing $15.

High-altitude hikers may consider a *pressure cooker.* At sea level, water boils at 212°F; at 5,000 feet the boiling point is 203°F and cooking time is increased by half or more; at 10,000 the boiling point is 193°F and cooking time is nearly quadrupled. Those who frequently

Top: *Typical four-man cook set. Everything nests into the large kettle for carrying.* Bottom: *Typical two-man cook kit, disassembled.*

camp at 10,000 feet, as in the Wind River Range, High Sierra, Colorado Rockies, Peru, and Nepal, may appreciate the pressure cooker's ability to cut cooking time approximately in half. A 4-quart cooker suitable for four people, of heavy-duty aluminum, with two perforated separators and a solid one for segregating foods, 6½ inches high, 6½ inches in diameter, weighs 2¾ pounds and costs about $35.

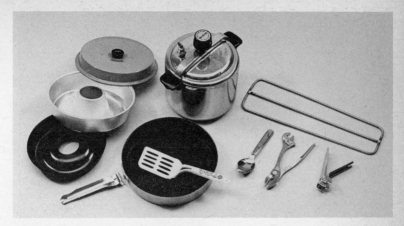

Kitchen accessories. Clockwise from left: *Optimus Mini-Oven (three pieces), pressure cooker, grate, pot gripper, pliers, stirring spoon, Teflon-coated aluminum fry pan with nylon spatula.*

EATING TOOLS

Any number of methods convey food from pot to mouth. There are hikers who cannot eat happy unless all solid elements of the entire meal are spread before them at once on a *plate.* The lids of billies and other kettles can be employed, or the plates included in cooking sets and kits, or pieces of aluminum foil, or plates of plastic or aluminum. Other hikers cannot abide cereal except in a *bowl*—the shops have them, mainly of plastic.

Most experienced hikers do all their eating from a *cup*—whether the food is soup, coffee, steak, pancake, or salad. While plate-eaters move now to this item, now to that, back and forth, everything getting cold, cup-eaters go one course at a time, finishing this before starting that. Plastic cups, light and cheap, are most popular; stacking (nesting) mugs of large capacity weigh ¾ ounce, cost 40 cents. A measuring cup with quarter-cup graduations doubles as a chef's tool, saving guess-work about quantities of ingredients and avoiding watery puddings.

A traditional favorite is a stainless-steel cup with wire handle (called "Sierra Club cup" in California, and among Northwesterners of long memory the "Ome Daiber cup"). It can serve as a small pot, such as to heat water for a spot of tea. Weight is 3 ounces; cost, about $2. The capacity is just over 9 ounces—a good thing for the cook to remember (1 cup equals 8 ounces).

Plastic cups have the enormous virtue of the "cool lip" but may absorb and retain tastes of certain foods; steel cups, cool at the rim but not elsewhere, are easy to keep clean and pure; aluminum cups are a disaster—when the soup is hot the edge burns the lip, and when the edge is cool enough for the lip the soup is cold.

The *pocket knife* every hiker must carry (see Chapter 15) serves all ordinary cooking and eating needs; if it lacks an effective *can opener,* a separate one must be included in party gear.

A *spoon,* stainless-steel or plastic, transports food to the mouth. Some hikers carry a *fork* as well, in order to spear their meatballs. *Chopsticks* are sporty.

FOOD CONTAINERS

Mountain shops stock many kinds of plastic (mainly polyethylene) bags, bottles, and jars for hauling foods, including water.

Strong, light, transparent *poly bags,* in sizes from 5-by-8 to 15-by-18

Eating tools. Top row: *Plastic plate, bowl, and cup.* Bottom row: *Cutlery, pocket knife, and stainless-steel cup.*

inches, costing pennies, have many uses noted in Chapter 4 and elsewhere in this book. Cheaper and lighter sandwich bags and those in which bread and produce are sold can be doubled for fairly decent durability. Bags may be closed by rubber bands or, better, paper-wrapped wires—several of which should always be in every hiker's pocket to replace the ones that disappear into thin air.

Poly boxes, square or round, with snap-on or screw-on lids, are good for lettuce, grapes, tomatoes, peanut butter, and other crushable or sloppy foods. *Poly vials* handle pills and spices and secret ingredients. *Poly squeeze tubes* are excellent for jam, honey, peanut butter, margarine, and other oozy foods—except in cold weather, when contents refuse to squeeze. The tube has a bottom clip to permit refilling and washing.

A plastic two-compartment *salt-and-pepper shaker* is convenient. If a larger supply of salt is carried separately, as customary on long hikes, the other half of the shaker can be filled with garlic salt, lemon pepper, cinnamon, or some other favorite spice.

A major use of flexible, translucent-white *narrow-mouth polyethylene bottles* with screw-on caps is as canteens; only a few traditionalists nowadays carry the old "canteen-shaped" canteens of aluminum or rigid plastic. The bottles come in shapes from oval to round, capacities from 2 ounces to 32 ounces (1 quart—the most popular canteen size), prices from 20 to 90 cents, weights from ½ to 3½ ounces. In the kitchen they serve as containers for liquid detergent or cooking oils or the ingredients of an apertif, as shakers for mixing the morning orange juice, and so on.

Wide-mouth polyethylene bottles, round or square, are intermediate between narrow-mouth bottles and poly boxes and do some things as well as either and some things better. Their advantage over boxes is a screw-on lid far less likely to let honey butter and margarine and other sometime-liquids escape. Their advantage over narrow-mouth bottles is ease of access: fresh eggs can be broken inside, carried a couple of (cool) days without spoiling, then fried with yolks un-broken; juice powder can be dumped in without spillage; peanut butter and mayonnaise can be reached with a spoon; snow can be crammed in quickly and easily. Sizes range from 1 pint to 2 quarts, weights from 2 to 5 ounces, prices from 50 cents to $2.

Dishwashing gear and food carriers.

Wide-mouth polypropylene (Nalgene) bottles cost more but don't absorb contents as polyethylene does. The much denser plastic becomes brit-tle at 0°F, compared to –100° for polyethylene, and thus must be handled gently in bitter cold.

Desert or hot-mountainside camps may be bone-dry, requiring that water be brought from far away and in large quantities. In fragile ecosystems a major source of damage to vegetation and soils is the back-and-forth trampling from camp to creek. Increasingly, therefore, hikers carry some such article as a *large collapsible plastic water bottle.*

Capacities range from 4 quarts to 5 gallons, weights from 2 to 7 ounces, prices from $1 to $2.

DISHWASHING

The tools of dishwashing are simple enough.

First is some device to loosen food particles (and charcoal) from utensils, particularly cooking pots. Oldtimers did the job with sand and gravel; much neater is a plastic or metal scouring pad.

Second is a means of cutting grease. Hot water alone serves very well but a small amount of soap or biodegradable detergent, liquid or solid, speeds the process, and minimizes consumption of hot water, which may be in short supply when the cooking has been done on a stove for which the fuel has been carried a long, long way.

Note: If aluminum utensils are not thoroughly cleaned and dried, acids will form that dissolve the metal with startling speed.

Final note: None of the above is to be done beside the lake or creek. Carry the water up in the woods or out on the moraine and wash dishes there.

14:	FOOD

ONCE upon a time in the Great Depression a CCC crew was building a road near Hood Canal. Several of the guys, all from Eastern cities, began wondering about the interior of the Olympic Mountains and decided to spend a holiday exploring. None had ever seen a mountain or trail before, so they asked an experienced hiker how such a trip should be done. After hearing the complexities of packboards and food lists and boiling oatmeal and rice on campfires a mile above sea level, they said, "The hell with it, we won't take any food. We're only going to be gone three days."

Off they went in Olympic wilderness, fifty miles up and down valleys and over passes and along ridges, and nothing to eat. In the Depression, many Americans learned that a mere three days of fasting wouldn't hurt. In fact, a person in average health can miss a lot more meals than that without harm; from a perspective of history and a glance around the world one might say that on the ordinary hike of up to a week or so, food is a frill.

To make a fast retreat before the gathering wrath of mountain rescuers: lacking a fairly constant supply of calories, the body slows down and weakens and becomes prone to stumble, the mind tends to make errors in judgment, and the system loses resistance to cold. Hikers should keep stoking for reasons of safety if not pleasure.

298

Still, it is true that most backpackers worry excessively about food. The first common mistake of novices is to haul too much of it—twice as much as they can eat and four times more than they need. The second mistake is to fret about the proper mix of protein, vitamins, and minerals—not realizing that on any hike up to a week or two in length, the only important physiological need is calories (unless one tends to suffer from constipation and requires a certain amount of roughage, in which case a cup of prunes a day keeps the suppositories away). To be sure, with an exceptionally bizarre diet, minor vitamin deficiencies could occur, perhaps causing night blindness, but in so

BUT, DEAR... WE'RE ONLY GOING FOR TWO DAYS!

short a time there is absolutely no risk of scurvy, beriberi, or rickets. And anyway, whatever foods are carried (unless one tries to subsist solely on sugar cubes) will have enough of the essential elements to prevent significant imbalance. As for fears of a deficiency in protein, even during strenuous exercise the body uses relatively little for muscle replacement; Americans happen to like and be able to afford protein and consume vastly more than the world average, but most of it is converted to energy (and fat), not muscles.

Before leaving the point, let it be noted that Americans of the affluent class that does the bulk of the backpacking generally can well afford to drop surplus pounds in the wildlands by deliberate undereating—which reduces not only body but pack weight.

The above discussion omits something: it's a pleasure to eat. And never more so than on the trail. Indeed, some long-time backpackers confess they are not sure whether they eat to hike or hike to eat. Though perhaps never in city lives having visited a gourmet restaurant, and at home hardly able to recall at breakfast what they had for supper, they will rapturously describe the famous hoosh they created at Pretty Meadows on a magic evening twenty-five years ago.

Whether necessary or not, then, eating is a diversion only the most ascetic totem-seeking hikers forgo. But what to eat? There is the question with a thousand answers, all correct. The choice is almost entirely determined by personal tastes, including passionate likes and dislikes that develop with age and experience. Assemble a seminar of old crocks and ask them to reveal the secrets of their trail success, and they'll talk boots and pants and packs—but eventually will end up in loud debate about the virtues of Logan bread versus pilot bread versus pumpernickel and how many smoked oysters per man are essential for a nine-day trip. Then they'll settle down to swapping recipes, which leads to arguments about brown versus white sugar, the ideal way to rehydrate a meatball, and whether the one-pot supper is the greatest invention of mankind or a sign that civilization is rushing toward total and richly deserved collapse.

Indeed, try to plan a week's menu that will perfectly satisfy each of four trail veterans, and chances are the party never will leave town. Two may insist on Thuringer sausage, one can't abide anything but salami, and the other vows to boycott all lunches lacking Goteborg. More has been written about food than all other aspects of wilderness travel combined. Most manuals have an enormous lot to say, and myriad books and booklets and pamphlets are devoted exclusively to trail cookery, offering googols of recipes for kabob, gorp, charcoal bread, fried grass, boiled owl. The number of cookbooks written is roughly equal to the number of camp cooks; the number published is only slightly less; the number stocked by backpacker shops is limited solely by the need to allow a bit of space for boots, packs, and all that.

The plethora is a delight to novices flitting from dish to dish, restlessly questing ambrosia. However, as they mature they typically decide that the spice of variety is overpraised and settle into a single menu of a few dishes, repeated over and over, liked better every passing year. (Arctic explorers used to eat pemmican and pemmican alone months at a time; upon returning to headquarters and sitting down to meals of moose steak and peas and potatoes and biscuits they sighed for—pemmican.)

The following exposition does not probe deeply into trail cuisine and is not intended for the experienced backpacker, who already knows what he likes and is certain to object more or less violently to whatever is said on the subject. Rather, the treatment is aimed at the absolute novice and is designed solely to assist in selecting the first trail meals. Having fed himself a few times in surroundings beyond electric stove and refrigerator, he will soon make stupendous discoveries, become as opinionated as the veterans, and start pressing recipes on strangers encountered in wilderness camps.

THE SHORT AND THE LONG OF IT

Opening a can is within the capacity of a majority of beginning hikers, given a can opener. Nearly all are able to strip a banana and assemble a jelly sandwich. No higher skills are required to make out well enough on short trips. As miles and days mount, though, cookery becomes slightly less simple—but nowadays never really complicated.

DAY HIKE

For an afternoon stroll a chunk of chocolate or an apple or packet of nuts may add to the pleasure of a rest stop; food, however, is purely optional.

On a full-day hike the only meal is lunch, usually consumed in several installments from second breakfast through high tea—and supper and breakfast, too, if an accident or loss of route forces an unplanned night out. Any menu will do—sandwiches, crackers and cheese, smoked salmon, grapes, cookies, carrot sticks, cherry pie—whatever the people enjoy. Any amount will do as long as there is enough for a possible emergency—too much is unlikely to damage the back. (Unless the example is followed of a group of climbers who once hoaxed an Eastern photographer at a lunch stop high on the Nisqually Glacier of Mount Rainier, and through him the readers of *Life* magazine, by casually pulling watermelons from rucksacks and slicing them up as if this were standard alpine fare.)

Even in well-watered (and pure-watered) country the party should have a canteen supply, if not to drink (perhaps mixed in the cup with lemonade powder) then for first-aid purposes. For thirst alone, canned fruit juices or carbonated beverages are delightful; they also give a quick shot of sugar to cure an acute case of that pooped feeling. Gatorade and the like (Gookinaid ERG, for "electrolyte replacement with glucose") replenish the sodium, calcium, and magnesium salts sweated out in heavy exercise, attacking other basic causes of the poops, as well as curing leg cramps better than salt tablets.

Do not drop along the trail or toss in the brush candy wrappers, orange peels, or cans. And don't bury them. *Pack it out! Pack it ALL out!*

OVERNIGHT

The same rule that applies to day-hike lunches extends to weekend lunches—and breakfasts and suppers. The rule is: there is no rule. Too little food doesn't cause intolerable misery and indeed adds zest to hamburgers and milk shakes at the drive-in Sunday night. Too much rarely leads to a permanent stoop.

However, a basic choice must be made prior to the trip: between walking far and fast or eating in the mode of the last days of Pompeii.

At one extreme are meals essentially a succession of quick lunches; ham sandwiches make a satisfying supper, and unheated hash fresh from the can resembles dog food but is amazingly tasty, especially with a splash of ketchup. To quote a maxim of climbers: "Though the food is cold, the inner man is hot." Civilized stomachs are conditioned to feel vaguely incomplete lacking at least one hot meal a day; amid grand scenery the sensation passes.

At the other extreme is wilderness feasting, where backpacking miles have as their goal the sharpening of the appetite. Sybarites may devote the afternoon and evening to a supper of: aperitif of choice and hors d'oeuvres of sesame crackers spread with truffled pâté; tossed salad or slices of lemon-washed avocado; Cornish game hen foil-roasted in coals and served with corn on the cob; biscuits baked in a mini-oven and topped with frozen strawberries and whipped cream; wines and brandies and cheeses at the discretion of the maître d'.

The average weekender meals fall someplace in the middle. For example, supper may be cherry tomatoes, soup, canned beef stew, bread and butter, stir-and-serve pudding, and instant coffee, tea, or milk. Breakfast may be orange juice, oatmeal "cooked" in the cup by addition of hot water, and instant coffee-cocoa. Thousands of other menus have been published. Ad infinitum, ad nauseum.

LONG BACKPACK

Beyond a 3-day weekend, eatery demands thought. Depending on the backs and appetites involved, somewhere around 4 or 5 days and certainly by 6 or 7 days, the distance from the road forces a qualitative change in cuisine.

Above all, it becomes essential to *go light.* An extra half-pound per person per meal matters little on a weekend with a maximum of 4 meals, matters much when the meals number 12 or 27—6 or 13 extra pounds on each suffering back makes for a slow and painful pace.

Through use of dried foods and those naturally low in water content, shucking cardboard packaging, and moderately careful menu planning, it is possible to feed the average hiker to repletion on 2 pounds of food per day. By more precise planning, the job can be done with 1½ pounds. And if party members are willing to leave a bit of lard along the way and endure pangs while stomachs shrink, with 1 pound. At this point, though, about the fifth evening the hiker will look into the setting sun and see not the drama of day's end but only a great fried egg dripping hot butter.

This general rule concerning pounds of food per person has so many exceptions that it is hardly a rule at all. Exercise stimulates the appetites of some, who grow ravenous several days out and go mad

at the aroma of peanut butter and begin to lust after chipmunks and prowl tidal pools for edible seaweed. Others eat less the harder they work—perhaps because their systems, freed from neurotic over-stuffing, are slimming down for the sane life of the wilderness.

And of course, an 80-pound human requires less fuel than a 250-pounder. Although, contrarily, a person with hyperactive metabolism, the sort who eats and eats and is always skinny, needs more food than the person whose inner plant is so efficient that a single kipper adds an inch to his girth.

And again, on extended backpacks as on day walks, the choice must be made between lightness and luxury. On long trips, lightness dictates most decisions, but there are no words to praise salted cucumber slices six days from the road; the extra ounces of such an occasional special treat may be worth the strain.

Cooking time is another consideration. When the intent is to cover a lot of ground, walking every day from early morning to late afternoon, and/or when all cooking is to be done on a stove, most meals should be medium-fast and some instant-quickies, requiring only hot water for supper and cold water for breakfast. On less frantic trips, though, a few meals should be fancy—for rest days or days of rain at camps where wood fires can be built. For example, the ingredients of a pancake-bacon-eggs breakfast contain no surplus water and are very efficient in the ratio of weight to calories. A pancake breakfast ordinar-

ily lasts to lunchtime, but when mists are driving through the flowers, or rain drizzling among the trees, or the camp is paradise, and there is no need to march on, who cares?

For obvious reasons the subject of foods for long backpacks is the most controversial among veterans—and the most baffling to novices. Thus, to guide through the confusion, a new section must begin. In fact, four sections, one after the other.

LONG-HAUL FOODS: SUPERMARKET

Forty-odd years ago, before food processors ran amok, the diet of the long-distance backpacker was restricted and his cookery a formidable art. Few dried foods were available (it was possible to get quite sick of prunes and chipped beef) and those naturally dry were not treated for quick cooking. Pasta (noodles, macaroni) was relatively easy to make digestible, but rice took an hour or more at high altitude and usually ended as a gruel punctuated by tiny pebbles; beans were an overnight project. Even oatmeal and farina required an eternity of smoke-swallowing and stirring and generally burned on the bottom.

Nowadays, however, supermarkets are cornucopias of low-in-water, fast-cooking products. By prowling the aisles and checking cooking times carefully, avoiding tempting packages that call for a 400° oven, the backpacker can assemble any number of lightweight, nutritious, delicious, alacazam meals. To stimulate the imagination, following are some of the innumerable supermarket foods suitable for long-haul backpacking.

For breakfast: quick-cooking and instant-in-the-cup oatmeal and farina; compact no-cook cereals such as Grape Nuts; pancake flour; bacon; dried fruits; powdered juice mixes; "instant breakfast"; sugar; dried milk; instant cocoa and coffee.

For lunch: dense and durable breads and crackers; margarine; cheese; peanut butter; jam and honey; candy; nuts; dried fruits; sausage; powdered juice mixes.

For supper: dried soups; instant potatoes and dry gravy mixes; quick-cooking noodles with cheese (Kraft Dinner); super-fast-cooking Oriental noodles (Top Ramen); Minute Rice, which requires no boiling, only steaming; canned meats and fishes; hard sausage; chipped beef; cheese; instant puddings; cookies; instant coffee; tea bags.

The big problem is deciding how much of any particular food is enough for a certain number of people; the "Serves four" on a package may mean four finicky mice. Trial-and-error experience gained on short hikes, where mistakes in calculation are not serious, is the best way to learn how to buy. If a shortcut is wanted, exact amounts of ingredients required for myriad menus are given by backpacker cookbooks.

Before we leave the supermarket, a word needs to be said in defense of canned meats. First, they cost enormously less than the freeze-drieds lauded below. Second, because the freeze-drieds contain little or no fat (4,000 calories per pound, compared to merely 1,600 for protein) they may offer less nutrition per ounce on the backpacker's back, even taking into account the weight of canned meat's water and metal. The advantage is greatest, of course, with fatty Spam-like meats and oil-packed fish.

DRIED FOODS

Time out now, before proceeding from supermarket to backpacking shop, for a bit about the background of dried foods, which gener-

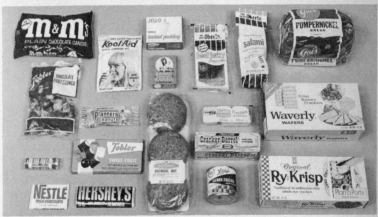

A sampling of long-haul foods available in supermarkets. Top: *Breakfast ingredients.* Center: *Lunch things.* Bottom: *Supper stuff.*

ally weigh merely a third or a quarter or less of what they did before processing.

Man's earliest means of preserving food was sun-drying, dating to prehistoric times and the original method of making raisins, prunes, dried peas and beans, beef jerky, and the like. Freezing came perhaps not much later as man moved into lands of cold winters. Probably the first use of artificial heat was in smoking meat and fish. The technology of preserving without tinning advanced little beyond this level until the twentieth century, when experiments with other techniques, stimulated by military requirements during and after World War II and the police action in Korea, led to the current state of the art.

HOT-AIR DRYING ("DEHYDRATED" FOODS)

Hot-air drying was once done in ovenlike chambers by the batch, requiring much handling and consequent expense. An improvement was *tunnel-drying,* where foods are placed on trays and passed slowly through a long tunnel in which hot air blows end to end; emerging after 6 hours or less with moisture content below 10–12 percent, the food is transferred to finish-drying bins; moisture is there reduced to less than 5 percent, the point necessary for storage stability. Demanding more complicated equipment but offering greater efficiency and economy and providing better quality control and thus gradually replacing tunnel-drying are various *continuous processes.* An example is

THIS WILL FEED BOTH OF YOU FOR FIVE DAYS

spreading the food on a wire-mesh belt that moves through a chamber perhaps 120 feet long; the air blowing through the food from various inlets may be very hot early on, then cooler. In 3–4 hours for large vegetable dices and 30–45 minutes for leafy vegetables, moisture is usually less than 5 percent, often eliminating the need for finish-drying in a bin.

Dehydration of highly concentrated fruit or vegetable purees, such as mashed potatoes, yams, applesauce, tomatoes, and so on, is by *drum-drying,* the "mash" spread on the stainless-steel outer surface of a large, internally heated, rotating drum, automatically scraped off into a hopper, and spread on another drum, and so on, until done.

Some fruits (apples, apricots, peaches, prunes) may be processed by *vacuum-drying,* basically with hot-air methods but in a partial vacuum to avoid excessive oxidation and resulting discoloration. The older and still-common and less-expensive alternative is to replace the air in the chamber with sulfur dioxide gas; the taste and odor inevitably linger.

Spray-drying, conducted in a tall tower into the top of which tiny droplets are sprayed, dehydrating as they fall through heated air, is customary for powdered milk, coffee, and vegetable and fruit juices.

Upon rehydration, foods treated by hot-air methods generally do not closely resemble the original in appearance or flavor, largely because when a plant or animal is air-dried to less than 10–15 percent of its natural moisture, the cell structure tightens up irreversibly. A stewed raisin is nothing like a grape, and rehydrated spinach flakes are only distant cousins to leaves fresh from the field. But then, a raisin is excellent eating in its own right, and some hikers prefer trail spinach to garden spinach. Air-dried foods can be delicious and have the advantage of much lower cost than the freeze-dried.

INTERMEDIATE-MOISTURE FOOD

On the horizon for the backpacker, though already on the floor for consumers of "moist and meaty" dog food, is "intermediate-moisture food," prepared by (1) removing enough water to prevent growth of mold and fungus, while (2) leaving in enough water to preserve the texture. This residue must be physically combined with a "humect-ant" to prevent growth of bacteria; sugar is the one used in dog food, which thus is very sweet for human tastes. If research finds better alternatives, the trail kitchen may be enriched. Meanwhile, there's "moist and meaty"—and to stop smiling for a moment, social workers testify it's already a regular item in the diet of elderly Americans on miserly pensions.

Also still on the horizon—and firmly held there by government regulations—is the fulfillment of a hiker's fantasy—Beer Kool-Aid. The Japanese have perfected a method of encapsulating alcohol in powder form. Resulting products, available now outside the United States, can be reconstituted on the trail to make beer (using solidified carbon dioxide for the bubbles, as in Pop Rocks), hot spiced wine, martinis, or, for the morning after too many of these, Bloody Marys. But until a host of bureaus and boards have pondered and approved, American hikers must keep a stiff upper lip. (However, as the Noble Experiment proved, old Adam will not be forever denied—should the feds delay too long, there may again be fleets of swift black boats arriving by night on secluded American beaches.)

VACUUM SUBLIMATION (FREEZE-DRIED FOODS)

Vacuum sublimation, called the greatest breakthrough in food pres-ervation since the tin can, combines the flavor-retention of freezing with the lightness of dehydration.

The food, cooked or raw depending on the product, is flash-frozen so that ice crystals cannot grow large enough to distort the cell structure, then placed in a high-vacuum chamber at very low temperature, perhaps down to $-50°F$, and exposed to radiant heat. The combination of heat and low pressure forces some 97 percent or more of the moisture to sublime—that is, pass directly from solid to vapor without ever becoming liquid, again preventing damage to the cells.

For millenia the Incas of the high, cold, sunny Andes successfully freeze-dried potatoes, and Indians of Alaska in winter did the same with salmon. Not until recent years, however, mainly as a result of military needs, has a modern refinement of the technique become economically practical.

Partly due to the inefficiency of batch-handling, freeze-drying is currently the most expensive of any method of food preservation; if engineers would quit fooling around and perfect an assembly line, the cost would drop considerably.

Not even high prices discourage affluent backpackers, who like freeze-drieds because they rehydrate quickly to virtually pristine shape and flavor, retain more nutritive value than air-drieds, and if correctly packaged and stored in cool, dark places, keep indefinitely. The technique works beautifully on meat and fish, most fruits and vegetables, coffee, and a great many other foods—though not all; cheese, for example, crumbles to dust.

PACKAGING

Many dried foods are shipped from manufacturer to retailer in large tight-closed tins and packaged in poly bags shortly before sale. (Some shops sell full tins of vegetables and fruits for big-time eaters.) A few dried products last for months in the poly, but because the plastic is not absolutely impervious to passage of air, many start to deteriorate in a matter of weeks. Dry fruits and vegetables stored in a cool, dry spot—ideally a refrigerator, otherwise a corner of the basement—may last a year or more before providing odd new taste sensations.

Eggs packaged in poly definitely must be used the same season purchased. So should such foods as flour and beans; they will not spoil but over a long period may develop weevils, which do not lessen food value, and indeed increase the protein content, but are widely considered unesthetic.

Though aluminum cans are occasionally used, the most common container for freeze-dried meats and meat products and some vegetables is the *shrink pack,* where the food is placed in laminated aluminum foil, the air drawn out by vacuum, and the sealed foil covered by an outer layer of tough plastic. The package is very durable if protected from puncturing and preserves contents indefinitely. Even a tiny, perhaps invisible hole, however, permits freeze-dried meats to rehydrate, in which event they quickly spoil; if the food stinks or looks strange, it must *not* be eaten.

LONG-HAUL FOODS: BACKPACKING SHOP

Where the supermarket leaves off, the backpacking shop begins, offering dried foods and specialties with limited appeal, if any, for city use but enabling a variety, convenience, and quality of wilderness eatery inconceivable to oldtimers.

Generally, because of special processing (particularly freeze-drying) and packaging, a menu entirely drawn from backpacking shop supplies is considerably more expensive than one depending partly on the supermarket. The hiker must let his pocketbook be his guide.

SEPARATE INGREDIENTS

A wide range of fruits, vegetables, meats, and miscellaneous foods are packaged separately, to be eaten alone or in combination with others, such as:

Air-dried and freeze-dried fruits and vegetables, from apples to peaches, from beets to peas and carrots (but rarely, nowadays, yams or spinach).

Freeze-dried meats, from meatballs and hamburgers and diced beef and ham and chicken to beefsteaks and porkchops and tuna salad.

Beef jerky, dehydrated bacon bar and meat bar, powdered eggs, freeze-dried cottage cheese, meat-flavored vegetable-protein (soya) chunks.

Fruit pemmican, English mint cake, maple-sugar candy, fruit-nut bar, powdered beverages, pilot bread, yogurt.

And more.

COMPLETE DISHES

A number of firms (Dri-Lite, Seidel, Rich Moor, Chuck Wagon, and Oregon Freeze-Dried Foods, with the Mountain House label) package complete main courses and side dishes that are delicious and nutritious or at least edible and so simple to prepare as to be virtually

312

foolproof; some require only the addition of hot or cold water to be ready to eat. To cite a very few from a great many:

For breakfast there are omelettes, pancakes, cereals, sausage patties, hashbrowns.

For supper there are rice-beef-vegetable mulligan, beef stew, chili, lasagna, beef Stroganoff, beef Stromboli, beans and franks, chop suey, shrimp creole, creamed chicken, Boston-style beans, ham and potatoes, noodles and beef, cheese Romanoff, turkey Tetrazzini, beef almondine, tuna à la Neptune. And for dessert, puddings and gelatins, apple compote and raspberry cobbler—and no-bake pineapple cheesecake with graham-cracker crust!

And drinks, snacks, and goodies galore.

Many of these dishes cost two or three or five times more than the hooshes (nowadays vulgarly called "glops") a hiker concocts from supermarket foods—which doesn't matter to the wealthy or occasional camper but certainly does to the impoverished, inveterate long-distance walker, who mostly eats at the Kraft Dinner level and considers freeze-dried hash a holiday treat.

It must be noted that most of these foods are unappealing in the city, barely tolerable on weekends, and don't become genuinely appetizing until about the fourth day on the trail. Moreover, an increasing number of disenchanted hikers report that despite the ravishing names, after a while they all taste the same.

COMPLETE MEALS

Several of the firms mentioned above provide the ultimate in convenience by packaging complete meals carefully tailored to the high-calorie, low-weight, easy-cooking requirements of the hiker and accompanied by exact directions which can be followed by anyone able to boil water and scramble an egg.

Among the fans of complete meals are Scoutmasters and other trail bosses who have neither the energy (or perhaps experience) to puzzle out a menu and shopping list for a dozen or a score gaping young mouths; using the shortcut, they can buy food for a week in minutes and feed the troops very well.

A sampling of long-haul foods sold by backpacking stores. Top: Separate ingredients, some normally eaten alone, others commonly mixed in hooshes. Center: Complete dishes, all required components in the package. Bottom: Complete meals, the easy way out for confused and wealthy novices.

This convenience, of course, has a price, and after the beginner has developed personal eccentricities he doubtless will prefer to structure his own menus. However, through packaged meals he receives on-the-job training in backpack cookery taught by experts.

THE CUISINE OF AN OLD CROCK

The eating habits of ancient mountaineers really are better left to silence. For example, the man who led Recreational Equipment Inc. through its early decades was noted for climbing a boggling number of tough peaks in typhoons and blizzards—and notorious for feeding himself three meals a day by reaching into a huge and greasy sack of sandwiches from home; by the fourth or fifth day of a peakbagging expedition, companions insisted he go off to a separate glacier to eat.

Nevertheless, readers have complained that previous editions of this book failed to satisfy their prurient curiosity about private habits of old crocks. Following, therefore, is the typical menu of one such in his forty-second summer since days as a Tenderfoot cooking kabob on a stick and hunter's stew in a coffee can.

Breakfast

When alone or wishing to get out of camp and on the peaks at the crack of nine o'clock, Old Crock eats the identical breakfast every morning: a packet (two if ravenous) of instant oatmeal stirred in the cup with hot water, Milkman, and brown sugar. Two cups instant coffee with white sugar and nondairy creamer. Companions have black coffee, coffee-cocoa, or plain cocoa.

When the party includes Mrs. Old Crock, who invariably arises mad to cook, breakfast starts with coffee, moves to bacon, progresses to a primitive (but good, but good) omelette of powdered eggs, cheese, bacon-flavored soya, and mushrooms (gathered fresh or reconstituted from an earlier harvest dried at home—Mrs. O.C. spends all winter fiddling with her food-drier). Finally, the box of Bisquick comes out and hot cakes begin, topped with margarine and strawberry jam, brown-sugar syrup, or (in season) huckleberry syrup. It's then time for lunch.

Lunch

The everyday staple is Royal Kreem, preferred for tastiness over Sailor Boy pilot bread, which is, however, more durable. Spread with margarine, peanut butter, cashew butter, strawberry jam, yellow or white or blue or cream or stinky cheese, hard salami, smoked oysters, spiced herring—not all at once.

For sweets (again, not all at any one meal), Callard and Bowser licorice and toffee, Cadbury chocolate, home-dried fruits, candied papaya and pineapple slices, and a sack of "squirrel food" (the original and legitimate name, though now incorrectly called "gorp," a wretched neologism) of M&Ms, candy corn (which Mrs. O.C. can't abide), and cashews (which Young Crock abhors), and absolutely no raisins (which Mrs. loves but Mr. calls "dried flies").

A jug of punch from a packet of Wyler's—the favorite flavors are cola and root beer, which, however, can only be obtained from Carter's Delicatessen on University Way. (Note: Though the supermarket is the main source, and the backpacking shop supplies several key items, any long trip requires crucial items only available at Puget Sound Consumers Co-op and an array of delicatessens, including Brenner Bros. for Jewish foods, Uwaijamaya for Asian, and Liebchen for German and other European. Of course, in other areas the names are different.)

Supper

The first course is soup from a country that knows how to make it right—Germany, Switzerland, France, Norway, Japan, or Israel, among others, not including the United States.

Because when denied greens Mrs. O.C. gets down on all fours and attacks the flowers, the next course flatly renounces the Law of Dry and Light. Early in the trip there is a nightly salad of lettuce, tomato, avocado, marinated artichoke, and oil-vinegar-spices mixed at home. When these are gone there are cucumber slices in vinegar.

The main course is a hoosh (or "glop"). The current favorites:

Top Ramen noodles: beef-flavor, with a can of corned beef; or

Oriental-flavor, with cans of shrimp; plus a dollop of soy sauce and a bit of sesame oil.

Kraft Dinner with extra cheddar cheese sliced in and a fresh green pepper, diced. Season in the cup with lemon pepper.

Minute Rice with cans of tomato paste and tuna fish; Minute Rice and tuna fish and packets of dried crab soup and lobster sauce.

Spam-Yam-Bam non-hoosh dinner, the Spam fried separately, the yams reconstituted from canned yams dried at home, boiled with brown sugar to taste.

Hungarian goulash soup, beef soya bits, that box of Bisquick brought out to make dumplings—and loud yowls of ecstasy echoing from the cliffs.

Now that dried spinach, the traditional staple, has been ruthlessly removed from the market, side dishes (not every meal) may be dried carrots; peas topped with hollandaise sauce made from a packet; or—hang the expense—freeze-dried cottage cheese.

Dessert is usually instant pudding (pistachio the favorite) with Dream Whip topping from a packet. One or two nights, store cookies instead. At least once during a week, out comes the Bisquick and a roll of aluminum foil and Mrs. O.C. bakes cookies over coals of the campfire: packet of spiced instant oatmeal with home-dried apricots, Milkman, margarine, and cinnamon.

For hot drinks in the evening cool: coffee, real or caffeine-free,

Postum, instant cocoa, tea, fruit soup, peppermint tea. Cinnamon sprinkled where appropriate.

And so to bed.

NATURAL FOODS

Many a hiker who flees the chemical-filled air and water of the city is chagrined to find, upon reading ingredients on a food package, that he is consuming the equivalent of the Houston Ship Canal. A search for the pure and "natural" can be arduous. Bewaring of possible mumbo-jumbo and ripoff prices, a person can often meet needs for a low-sugar, low-sodium, nonchemicalized, vegetarian, or whatever, diet at a health-food store. Large supermarkets typically have small sections catering to special dietary needs and desires. A few communities have consumers' co-ops whose members pool buying power to obtain natural foods at low cost; they may have connections with farmers (retired hippies or other counterculturists) who grow fruits and vegetables by "organic" means. Some backpacking shops feature such natural foods as lentil soup, curried bean pilaf, Loch Ness stew —good to eat and good for you.

WILD FOODS

Living off the country cannot be condoned or encouraged now that people-pressure is crushing the small scraps of wilderness remaining in North America. Still, in proper places at proper times hikers may gently crop the wildland without harm.

Fishing in lakes and streams is an obvious example, and gathering clams and other shellfish from ocean beaches. A person may harvest all the edible berries he can find without upsetting the natural order (though perhaps a bear) and thus explode a tart moisture in a dry mouth, or by saving a cupful for camp, boil up a topping for pancakes.

Mushrooms sautéed in margarine add a gourmet touch to any outdoor supper. With a little study a half-dozen supersafe varieties can be learned.

Similarly, a number of greens may be harvested for a wildland salad

—miners' lettuce and sorrel are famous. For fresh vegetables there are such delicacies as boiled nettles and skunk-cabbage leaves—picked at the proper stage. *Stalking the Wild Asparagus* and sequels, by Euell Gibbon, are story-style introductions to enlivening the diet. The edible plants native to various parts of America are described in a number of regional booklets sold in bookstores and backpacking shops. The backpacker does well to know some of the common edible plants in the area of his customary travels, not only to vary menus on long trips but to gain the increasingly rare experience of eating absolutely natural, completely unchemicalized, perfectly organic foods.

ENOUGH! The wallet is empty, the pack full, the back bent.

And yet *not* enough because to travel trails happy and secure, the hiker needs still more gear.

Don't panic—these last few bits cumulatively weigh not many pounds and cost not too many dollars.

But don't omit them—all are more or less essential either for safety or comfort or efficiency.

THE TEN ESSENTIALS

Back in the 1930s, when the Mountaineers began presenting an annual Climbing Course, the faculty soon discovered that while students were eager to haul axes and ropes and pitons, they saved weight by eliminating less glamorous stuff. Novice Homer and Novice Chuck, inseparable companions, would arrange for one to carry a flashlight, the other a map and compass. Then the party scattered on the descent from a peak, and the buddies were separated from each other and everyone else. Darkness came and Homer could see to walk but didn't know which way to go; Chuck knew which way to go but couldn't see to walk.

From innumerable such incidents, many miserable and not a few tragic, the Mountaineers drew up a list of Ten Essentials to be carried by every climber on his person or in his pack at all times. The list was really just a teaching device, since no experienced wilderness climber then or now would ever be caught without the Ten.

The rule is absolute for climbers; for hikers there is a sliding scale of necessity. The afternoon walker on a broad, well-marked, heavily populated trail often can do without a single Essential. The overnight backpacker who sticks to turnpikes may need only several. Those who probe deep into wilderness, away from quick support of rangers or other hikers, and especially those who strike off cross-country, must have the full Ten.

A further qualification. A family that invariably stays together in a tight bunch may need some of the Ten only *as a group.* The more independent the party members, the more important that *each person* carry all Ten.

ONE: EXTRA CLOTHING

Chapter 9 sufficiently makes the point, which is to have in the pack more clothing than seems necessary when setting out on a sunny morning; the afternoon may be windy and rainy, the night stormy and

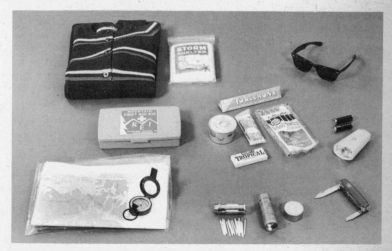

The Ten Essentials. Top row: *Extra clothing (here, a sweater and a storm shelter), sunglasses.* Middle row: *First-aid kit, extra food, flashlight (and extra cells).* Bottom row: *Map, compass, matches, fire starters, knife.*

freezing, and though the hiker doesn't intend to be on the trail then, a sprained ankle may leave no choice.

In wet, cold country each person must have *wool* or other *warm-when-wet* clothing and some sort of protection from moisture of sky and ground (such as a light sheet of polyethylene) in case circumstances force a bivouac without camping gear.

TWO: EXTRA FOOD

The day-hiker's lunch may have to be stretched to a supper, a breakfast, another lunch—while the lost route is being found or the rescue party summoned. Thus the lunch must be substantial; the test is that on any trip *without* misfortune there should be food left over.

A can of fruit-nut pemmican stowed permanently in the pack serves the purpose; few people will eat it in anything but an honest-to-gosh emergency. One Northwest climber carries a packet of dry dog food.

322

THREE: SUNGLASSES

In forest travel, sunglasses are not essential; they surely are in desert country and open alpine regions, such as massive screes or felsenmeers (boulder fields) of light-colored rock. The extreme case is snow, where sunglasses are mandatory on bright days to prevent discomfort, pain, and even *temporary blindness and permanent damage.*

For ordinary hiking, any model that filters out about 65 percent of available light will do. For extended snow travel, more care must be taken in selection. First, side shields are important. Second, glass lenses are recommended because they filter out both ultraviolet and infrared rays; some cheap plastic lenses are virtually useless and even the best, made of CR-39, don't stop infrared. Except in fog, where yellow lenses improve contrast, helping distinguish holes from bumps, green or gray-green are best because they don't alter the color balance of visible light. Persons who wear prescription glasses should be careful to buy sunglasses that fit comfortably over regular lenses; few do, and none of the clipons are dark enough or have side shields, and that's why myopic snow-trompers usually end up having an optician make them a pair of prescription sunglasses.

FOUR: KNIFE

Except for small children, each hiker should carry a knife. Uses include eating (opening that can of pemmican), first aid, whittling kindling to start a wood fire (for cooking or for emergency warmth when trapped in storm or night by accident or loss of route).

No backpacker needs a "hunting knife" or cutlass or scimitar. Big blades are for hunters, fishermen, and guerrillas.

While we're on the subject of weaponry—the backpacker has no business hauling an ax or hatchet; they are heavy, unnecessary, and inevitably lead to clear-cut logging of campsites. And just as an ax triggers a compulsion to chop-chop-chop, a lightweight folding saw may cause even the sensitive hiker to engage in an orgy. It was a symptom that a frontier town was coming of age when the sheriff required transients to check their guns at his office, and it is high time now for wildland walkers to check their steel at the trailhead. If Sonnyboy is going out of his mind for a chance to try his new hatchet, keep him away from the trees, send him off to whack at billboards.

Returning to knives, the most popular is the Boy Scout type with single blade, can opener, combination cap opener and screwdriver, and awl, costing from $2.50 to $10 depending on the quality of materials and manufacture. The cheapest is best for children, who lose knives instantly.

Many prefer the Swiss Army knife, strongly constructed of stainless

steel and thus not rusting shut. Various models, more or less elaborate, range in price up to $25 or so; generally sufficient is the $10 one with two blades plus can opener (which works much better than the Boy Scout design), cap opener, and screwdriver. Note: Victorinox makes "the original" and Wenger "the genuine," and both have been doing so under Swiss Army contract since 1903. Though the companies say otherwise, their products are virtually identical and of the same high quality—the Swiss Army insists on it.

The "Japanese Army knife," including fork, spoon, toilet kit, fishing pole, and portable sawmill, entertains kids.

The hiker should own but not necessarily carry a whetstone for occasionally sharpening the blade.

FIVE: FIRE STARTER

Even where the wood fire is obsolescent or forbidden, it continues to have a role in emergencies. To be able to start a fire when one is urgently needed, as in a rainstorm when the hiker is lost and the wood wet, each person should carry Fire Ribbon or a few candle stubs or fuel tablets (see Chapter 13).

SIX: MATCHES

To start the fire starter, matches are required. In addition to those carried for routine purposes, each person should have an emergency supply, either waterproof or in a waterproof container; windproof matches can be lifesavers in foul weather. So can a butane lighter.

SEVEN: FIRST-AID KIT

Ideally, every hiker venturing more than a few miles and hours from civilization should have first-aid training and a complete kit; certainly anyone who spends much time in the backcountry should avail himself of instruction offered by the American Red Cross or mountaineering clubs, and assemble a kit with sufficient materials to cover a wide range of eventualities. If unable to take formal instruction, he should study such books as *Mountaineering First Aid,* by Dick Mitchell, describing contents and use of the first-aid kit, and *Medicine for Mountaineering,* by James A. Wilkerson, a detailed "doctor book."

At the very least, the novice must be equipped to handle common ailments of the trail, some of which can be disabling even though not "serious" in a medical sense. If each hiker carries a small kit, supplies can be pooled for crises; if the group (say, a family) carries only a single kit, it should be correspondingly more elaborate.

The following items constitute a *very minimum, one-man* first-aid kit:
  Band-aids—several, for minor cuts
  Gauze pads—several, 3 inches and 4 inches square, for deep wounds with much bleeding
  Adhesive tape—a 1-inch or 2-inch roll for holding bandages in

place, covering blisters, taping sprained ankles, etc.

Salt tablets—to prevent or treat symptoms of heat exhaustion (including cramps) when sweating heavily

Aspirin—for relieving pain and reducing fever

Needle—for opening blisters, removing splinters

First-aid manual—a booklet discussing diagnosis and treatment (supplied with kits at backpacking shops)

Such a kit can cope with only the simplest problems; after a hiker has gained a bit of sad experience he will want to add many of the following:

Moleskin or molefoam—for covering blisters

Razor blade, single-edge—for minor surgery, cutting tape and moleskin to size, shaving hairy spots before taping

Gauze bandage—a 2-inch roll for large cuts

Butterfly Band-Aids—for closing cuts

Triangular bandage—for large wounds

Large compress bandage—to hold dressings in place

Iodine-based purification tablets—for treating drinking water of doubtful purity

Antacid—for settling stomachs upset by overexertion, unaccustomed altitude, and the cook's mistakes

Wire splint—for sprains and minor fractures

Elastic bandage—3 inches wide, for sprains, applying pressure to bleeding wounds, etc.

First-aid cream—for sunburn, itches, scrapes, and diaper rash

Antiseptic—Bactine, Zepherine Chloride, or other, for cleaning minor wounds

Antihistamine—for allergic reactions to bee stings

Oil of cloves—for toothache

Darvon—for severe pain (prescription required)

Antidiarrhetic pills—for terrible cases of the trots (prescription required)

Laxatives and/or glycerine suppositories—for prune-resistant constipation in persons congenitally suffering from this affliction

Snakebite kit—see Chapter 5

Backpacking shops stock small kits containing some of the above items, weighing from ¼ to 1 pound, costing from about $6 to $15. The beginner should purchase one of these for a start and build from there.

EIGHT: FLASHLIGHT

Hikers often carry candles for camp use and many climbers like headlamps which free the hands; the standard "essential," however, is a two-cell flashlight.

The tool is secondarily for camp convenience and primarily to permit continued travel when caught by darkness. With the exception of small children who never will be far from parents, each person must carry his own light. (One in the party is not enough even if the group stays scrupulously together; most modern flashlights are notoriously undependable.) The obscurity of a forest night is total and the only safe way to navigate an unlit trail is on hands and knees, which makes for a very slow pace; off the beaten path, forget it.

Almost every year, somewhere in America, a benighted light-less hiker keeps walking in an attempt to reach his destination, perhaps minutes away, and steps off the path, over a cliff, into eternity. And every year other hikers wisely give up the attempt and sit out long shivering hours while relatives worry and rescue parties mobilize; these hikers nevermore leave the flashlight home to save weight.

Liked very much by some (but hated by others) for ordinary hiking is the Mallory AA Compact Light, weighing (complete with two AA alkaline cells) only 3 ounces and costing about $2. At moderate temperatures the cells give continuous useful light (enough to walk a trail by, that is) for about 3–4 hours; a spare bulb should always be carried and at least one extra set of cells—more for hikers who habitually read in the sleeping bag. To prevent power wastage in the pack, the switch should be securely taped in the "off" position. Though many people think the little Mallory quite rugged, others find it goes haywire at a frown; since it is unfixable except by practiced technicians, and not at all in a midnight storm, hikers may wish to take two,

Two popular "light kits." Left: *C-cell metal-case flashlight with spare bulb and two extra zinc-carbon cells.* Right: *A matched pair of AA-cell Mallory flashlights (in case one fails) with spare bulb and four extra alkaline cells. Each kit supplies enough hiking light for an entire night.*

plus two extra sets of cells, sufficient illumination for an entire night if need be; the total weight of this versatile package is 10 ounces and the cost about $7.

More widely popular are the bigger C and D flashlights, preferred for the larger beam and possibly greater durability—though as a commentary on contemporary manufacturing practices, no inexpensive flashlight made today is as tough and trustworthy as the typical product of the past. A typical C-size with two heavy-duty zinc-carbon cells plus a spare pair (yielding somewhat longer useful light than the doubled-up AA Mallory package) weighs 10 ounces, costs about $6. Pessimistic hikers who used to carry two C lights and gloomily hoped one would work in time of need report that life is brighter now that they've switched to the Kel-Lite, ruggedly made for policemen, who hate to be left in the dark. A price is paid—the C size, with alkaline batteries plus a spare pair, weighs just under 1 pound, costs $20.

Which are the best cells, the Eveready heavy-duty zinc-carbon (note the "heavy duty," denoting cells with 50 percent greater life expectancy than the standard zinc-carbon) or the alkaline? Certainly the alkalines are superior for prolonged use (night-hiking, reading in the bag) and for cold weather. At 70°F the C alkalines provide useful light for perhaps as long as 15 continuous hours, compared to no more than 4 or 5 for zinc-carbon; at freezing the differential is greater, some 8 hours to about 2. Other statistics could be bandied about to prove alkaline cells are the only ones worth carrying—as, indeed, many hikers believe.

Others, though, cite faults. The alkalines cost twice as much and weigh a third more; even so, they still would have a clear advantage in terms of useful-light-per-ounce were that the whole story. But alkaline cells abruptly blank out when exhausted, unlike the zinc-carbons, which go from bright to dim in a straight-line dwindling, warning when darkness is imminent. And once in a while alkalines have a mysterious tendency to drop dead very prematurely. When slightly damaged, they may leak gelatinous filler, losing all power and fouling the flashlight or pack.

A key matter is the definition of "useful" light. Cells that by manufacturer's standards have fallen below the minimum "useful" voltage in fact suffice to follow a forest path. The lower the voltage accepted as "useful," the less the longevity advantage of the alkaline.

Lithium batteries have a tremendously longer life than alkalines and weigh half as much. The price—seven times higher—would still be a bargain were it not for the unreliability and leakage. Though very promising, at present they must be considered experimental.

A thing to remember at low temperatures: cells apparently dead can be warmed to 70°F or so in pockets or by a fire (carefully—when too hot, they explode) for additional life.

The bulb used affects battery life. Figures given above assume a PR2 bulb, rated at .8 candlepower, sufficient for prowling around in bushes. However, a PR4 bulb, with .4 candlepower, adequate for camp chores and walking trails, approximately doubles the time of useful light.

NINE: MAP

The kinds of maps and their use and where to obtain them are discussed in Chapter 16. Here, suffice it to say that a party, and preferably each individual, must have a map of the area being traveled —and know how to read it!

TEN: COMPASS

The natural companion to the map is the compass, use of which also is treated in Chapter 16. The hiker should avoid the expensive precision instruments intended for complex navigation; he can do very well with a simple compass costing around $3 to $7 as long as it has a clear base with grid lines that can be aligned with a map reference line for orientation.

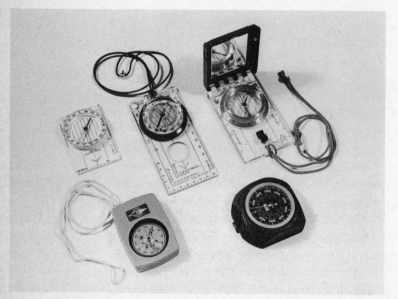

Representative compasses popular with hikers. Top row: *Silva Polaris, Suunto Boy Scout, Silva Ranger.* Bottom row: *Suunto KB-20, Thommen altimeter.*

The *altimeter,* to climbers and cross-country roamers a routefinding aid often more valuable than a compass, is hardly necessary for ordinary trail hiking but makes a nice conversation piece (and also serves as a barometer). Instruments calibrated to 16,000 feet or higher in 100-foot graduations are available for about $15—and $50—depending on the continent where made.

OTHER (FREQUENTLY) ESSENTIALS

There is another category of items whose lack rarely imperils life or limb but can lead to major discomfort or inconvenience.

WHISTLE

Rescue authorities wish every lost hiker had a whistle, since the shrill blast carries farther than a yell and takes less effort. Parents often issue whistles to offspring—after sternly emphasizing they are *not* for scaring birds and aggravating neighbors, but solely for emergencies.

SUNBURN PREVENTIVE

See nature boy strip to shorts and T-shirt in morning and walk meadows or desert or beach, joyously soaking up rays from the life-creating sun. By afternoon he notes that his skin feels warm even when a cool wind blows, but is unaware of catastrophe until, in camp that evening, companions cry out aghast at the sight of him. Through the night he lies sleepless on his bed of pain. In morning he cannot move legs or head without wincing, and to hoist pack on back is to scream and whimper. He will not again seek oneness with the solar furnace, this miserable nature boy. Next time he wants a tan, he'll buy it at the drugstore.

In woodlands and poor weather a hiker is unlikely to receive more radiation than his skin can readily tolerate. But in all-day brightness, especially at high elevations and/or in snow, a burn can become a true medical emergency, requiring first aid with soothing creams and pain-killers and sedatives plus aspirin to reduce fever, possibly an un-planned layover, or in the extremity, evacuation to a hospital. Persons with dark complexions or deep tans slowly acquired can stand more sun than those with fair skins freshly exposed after months of encase-ment in city clothing, but not as much as they think; even blacks can become gravely sunburned.

During the first bright trips of summer a hiker should cover up with shirt and trousers after no more than 2 hours or so; gradually the time

of exposure can be lengthened, perhaps to a full day. The uncertain beginner should apply sunburn preventive to exposed areas at the very start of an extended walk in the sun and every hour or so during the day and definitely *not wait* for "hot skin" or "red skin"; by then it's already 2 hours too late to avoid agony.

Unless a hiker spends a lot of time in snow or is supersensitive to sunlight (a condition likely discovered early in life) he doesn't need the clown-white or glacier cream favored by climbers and skiers. The standard screen, the active ingredient in most current preparations, is para-aminobenzoic acid, PABA for short. At a concentration of 5 percent the ultraviolet is totally blocked and the skin neither burns nor tans. Lower concentrations for "tanning without burning" (an impossibility) suffice for most hikers most of the time. The main thing is to have *some* burn preventive—and to *use* it. Experience (a certain amount painful) tells how much protection is required. Preparations are usually labeled with their SPF (Skin Protection Factor), ranging from 2 to 15; individuals with sensitive skin ordinarily prefer a rating of 8 or higher. Some people learn to their chagrin that they have an allergic reaction to this ingredient or that; perhaps worse, they may have a phototoxic reaction, the cream itself giving them a bad burn with any sun exposure whatsoever.

A person whose lips are prone to burn and chap should carry a lip salve or Chap Stick. (Lipstick works fine for women, but men risk misunderstandings.) Similarly, people with flaring nostrils may appreciate one of the preparations available to prevent interior burns that cause runny noses.

INSECT REPELLENT

It is possible for hikers to be totally incurious about the water ouzel, golden eagle, varied thrush, and hummingbird. However, none is so stolid of soul and tough of skin as to lack a lively interest in mosquitoes, flies, gnats, no-see-ums, ticks, chiggers, and others of the afflictions visited upon man as a consequence of his fall from grace. These instruments of the Lord's anger, which drove Adam and Eve from the Garden of Eden, are considered at gruesome length in Chapter 5.

Though no repellent answers the hiker's prayer for a zone of quiet, application can reduce the incidence of bites; the attendant cloud of wings just has to be lived with.

Still on the market and still with faithful adherents are liquid and rub-on stick repellents, dating from World War II, whose principal active ingredient is ethyl hexanediol; there are also arcane potions concocted by North Woods medicine men and transcending science. Vitamin B-1 taken orally has long been thought by some hikers to drive bugs away, and has long been known certainly by all hikers to give a sweating body a distinctive aroma that drives people away; marketed as an "oral repellent," the tablets are priced many times higher than those sold in drugstores as just plain vitamins. The nicotine reek of tobacco addicts is also reputed to offend bugs and other nonsmokers.

For all that, in the late 1950s the bug experts of the U.S. government concluded after extended research that *N, N, diethyl meta toluamide* is the most effective known chemical (safe for application to the human body) at discouraging insects. Because no successor is in sight, and because once a candidate is identified, the federal safety tests take years, the status is likely to stay quo for decades. Diethyl toluamide is not without flaws—it attacks the plastics in watch crystals, glass frames, and handles of Swiss Army knives, and is a suspect in cases of mysterious allergic reactions.

The most potent form is Vietnam-born "jungle juice," a 71 percent solution in alcohol, 2 ounces of repellent (not counting bottle weight), costing about $1. The alcohol quickly evaporates, but the odorless, invisible chemical remains and works for hours unless washed off by sweat or rain. The compound is so strong in this concentration that care must be used around the eyes, where it may be carried by sweat and sting like fury. It may also irritate the tender skin of infants.

The concentration is 28½ percent in Off, the cost for 1 ounce (of repellent) about $2, a fifth the power per penny, but the oil base is preferred by some hikers.

Even at its mere 19 percent concentration, Cutter copes very well, and even despite the cost of nearly $2 for 1 ounce of repellent (a seventh the power per penny of jungle juice), it is the popular favorite, largely because the cream base feels so nice.

Aerosols and foams have more gas and package than repellent and weigh and cost too much for backpacking.

Tundra in mosquito time, forests in fly time, may drive a hiker to cower in a tent barred at every opening or cover up completely with clothing supplemented by a *head net.* More commodious for sitting around camp or trail, and highly recommended for tentless sleeping, is the *"habitat,"* a piece of no-see-um netting wide and long enough to drape over head and torso; from within, dreaming peacefully or nibbling pilot bread and peanut butter, one looks smugly out to the wing-crowded world. Praised by walkers and canoeists in the Far North, where mosquitoes work around the clock in numbers endangering sanity and life, is the *"shoo-bug jacket,"* a light fishnet garmet with elastic at wrists and waist and a drawstring hood. To prepare for use, place the jacket in a ziplock plastic bag, pour in a bottle of jungle juice, and zip the bag tight for 6 hours, during which period cotton fibers interwoven in the nylon fishnet soak up the juice. The treated jacket frees the wearer from bites for up to 2 weeks without a recharge. It is not manufactured at present, but a handy hiker might improvise a substitute from a cotton shirt and whatnot.

REPAIR KIT

A hiker awakes to find that during the night a goose apparently died a violent death inside the tent; then he notes the rip in his sleeping bag, exactly where he dried it by the campfire. On the trail he carelessly dumps pack from weary back, the frame hits just right (wrong) on a rock, a joint separates, and there seems no solution but to send out for a wheelbarrow. Nearing the road, he lengthens stride and overstrained pants rip and modesty forbids him to enter mixed company.

These are only a few of the ills the best of gear is heir to, reasons experienced backpackers carry some sort of repair kit. Following are typical components and examples of uses:

Cloth tape—for repairing tarps

Ripstop tape—for mending ripstop nylon parkas, sleeping bags, and tents

Thread—a spool of heavy cotton-covered polyester for mending clothing and sewing on buttons

Needles—several in various sizes

Awl and very coarse thread—for sewing packbags, tent floors, and other tough fabrics

Safety pins—several large ones and lots of little ones for such emergencies as a zipper that goes off the trolley

Clevis pins and wires—for packframe problems (see Chapter 10)

Nylon cord—⅛-inch or so, for lashing together broken packs and sick boots

Light steel wire—for field reconstruction of gravely wounded packframes

Pliers—for manipulating recalcitrant materials, in addition to kitchen use and expedition dentistry

TOILET KIT

A folk hero brags in an old ballad:

> I clean my teeth with river sand,
> Comb my hair with a tree,

> Wash my face whenever it rains,
> And let my wind blow free.

His gamy descendants know neither soap nor comb nor toothbrush nor handkerchief from start of trail to end, when they again submit to cleanliness and godliness.

Admittedly, years of wildland wandering are necessary to live content unsoaped and uncombed, and TV training is so ingrained that most people can never blow their nose in the old way, finger against nostril, without feeling nasty. And in an age when sweating in public is virtually a penitentiary offense, who dares spit anymore? Women especially, because of the sexism (sugar and spice) too many of them share, adjust very slowly to an environment of natural, healthy dirt.

Eventually the steam roller of the Neatness Industry must be halted and a compromise found that allows people to pass downwind of each other without being stunned, yet permits rivers to flow suds-free to unpoisoned oceans.

Granted, a clean body, even if it does not lead to a clean mind, has certain health values; the following simple toilet kit is environmentally tolerable if used in moderation:

> Toothbrush and paste in carrying case
>
> Soap or biodegradable detergent—a plain old bar or a tiny bottle of concentrated liquid solution—either of which doubles for dishwashing
>
> Small cloth towel, reusable paper towel, or a packet of Handi-wipes
>
> Polished-steel mirror
>
> Comb
>
> Handkerchief—if not for nose-blowing, for cleaning glasses, wiping sweat, binding wounds

Finally, a word about what was formerly called the Eleventh Essential. Toilet paper, which started to be widely used only in the past century, can be dispensed with by employment of available greenery —avoiding, of course, the likes of poison ivy. Whereas human wastes are biodegraded in weeks, the paper may last for years in a dry climate

—and not out of sight, because little critters dig it up and the winds blow it here, there, everywhere.

NOT ESSENTIAL BUT SOMETIMES NICE

By now the beginner may well be yearning to cry a pox on it and follow the fabled youth who gear-less, food-less, nearly naked, and supremely free, crossed the Olympic Mountains on a very cheap trip. Patience. A final few words about this and that—frills, really, but potentially adding enjoyment.

Cameras and fishing gear are examples.

In later chapters (namely, 17 and 19) a bit will be said about how ice ax, rope, snowshoes, and cross-country skis can expand hiking horizons.

Binoculars aid in puzzling out cross-country routes, identifying distant peaks, and gaining close-up looks at birds and animals. A good choice for backpackers is a set with a magnification of 6 or 8, weighing about ½ pound, costing about $75—or $300. A monocular can be had for ¼ pound and $30, or ⅛ pound and $15. A telescope is available for ½ pound, $20. At the other end of the scale are an 8-power hand lens for 3 ounces and $5, a 40-power pocket microscope for 1 ounce and $6.

Curious about wind velocity? Air temperature? Moisture? A wind gauge weighs 2 ounces, a pocket thermometer less. A rain gauge is 4 ounces, good for up to 5 inches, a typical night's quota in the Olympic rain forest. A hygrometer, 3 ounces, measures humidity, a subject of unfailing interest from the Rockies east to the Atlantic Ocean.

Philosophers may leave watches in the car to symbolize renunciation of city routine, and trust to sun and moon and stars to measure the passage of time, close enough for ordinary trail purposes. However, approximations can be far from the mark when heavenly guides are obscured by clouds; especially if boats or buses are to be met or many miles covered between dawn and dusk, a party generally takes along one or two watches. Climbers and other fanatics often carry an alarm wrist watch or lightweight alarm clock in order to be stirred to heroism before the birds chirp.

Toys are fun. Flying a kite from a tall peak gives a feel for the winds and sky, and except for mystifying eagles, causes minor disruption of the natural scene; on the beach, though, it may cause gulls and crows to riot.

What to do when confined to tent or tarp for hours or days by storm? Sleep, of course, until that's worn out. Talk, until hostilities trend toward confrontations. Then, a deck of cards for a game of hearts ("Smoke it out! Smoke it out!") that harmlessly releases tensions, or a pocket chess set which does the same at a lower noise level.

A few days from the city, compulsively literate folk become inordinately fascinated by lists of ingredients on food packages, a symptom of printed-word hunger. The syndrome can be controlled by carrying a paperback book, preferably with maximum words for minimum paper and slow enough going not to be run through hastily. An Ian Fleming or Stanislaw Lem fills a mere afternoon; for little more weight a single volume of Gibbon's *Decline and Fall* occupies the entirety of a three-day blow and then some; a Bible is unsurpassed in weight-to-content ratio; what with memorizing soliloquies and reciting them to tentbound companions, a collection of Shakespeare's tragedies can last a whole expedition, or even end it.

In bad weather and good, knowledge of wildlands is enlarged and appreciation deepened by guides identifying birds, animals and their tracks, flowers, trees, mosses, mushrooms, rocks and minerals, planets and stars. An Audubon bird call lets a hiker talk back, as does a beautifully crafted Brazilian bird whistle.

The scene may stimulate cravings for artistic expression with watercolor pad and paints.

Finally, a notebook and pencil stub have many uses. For leaving notes when the party is traveling in two or more sections. For keeping a trip log or diary. For composing letters to the makers of this book, sneering at the freaks of an old crock and condemning stupid mistakes.

16:

MANY hikers, even some with years of trail experience, stay on course entirely by watching the heels of the companion immediately ahead and never need any routefinding skill except that of boot identification, to avoid switching to the wrong boots at a crowded junction and following a stranger up the wrong valley.

However, the method has serious faults. The heels may disappear around a bend and be seen no more. They may themselves be lost. Finally, even should the heel-watcher always get where he wants to go, he never feels independent and self-reliant, always is somebody's caboose.

Mastery of wilderness navigation requires considerable ~~...~~ nd study and is too complex for extensive treatment in these page. A text recommended for anyone who expects to leave turnpike trails for byways is *Be Expert with Map and Compass,* by Bjorn Kjellstrom. But even the raw novice should learn the fundamentals discussed here in order to have a fighting chance to reach his objectives—and return without the assistance of a search party.

TOOLS OF THE TRADE

The basic equipment of routefinding is built into the human body; the skilled navigator, by use of eyes and ears and other senses, and through habits of always watching where he's going and where he's been, constantly filing mental notes about landmarks, maintains a sort of internal gyroscope.

However, the instrument occasionally gets out of whack, particularly in fog or darkness and unfamiliar terrain, and other tools must be brought into play.

COMPASS

The compass needle always points north—right? Wrong. The needle has two ends and one points south; to avoid very gross errors, the distinction between the ends must be kept in mind.

The north end of the needle always points north—right? Wrong. It does not point to *true* north—that is, the North Pole—but to *magnetic* north—that is, the North Magnetic Pole, located about a thousand miles to the south in the Canadian Arctic. The difference between true north and magnetic north is the *declination,* and unless this is known for the area being traveled, the compass merely confuses the situation.

For example, the current declination in the state of Washington is approximately 22° east (that is, the needle points 22° east of true north) and in the state of Maine approximately 20° west. Some maps give the local declination but some don't, in which case the information must be obtained elsewhere before the trip. Trail navigation is not so precise that the hiker must fret about declination down to the last several degrees. However, failing to distinguish between east and west, and thus adjusting for declination in the wrong direction, is a good way to see a lot of unexpected country.

Before it is used, the compass must be oriented. Set it on a flat surface or hold it carefully in the hand, making sure no metallic objects are close, since their slight magnetism may distort the reading. When the needle stabilizes, rotate the compass to the proper declination—that is, for Washington, until the north-pointing end of the needle points 22° east (right) of the north symbol on the dial, and for Maine, 20° west (left) of the symbol. The compass is now oriented and the north symbol on the dial indicates true north.

Compasses oriented for various parts of America, showing declination.

True north can also be found by spotting the North Star on a clear night. True south can be found with a watch: point the hour hand (standard time—not daylight saving) at the sun; true south lies halfway between the hour hand and 12.

Through experience a hiker learns to identify certain characteristics of his home hills with certain directions—a greater frequency of cirques, avalanche paths, and snowfields on north and east slopes, or dry-habitat trees and shrubs on south and west slopes. But the lore is much less dependable than always carrying a compass and always knowing the local declination.

ALTIMETER

In areas accurately contour-mapped, knowing the elevation often permits climbers and off-trail ramblers to puzzle out their position even in thick fog. The altimeter has less utility for the average hiker but may serve such purposes as gauging progress when he ascends a trail in dense forest.

An altimeter does not directly indicate distance above sea level but rather, being in fact a barometer, measures atmospheric pressure, which varies not only with altitude but with weather changes. Readings are therefore approximate; while sitting in camp, a party may be informed by the altimeter it is gaining elevation at a mad rate—unsettling news, meaning air pressure is falling rapidly and a storm is roaring in.

BINOCULARS

In cross-country travel a close-up look at distant terrain is extremely valuable in choosing a route or campsite, identifying landmarks needed for orientation, finding a skimpy trail invisible to the naked eye. Trail hikers use binoculars more often for nature study.

MAPS

Anyone who paid moderate attention to geography lessons has at least a rudimentary ability to interpret maps, sufficient for the elementary demands of trail travel; though only field practice makes perfect, mainly a novice needs to know which maps to use and where to get them.

A *planimetric* map shows lines (roads, trails, rivers, and perhaps ridge crests) and points (camps and peaks) in their horizontal relationship but without "depth." A familiar example is the highway

map normally required to escape civilization.

A number of federal and state land-managing agencies and some private firms publish planimetrics. Most widely used are those from the U.S. Forest Service, given away or sold at ranger stations and (by mail) headquarters of National Forests, normally obtained by a hiker along with a wilderness permit. Government planimetrics are revised fairly frequently and provide the most up-to-date information about roads and trails and other works of man.

A *topographic (contour)* map contains all the data of a planimetric, and in addition portrays the vertical shape of the terrain with *contour lines* —lines upon which every point is the same elevation above sea level. With experience a hiker develops stereoscopic vision that allows him to look at a topographic map and clearly distinguish ridges from valleys; however, even a novice can readily learn from the contours such crucial matters as whether a planned camp is at 6,000 feet rather than 2,000, or whether the trail ahead gains a lot of altitude or very little.

Topographic maps of the United States are produced and sold by the U.S. Geological Survey. For areas west of the Mississippi River, order from U.S. Geological Survey, Federal Center, Denver, Colorado 80225; for areas east of the Mississippi, from U.S. Geological Survey, Washington, D.C. 20242. Index maps of the sheets available for individual states are free on request. The newer Forest Service maps of dedicated wildernesses are also topographic.

Topographic maps of Canada may be purchased from the Map Distribution Office, Department of Mines and Technical Surveys, Ottawa, Ontario.

Backpacking shops stock selections of topographic and other maps in their areas.

Pictorial relief maps, giving a bird's-eye view of the land, and sketch maps published in guidebooks and alpine journals often offer supplementary data not found on the basic maps.

Rare is the map that merits absolute, unquestioning trust. Several factors determine the reliability. First is the reputation of the producer, the U.S. Geological Survey standing at the summit and other agencies at varying positions downward. Second is the date of the

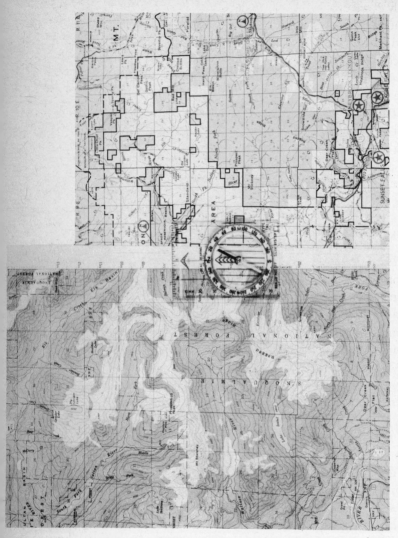

U.S. Geological Survey topographic (contour) map and U.S. Forest Service planimetric map, covering approximately the same area. Both are properly oriented by the compass.

survey on which the map is based, usually noted on the sheet. Particularly in areas being heavily logged, such as multiple-use zones of U.S. National Forests and most of Canada, roads are constantly being built and trails obliterated, and maps more than several years old may be ancient history. Third is the scale, since the larger the area represented by a map, the smaller the amount of fine detail and the less painstaking the preparation.

Though maps are inexpensive and can easily be replaced in the city, not so during a wildland storm, precisely when hikers may be wondering where in tarnation they are and how to get out; maps should thus be protected by being carried in a polyethylene bag—in windy, rainy weather the map can be folded for reading without removal from the bag.

VERBAL INFORMATION

Maps condense an enormous amount of data in small space but cannot tell all a hiker may wish to know about a trail—the special attractions that make it worth walking, the best season, the legal and the preferred campsites, the rules and regulations, the confusing junctions, and so on. For this there are hiking guides, more every year; few portions of the continent now lack "cookbooks."

Climbing guides should not be overlooked from a sense of humility; in describing approaches to basecamps for summit ascents, they often provide excellent recipes for trail trips and off-trail roamings. However, the hiker must not be tempted beyond his abilities; when a climbing guide says a route is "easy" it means easy for a trained climber, not every casual pedestrian.

Each guidebook must be checked for publication date, field-tested for accuracy, and accorded only the degree of trust it earns; some guides are sloppy ripoffs and even those of the highest integrity invariably include mistakes in observation, typographical errors, and data rendered obsolete by time and bulldozers.

Other valuable sources of verbal information are mountaineering and conservation journals, annuals, and magazines, which frequently print narratives of tempting hikes, descriptions of inviting country.

But only by talking (in person or by letter) to local folk—usually the rangers—can late news be learned—such as that spring floods took out a key bridge or that due to an exceptional winter the snow is still deep in meadows ordinarily in flower.

ORIENTATION

Rescue-wearied, sleepless rangers, besieged by worried relatives calling about overdue parties, sometimes suspect that a majority of travelers abroad on the trails know their location only to within several miles and that if a dense mist were to settle on the land, the backcountry mortality rate would approach that of the Black Death.

Even the hiker who intends never to stray—on purpose—from well-beaten paths must learn the basics of orientation (determining present position in relation to surroundings) and navigation (getting from one known point to another); getting from one unknown point to another is called "being lost" and requires no elaboration beyond that in Chapter 6.

Any honest veteran will admit that more than once he has been, if not lost, badly confused, and has felt the panic of disorientation. Once or twice is enough; the mark of the veteran is that whenever he walks a few minutes without knowing exactly where he is, legs automatically halt, suspicious eyes rove. And if a sure sense of direction does not come quickly, he pauses for orientation. The following brief outline is the merest introduction to the most elementary techniques of a complex science-art.

The first step is to *orient the map,* most easily done by lining up known landmarks with their symbols on the sheet. This failing, as in unfamiliar country, the compass is brought out. Spread the map flat and lay the compass on the sheet with dial north aligned with the true north arrow of the map (almost invariably true north is the top of the map). Rotate map and compass as a unit until the needle points the correct number of degrees east or west of dial north, in accordance with local declination. Compass and map are now oriented.

The next step is to *orient the hiker.* If he *knows the precise point* of his present location (river crossing, trail junction, mountain summit), any

visible feature (peak, pass, valley) can be identified by placing a stick (or other straightedge) on the map touching the known point, aiming the stick at the visible feature, and examining the map to see what features are intersected by the stick. Similarly, if the hiker wants to find the position of an invisible feature (hidden by trees or fog), he places the stick on the map to intersect his known point and the invisible feature, which then lies in the direction indicated by the stick.

Orientation is more complicated when the hiker *knows only he is somewhere on a certain line* (trail, river, ridge). He must be able to identify at least one distant feature—say, Bald Mountain. A simple procedure, not as craftsmanlike as the methods of Kjellstrom and other masters, is to place the compass on the map with the compass center exactly atop the symbol for Bald Mountain, orient map and compass as a unit, place the stick on the compass center and point it at the actual Bald Mountain. The intersection of the stick with the known line (trail, river, ridge) is the present location—*approximately*. A second distant feature is desirable for verification. Comparison of the surroundings with the map determines if the results are reasonable.

When a hiker *knows only that he is in a certain area* (perhaps on one of several possible trails, rivers, or ridges), at least two distant features must be identified and the technique is beyond the elementary; see Kjellstrom.

And if no distant features are visible, as in fog or deep forest? Or none can be positively identified? Time then for advanced navigation methods. Either that or sit down and wait for the search party, as discussed in Chapter 6.

STAYING ON COURSE

The beginner may say, "I don't need to bother about all this route-finding stuff because I'm always going to stick to trails." Well and good—if he can. But sticking to the trail, and finding it in the first place, isn't invariably a cinch.

For openers, in multiple-use public lands of the United States, and in the entirety of Canada outside National Parks, the trailheads often lie amid a maze of logging roads, either completely unsigned or, in some National Forests, marked only by cryptic numbers meaningless without the proper Forest Service map. Stops may be necessary at junctions to consult map and guidebook, which perhaps are obsolete because of new roads built and old ones abandoned. At length finding the presumed start of the wanted trail, a party may see naught but a chaos of logging slash, or perhaps several paths heading in different directions, and no signs. Again map and compass may be required even before leaving the road, and possibly short scouting trips.

Once his boots are pounding a broad, well-maintained, heavily used trail, usually the hiker must only avoid walking with eyes steadily on the path underfoot and failing to see a junction and hours later having to ask a stranger, "Pardon me, but do you know where I am?" Similarly, ground-watchers have been known to walk blindly off the end of a switchback and plunge stupidly forward into brush.

Many otherwise distinct trails require frequent reference to the map because they lack signs at junctions, or have signs so mauled by bears, chewed by porcupines, or shot up and chopped by idiots to be past deciphering. At any dubious junction the party should assemble, particularly if the rear-guard members are inexperienced or notorious, given two choices, for instinctively taking the wrong one.

Traveling old, little-used trails is more akin to cross-country roam-

I KNOW THE BOOK SEZ... "KEEP THE PARTY CLOSE TOGETHER"... BUT THIS IS — RIDICULOUS

ing than trail-following. On some the tread periodically vanishes in blowdowns, meadows, marshes, and rocks; on others frequently divides and redivides in myriad tracks beaten by deer, elk, goats, sheep, or cattle. There may be blazes on trees—but also "lost-man blazes" made by falling trees and rocks (and lost hikers). There may be cairns or ribbons—helpful if placed by people who knew where they were going. Often a hiker can steer through the maze by figuring where he would have built the trail if it had been his job. The second and third in line should pay as much attention to routefinding as the leader, who in forest may not see a blaze or sawn log off to one side and on a fogswept ridge fail to note diverging spurs.

When a path disappears and does not immediately resume, the party should *stop.* The temptation is to forge straight ahead, hoping to pick up the way, but if the trail turns sharply in the missing section every forward step leads farther into nowhere. With the party halted and assembled, two or three members (more just muddle matters) should fan out and scout for tread, blazes, sawn logs, and the like, staying in communication so that any of them can sound the recall; the scout who goes beyond intelligible voice range perhaps enjoys his solo exploration but may return to fuming companions who found the trail a half-hour ago and have been yelling their heads off.

Several rules are important when traveling sketchy trails and wandering away from trails, particularly in poor weather. *Keep the party*

together, every member in sight or sound of others at all times.

Maintain constant orientation, at every step observing close and distant landmarks, periodically relating them to the map.

Since half the fun is getting home, prepare for the return by noting prominent boulders and trees, cliffs and creeks. *Look over the shoulder* frequently to see landmarks as they will appear on the return. If terrain is complicated or visibility limited, mark the route at critical points with toilet paper or crepe paper draped on trees or shrubs. Plastic and nylon ribbons are more durable but *should not be used unless faithfully removed later on;* paper markers should also be picked up on the return, but if circumstances forbid, remember that toilet paper disintegrates in the first rain and crepe paper in the second, while "surveyor's tape" is a semipermanent and obnoxious addition to the landscape. Wilderness managers hate "tapers" because their pioneering encourages boot-built trails, often on fragile lands where there should be no trails.

A final rule: a good leader should take it upon himself to train less-experienced party members in routefinding—especially children who otherwise may never progress past heel-watching.

Enough. Already the discussion has far exceeded proper limits of the novice.

But everybody is a beginner sometime and the only way to master wilderness navigation is doing it. By maintaining constant orientation, probing cautiously, invariably keeping open the line of safe retreat, inexperienced hikers can venture some distance into uncertainty without unreasonable risk. Yet it should always be remembered how unpleasant it is, and potentially fatal, to be lost in wildlands.

17: WHEN THE WAY GROWS ROUGH

THE elements of walking and camping properly are learned on well-marked, well-manicured trails. Indeed, most hikers, immune to the charms of nastiness and danger, never stray from friendly turnpike terrain. They feel no need to prove their bravery and fortitude, which they do every workday driving freeways and breathing city air, and are happy to renounce high adventure for peaceful enjoyment of forests and waterfalls and gardens.

Others, though, having put a few hundred miles on their boots, hear the call of the wild so loud and clear, are so driven by a force stronger than good sense, that they climb above trails through brush, up rocks and snows, to tall summits. Such berserkers must look elsewhere than here for instruction; one place is *Mountaineering: The Freedom of the Hills,* the standard American text since first publication in 1960.

Between the modes of easy-trail hiker and wilderness mountaineer is the subject of this chapter—a middle way that leaves the beaten track but stops well short of "technical climbing."

Actually, no hiker is so timid that he will not occasionally abandon the security of tread to wander a meadow valley, a tundra ridge, an open desert, a wave-washed beach. But the more ambitious, studying maps, see how little wildland is traversed by trails—they wonder about all those other valleys and ridges, peaks and basins, streams and lakes. Thus they graduate from trail-pounder to cross-country rambler.

Without ever leaving trails, a hiker may be challenged to something more than hands-in-pockets walking. In maritime mountain ranges of the Northwest even turnpikes are completely snowfree only a few weeks of summer; ability to cross a lingering snow patch safely can make the difference between continuing to the planned destination or turning back disappointed. Similarly, trails frequently come to river banks and quit; the hiker must either ford or go home. And a good many paths, including some very popular ones, have been built solely by boots and hooves and nary a stick of dynamite, and are interrupted by short stretches of rock that require hands as well as feet.

Let it be sternly stressed that rough country is not for everybody and surely not for the beginner; when the next step can be taken only at the risk of becoming a statistic in the annual report of the local mountain rescue organization, the mandatory decision is: *Don't take it; turn back.*

Further, reading this chapter does not give certification as an expert wildland rover; for that one should seek personal tutoring from veterans, best done by joining an outdoor club.

However, by adding a few items to his outfit and learning a few simple techniques, a hiker who has served his trail apprenticeship can greatly increase his safe hiking range. These tools and techniques will not be described here in detail, but rather introduced, their potential suggested, and the reader referred elsewhere for more information.

ICE AX AND ROPE

A hiker may feel presumptuous even to think about carrying ice ax and rope, symbols of the climber, yet through their use he frequently can pass otherwise dangerous obstacles with no more risk than walking a broad trail. So what if somebody does accuse him of dressing up for a masquerade? It's his neck.

ICE AX

The ax at work is discussed in following sections; here, several remarks about the instrument itself.

The ice ax is a dangerous weapon; one was used to assassinate Leon Trotsky in his Mexico City hideout, and others have accidentally wounded and killed climbers on many a mountain. Fresh from the shop the pick and spike are daggerlike and the adze razorlike, this for high alpine needs; the hiker's first action after purchase should be to dull everything on a grinding wheel. Even then the ax retains considerable potential for mischief and should always be handled with care not to inflict injury on companions or self.

The various refinements of fancy models have no utility for the hiker, who should buy the simplest and cheapest he can find. The shaft should be just long enough so that with carrying arm hanging loose, hand gripping ax head, the spike firmly contacts the ground; however, length isn't too critical and several inches this way or that make no appreciable difference.

If a hiker is sensitive to the sneering and gawking occasioned by an ice ax miles from the nearest snow—even though, as noted below, the value is not limited to snow and indeed is very great on slippery driftwood of an ocean beach—he may prefer a steel-tipped cane that does much (but not all) the work of an ax and with less threat from errant metal.

The alpenstock cherished by oldtimers serves some of the same purposes, as does a bamboo staff or a sturdy stick picked up in the forest and discarded when no longer wanted.

ROPE

A snow patch, a steep bit of rock, a footlog, a cliff of slick grass may bother some members of the party not at all but force others near or over the line of mortal peril. The weeping and the whining, the silent fear frozen in a face, must never be ignored by the strong, the brave, the sure-footed. By tying a rope to the frightened and thus endangered child, wife, husband, or weary friend, they can often remove the risk of tragedy from what is, after all, a pleasure trip. The cost? A few extra minutes—nothing compared to the time spent on a rescue.

Even if the risk is merely imagined, the terror is real, and except in small, infrequent, controlled doses the average hiker gets no fun from terror.

Unlike the climbing rope, the "hiking rope" is intended strictly for short pitches where the only falls possible would develop relatively minor forces. A good choice is 60 feet of ⁵⁄₁₆-inch nylon weighing 1¾ pounds. The breaking strength is around 2,800 pounds, which may sound like overkill, but keeping in mind that a knot reduces the effective strength by as much as half, and that a 150-pound person in a free fall of 10 feet gains a kinetic energy of 1,500 foot-pounds, really is about the safe minimum.

Totally lacking any notion of how climbers tie into a rope and establish belays, a hiker can fumble up some way to attach the rope securely to the waist of a companion and find a solid stance for safeguarding his passage. Obviously the job can be done better with knowledge of knot-tying and rope-handling; for hiking (but not climbing) purposes, enough can be learned from books—see *Mountaineering: The Freedom of the Hills.*

WALKING ROUGH GROUND

When the route leaves trail for untracked forest, steep meadow, talus or scree or moraine, rock slabs, brush, marsh, or snow, the hiker accustomed to having decisions made for him by established tread tends to stop after each step to plan the next; the pace slows to a creep and the sun goes down with camp still hours away.

What centrally distinguishes cross-country rambling from trail-tramping is that the hiker must constantly look and think ahead, or *hike with the eyes,* a three-part process: periodically he halts momentarily to survey the area and choose the broad line of approach; while moving, he scans the terrain a dozen yards in front to pick the easiest going; simultaneously he examines the ground of his next several steps. With practice the long-, medium-, and close-range studies fall

into an automatic routine and the pace is almost as fast and rhythmic as on a trail.

To reveal a secret about the ice ax: even a climber uses it maybe 1 percent of the time for chopping steps in ice, perhaps 9 percent for security on snow, and 90 percent purely as a walking stick. Old climbers are accused of carrying axes on trails and beaches out of snobbery so they will not be mistaken for mere hikers, but in truth, take away the old climber's ax and he walks off balance, pawing the air with his empty ax hand, falling down a lot.

On any steep and/or slippery terrain, not just snow but also wet heather, mud, moraines and talus, stream beds, footlogs, brush, and driftwood, the ice ax (or cane, staff, or stick) *provides a third leg*. If a foot slips, weight can be shifted to the ax while recovery is made. To put it another way, the ax is an arm extension that allows use of one or both hands in maintaining stability.

CROSSING STREAMS

A trail is plainly shown on the map, clearly signed at the parking lot, and obviously maintained regularly. Does this not mean that the land-managing agency—U.S. Forest Service, National Park Service, or whatever—officially certifies that every step of the way is certain and safe?

No. Those blue lines on the map always remain the same but not the streams they symbolize. Maps, guidebooks, rangers cannot provide money-back guarantees that any particular blue line, though usually a peaceful dribble easily stepped across on boulders, may not become, however briefly, a hell-roaring torrent. During a recent several-year period more hikers were killed in the North Cascades by drowning—swept away while fording or after slipping from footlogs —than by falls from cliffs, falling rock, avalanches, hypothermia, and all other wildland hazards combined—and most were on "turnpikes."

The first lesson about stream crossings: a passage simple last week and simple next week may be fatal today. Whenever a solid bridge is lacking—and in backcountry, bridges are often the exception rather than the rule—the trail may be absolutely blocked for hours or days.

In the absence of a bridge, perhaps there is a footlog. Is it wide, dry, and level? Splendid. Or is it narrow, steeply tilted, slippery with spray? Beware. A helping hand may be enough to steady a small child or nervous friend; a rope tied to the waist of the insecure body and anchored from the bank will not prevent a fall but may permit a rescue. The wisest decision may be to give up the trip and try again later in summer, when the log is not water-drenched, the flood has diminished, and the consequences of a tumble are not so drastic, or the trail crew has arrived and felled a bigger tree.

With footlog lacking at the trail crossing and none to be found by searching upstream and down, the trip is not necessarily deadended. Quite broad and deep waters can be waded safely if not excessively rapid and cold—but probably not by the beginner who has yet to learn what "excessively" means. Gently flowing, relatively warm streams of lowlands and deserts are no problem when shallow; even when deep,

361

they are often easily swum, rafting the pack on an air mattress. But mountain torrents are something else, and any depth greater than 18 inches or so requires thought. Swift water only knee-deep may boil above the waist, half floating the body; unweighted feet cannot grip the bed and with the shift of a boulder underfoot the hiker becomes a swimmer—except swimming is impossible in turbulent foam composed equally of water and air. Drowning and battering aside, a person's life expectancy in snowmelt is a matter of minutes.

Fording big, rough rivers is as complex and hazardous as ascending cliffs and traversing glaciers and is far beyond proper ambitions of the novice. However, by starting with little creeks, moving to larger ones, studying and practicing, he can in time handle rather substantial waters. To begin the education, following are several rules not universally applicable but often helpful:

Generally cross not at the narrowest point, where kinetic energy is greatest, but at the widest. Up to a point, choose the slow and deep water in preference to the shallow and fast. On occasion, pitch camp by the stream and cross in morning; snowfed rivers are usually lower after a cool night than at the end of a scorching day; similarly, the flash flood from a cloudburst ordinarily subsides in hours.

Before any crossing not completely worry-free (tricky footlogs as well as fords), release the hip belt of the pack so the load can be turned

loose instantly; better to splash around later trying to retrieve the pack than be dragged under by it.

Wear short pants, or in the right company, no pants. If the bed is soft sand or rounded boulders and the water not too cold, barefoot wading is delightful; however, wear boots when rocks are sharp, footing treacherous, or water so icy that bare feet might lose sensation. Wet feet on the succeeding trail can be avoided by taking off socks, wading in boots alone, and on the far bank dumping out water and donning the dry socks. Boots can be kept completely dry by wading in heavy socks, adequate for intermediate situations, or in sneakers carried for the purpose.

In rapids, face upstream and move crabwise sideways, using the ice ax—or stout stick—as a third leg. Move each foot separately and place it securely, remembering the tendency of boulders to depart downstream at the slightest excuse.

The point has been belabored sufficiently that a party in doubt must give up the attempt, turn back. However, a ford unquestionably safe for a large adult may surpass the unaided capacity of a smaller one or a child. In such case the big can accompany the little on the crossing to provide support.

Rigging a handline is generally a mistake, since the give of the rope is certain betrayal in time of real need. When more than convoy-type security is wanted, the hiking rope is better tied to the forder's waist, an anchor on shore ensuring against his being swept away—all the way away, that is, the pendulum swing to shore remaining to be endured.

ROCK SCRAMBLING

Another scary subject is raised—to be quickly dropped, and without revealing the magic formula by which any trail-tramper can step into a telephone booth and emerge moments later as a human fly. For the sake of family and friends, rangers and rescue groups, and his own tender flesh and brittle bones, a hiker must quit, go back, seek another route or switch to another destination when confronted by steep rock from which a fall would be damaging. Let him keep in mind that the body, with hands and eyes at the upper end, blind and clumsy feet at the lower, is much better designed for going up cliffs than down; a common cause of scrambling tragedies is the daring novice managing to get high on a wall, finding he cannot proceed upward, and then finding he cannot descend what he has climbed; weariness, panic, and gravity do the rest.

However, many trails never improved by blasting powder, and many off-trail routes include brief sections of rock that seem dangerous but really are not, or at least no more so than merging from an on-ramp into freeway traffic. With practice, and always with caution, a hiker can negotiate short rock steps in ease and security by observing the fundamentals of what mountaineers call "balance climbing."

Keep body weight directly over the feet by standing erect. Legs do the work, just as in ordinary hiking. Hands are not for pulling the body up but for gripping holds that serve as anchors in case a foot slips. Leaning into the slope gives a false sense of security; it actually causes body weight to thrust the feet sideways, slipping off holds or breaking them out.

Support the body always by three points. At every moment, be connected to the slope by two hands and a foot or two feet and a hand. Thus, if a hold fails, two points of connection remain.

Test holds. Before trusting a foothold with body weight, or a hand-hold as an anchor, make sure it is firmly attached to the mountain.

Move smoothly. Smooth transference of body weight puts minimum stress on holds. A rhythmic pace (the rest step described in Chapter 1) maintains a reserve of strength for surprises and is conducive to mental composure. A jerky pace breaks holds, sets lungs to gasping and heart to pounding, and leads to doubt and thence to fear and panic.

Climb with the eyes. Constantly look ahead to spot the easiest line of progress, to study holds and plan the next sequence of moves, and to avoid climbing into traps.

To repeat with emphasis, these expressions of common sense do not amount to a mystical incantation, are nothing but words on a piece of paper until they become reflexive in mind and muscle through prac-tice.

Some hikers scramble better than others. In a party of mixed experi-

365

ence or ability, the hiking rope can eliminate terror from short stretches of steep rock (or heather or mud)—a strong and confident scrambler belays from the top, the inexperienced or weary or tiny companion is protected from a fall by the rope tied around his waist, and
perhaps on occasion (especially in the case of a child) given a helpful
pull to get up a section of thin holds. For reasons stated earlier, the
rope should *not* be used as a handline.

Fewer hikers are endangered, injured, and killed by falling from
mountains than by being fallen upon, and the most frequent menace
is not natural disintegration. Never, ever, should a hiker roll boulders
down a slope or throw them into an abyss for the thrill of it—how is
he to know who may be below? Never, ever, should a hiker scramble
carelessly, blithely loosing barrages. If despite caution he dislodges a
rock and there is the slightest possibility that people are below, he
must immediately sound the alarm by shouting "ROCK! ROCK!

ROCK!" In steep terrain with a considerable human population, on trails and off, the hiker must at all times be alert for attacks from above, watching and listening, and when appropriate, shouting, cursing, threatening.

SNOW TRAVEL

Snow is tricky stuff. In winter and spring it avalanches. Undermined by streams, it conceals pits. When steep, it provides toboggan runs often ending bloodily in boulders, trees, cliffs. Being cold and wet, it's ideal for hypothermia. All in all, a blanket endorsement of snow play could be interpreted by the courts as homicide. The novice who reads the few words here, rushes off to buy ax and rope, and with no more preparation than that invades the white wilderness is quite likely to become a statistic. Though *Freedom* offers more background, most

367

emphatically the subject should be studied under expert tutelage, as by enrolling in a climbing school offered by an outdoor club, youth group, college, mountain shop, or guide service.

The rewards are worth it. By mastering certain basic techniques, a hiker can enormously enlarge his realm of safe wandering, add months to his high-country hiking season, feel the exhilaration of walking on top of brush instead of fighting through it, and pretty much get away from the madding crowds.

As the beginner will be taught in any school, the most important tools of snow travel are the boots, used to kick platforms, and the most important technique is standing erect so that boots are not thrust sideways by body weight, breaking out platforms or slipping off them. The ice ax, however, serving as a cane—a third leg—is the tool that gives the stability and thus the confidence necessary to stand erect, and

provides an anchor when a foot skids, stopping most slides before they start and further reinforcing confidence—and on snow confidence is more than half the battle.

Alpenstock, cane, staff, or stick picked up in the woods can also act as a third leg. The ice ax, though, has a further value in putting on the brakes once a slide has begun. *Self-arrest,* where a person digs ax pick into slope, presses chest against shaft to give the pick purchase, and spreads legs and digs in toes, will not be elaborated on here. Suffice it to say that the technique must be learned by anyone intending to do much snow hiking—and cannot be learned from books but only by intensive practice under expert instruction.

The hiking rope has uses on snow when some members of the party are experienced and sure-footed and others are not. For example, a father with a background in climbing usually can safely convoy a small child over a snow patch hand in hand. But if he needs both hands for ice-ax control lest he himself slip, he does better to tie the rope to his waist and that of the kid. And if he has any doubts about being able to arrest a joint slide, the mother should stand on safe ground, belaying the child with the rope while the father does convoy duty. (Or mother and father may exchange these roles; climber females have been known to become attached to non-climber males.)

ROUGH ROADS TO FREEDOM

There are hazards in snow travel, rock-scrambling, river-fording, off-trail wandering generally, rough-country exploring particularly. Many dangers are more apparent than real and vanish like goblins in the light of experience. While gaining the experience, a hiker discovers unsuspected dangers and how to avoid some, and develops the wisdom and humility to turn back when faced by the others. With patience and caution and imagination he can, if he so wishes, escape the confines of trails, become a cross-country rambler, and to a very considerable extent enjoy what mountaineers call "the freedom of the hills."

18:        **SUFFER THE LITTLE CHILDREN**

"WE USED to go hiking all the time, but then we had the kids."

"We'd like to take the kids hiking with us, but they're too young."

"We'd like to start hiking, and will when the kids are bigger."

Such sentiments often are expressed by parents: experienced backpackers who consider wildlands too brutal for young innocents, or else that coping with children on the trail is too complicated; beginning hikers who still find the backcountry somewhat spooky; car-campers who want to venture away from roads but don't quite dare.

Let it be said at the outset that no editorial position is taken on the proper way to run a family. If the father wants to go hiking with friends and leave wife and kids home, and they don't mind—well and good. Parents with rotten kids may find vacations from them essential to sanity—the rotten kids, parked with grandparents, may enjoy the vacation from rotten parents. In no holy book is it written that a family must always go everywhere together; indeed, if the wife abhors hiking, the marriage is not enhanced by dragging her to agony—which any competent wife can force her husband to share.

No—this is not a homily on family living. The intent is merely to suggest to beginning hikers, and experienced hikers who are beginning parents, how they may take the children along with fun and games for all.

Certainly many parents so desire. Commonly they wish to raise offspring in their own life pattern. And much of the pleasure of parenthood is watching young ones discover the wide, wide world. Finally, on long backpacks a deprived mother can often be found off in the woods, weeping, and when asked what's wrong, wails, "I miss my baby!"

And what about the children's desires? At a certain age when Mommy is away overnight they fear she has abandoned them forever. Somewhat older, they protest the bitter injustice of their folks going off without them to wonderful secret places, they agitate for Children's Lib, full membership in the family.

No brief is made here for the wisdom or necessity of being totally child-centered; people do not give up all their rights, become third-class citizens, in changing status from "man and woman" to "daddy and mama." However, if they *want* to take the kids hiking, they *can*.

Almost invariably, worries are exaggerated. Children are tough little beasts, usually better able than city-pampered adults to withstand trail rigors. (Except bugs, which eat tender-skinned youngsters alive, requiring special protection.) Moreover, ordinarily they are accustomed to a totalitarian regime, to being forced into unfamiliar situations (after all, nearly everything in the world is unfamiliar to them), and stoically put up with a lot of guff. (Not so in extreme cases of the "permissive parent," but brats are a couple other books.) If introduced to trails early, they probably will grow up to be loyal citizens of the wild country—and better people for it and better Friends of the Earth (editorial opinion).

For many families the question is academic. No free baby-sitters, such as grandparents, are available, and no money for a hired baby-sitter; either the kids go along or nobody goes—or only the father, which is grossly unfair if the mother is a devout wildlander. (The fair alternative is for parents to take turns staying home.)

Hiking with children is a special subdivision of the sport, but not so complicated as some parents and pundits make it. The proper gear solves most problems, as already discussed. That, of course, brings up another problem which looms especially large in a large family—the cost of equipping children while growing, and growing, and *out* growing. To re-emphasize a point previously made, the budget can quickly be busted unless recourse is made to thrift shops and hand-me-downs and hand-arounds among several families of friends.

One bit more about equipment. Poorly fitting boots and badly adjusted packs give a child just cause for complaint and support his paranoid suspicions of an adult plot to destroy him. Protests must be heeded. For example, hurt feet require instant attention, applying moleskin at the first redness lest a real blister develop and Mommy and Daddy be haled into Children's Court.

So much for prelude. Each family must invent its own formula, write its own history. Following pages offer a mixed bag of hints drawn from the memories of real-life backpacking families—mainly my own and several others we know well, leavened with observations of strangers encountered on the trail and comments by a number of parents and experienced ex-kids.

TAKING IT EASY

The capacity of the average child to endure hardship is incredible. The prime examples are from family annals of Little League parents who brag that Junior carried a 12-pound pack 10 miles when only four, conquered Tiger Tooth at seven, and climbed all the 14,000-foot mountains of the nation before puberty. Aside from being a pain in the neck to other parents, the pace-forcers take a risk; Junior may grow up to be a famous climber but chances are 50-50 that once old enough to escape the lash, he'll turn in boots and pack on a surfboard.

However, Junior's exploits demonstrate that children can perform prodigies of exertion beyond the belief of overprotective parents, and normally with no harm. (Needless to say, strength and hardiness vary widely; doubts should be resolved by consulting the family doctor.)

Nevertheless, a child, just as an adult, gains most pleasure operating below maximum potential. Maybe he *can* do 6 miles in a day but hate it, yet enjoy 3 miles. Trips with kids generally should be shorter than for adults alone, and the pace slower. How much shorter? How much slower? The only way for a family to find out is on the trails; the rule is, take it easy at first, and as muscles and ambitions grow, still keep the effort not only within the *physical* limits but within the *fun* limits.

APPLIED CHILD PSYCHOLOGY

Why is it that a child can dash full tilt around a playground for hours, yet collapse on the trail in minutes, whimpering and complaining? Every child is a natural malingerer—it's the only defense against adult tyranny—but the deeper explanation is motivation. The kid is impelled in the playground marathon by a constant succession of immediate goals—racing Patty to the swing, chasing Ira up the monkey bars, Indian-wrestling Tommy, teeter-tottering with Nancy—meaningful goals, kids' goals.

But trail goals are adult goals, incomprehensible or impossibly remote. Describing wonders of the day's destination—the creek to play in, the boulders to climb, the special pudding for dessert—may stir interest, but when they are not instantly attained, the whining questions arise, "Are we almost there? Why do we have to go there?" What use telling a little child that camp is only an hour away—when he doesn't know what an hour is? Seeing eternal suffering ahead, no fun, he despairs and collapses. At which point Mama may cry, "You poor dear!" and Daddy may find a smug lump perched on his shoulders. Even very tiny kids quickly become adroit at this fraud.

To keep the poor dears happy and off Daddy's back, parents must

become equally crafty, and the secret lies in thinking as kids do—from minute to minute, step to step—and seeking or arranging a constant sequence of goals, forgetting the rules for covering ground efficiently. The family group may walk 10 or 15 minutes and rest 15 or 20. Or take a dozen steps and pause, a dozen steps more and pause again. This latter pace, of course, is cruel to burdened adults. The father therefore may pile most of the gear on his back and stagger steadily to camp, leaving lightly loaded mother to dawdle with the babe. Otherwise, say spokeswomen for Mothers' Lib, the father should alternate in the dawdling duty.

The stops and pauses are occasioned less by needs for rest than by

happening upon things that make satisfying kids' goals. Water is an unfailing delight; at an age when gorgeous panoramas mean nothing, a child never tires of tossing pebbles in a pond, floating sticks down a stream, building castles in a sand bar, mucking around in a mud puddle. Perhaps he spots a beetle and is fascinated by watching it creep; parents should then join the watching—perhaps suddenly to remember how once they too loved beetles and ants and ladybugs. And so with flowers and frogs, mushrooms and spider webs, a festoon of moss and a chittering chipmunk. (But drop the pack if the session promises to be long!)

Be alert to point out a hawk circling the sky, a towering cloud that looks like a dog—a knight—a witch—Aunt Prunella. Teach the mysteries and solemnities of the wildland—that the trail lies on the slopes of a volcano and all these rocks were once hot as fire, that the valley below was once full of ice. Answer questions—"Will the volcano blow up while we're here, Daddy? Will the glacier come back and cover us up tonight?"

When nature fails to offer continuity of motivation, stage an impromptu party by bringing from the pack a piece of candy, a favorite toy; chewing a chunk of toffee while playing with cars in trail dust is a worthy goal.

Devices of this sort suffice on leisurely trips. However, with darkness or storm approaching, or for other reasons, sometimes it is necessary to keep a kid purely and steadily walking. Adults then must dip into another bag of tricks to relieve boredom while maintaining motion.

Perhaps promise a party at the very next creek or viewpoint, with animal crackers and root beer, and thus gain ten or so minutes of constant advance. In the interim, a bit of trail candy is usually good for a few more steps.

Try games. Announce that the family is a train and have locomotive father and caboose mother and freight-car and mail-car children make appropriate locomotive and caboose and etcetera sounds. (But let kids call their own game—one time a little boy who always before had loved to play train continued glum; that particular day he didn't want to be part of the family train, yet became perfectly happy when permitted to be a Pepsi-Cola truck.)

Tell stories from folk literature, the family past. Or start a story and have each hiker add an episode in turn. Or extract a story by asking a series of questions—one time a boy walked most of a day without complaint while describing the dinosaurs he was going to invite to his birthday party, and those he was not, and the foods he would serve and the games they would play.

Try singing. One time a father was at the bottom of a nettle patch, awaiting his wife and three-year-old daughter, and was alarmed to hear the girl scream as she was attacked by vicious bushes, and was alarmed further when weird sounds arose from the greenery—until

he recognized the child's voice, and the mother's, joined in song: "I'm Popeye the Sailor Man, *toot toot!*"

In such ways do parents outwit offspring. But the wily child fights back. One time a father and mother patiently cajoled their three-year-old daughter three miles upward from a camp beside the Stehekin River nearly to Cascade Pass, turning back in the snow when the girl had a tantrum, apparently from exhaustion. On the descent the poor babe tottered, stumbled, fell, and Daddy carried her the last mile, fearing for the health of the comatose little darling. And immediately on reaching camp, Sleeping Beauty awoke and for hours on into darkness splashed in a river pool, gathered pretty rocks and neat sticks, and when the parents at last sought to stuff her in a sleeping bag, complained, "I'm not tired!"

Similarly, parents have often felt pangs of conscience about pushing the family to a highland camp—and once there the destroyed children have miraculously revived and spent hours running up a snowbank and sliding down. (Snow, incidentally, is even better than mud; any camp with a good supply makes a perfect holiday.)

So goes the psychological warfare, the struggle between long-range goals of adults and short-range goals of children. When the conflict is conducted with love and compromise, both sides win, everybody has fun. In later years the trails and camps may well be remembered as the best of times—the moments when the family was closest.

Obviously, "taking it easy" means one thing with infants and another with teenyboppers, and obviously each family and its trail adventures are unique. However, the following chronological discussion of hiking with children from babyhood through adolescence, though based on the experience of a few families, suggests the possibilities.

BABIES

A babe in arms can be taken on roadside picnics and car camps, and with proper protection from sun and wind and mosquitoes be perfectly comfortable. To be sure, the infant derives little if any pleasure from the outing but the parents do, and in the process gain confidence for more ambitious ventures.

When the baby is three months or so they can stow him in a child-carrier and on suitably mild days go for short or long walks, hauling the appropriate paraphernalia of diapers and bottles. Babies generally enjoy the lulling bounce and spend most of the time sleeping; in fact, if colicky, they sleep better on the trail than in a crib. Care is required to bundle the baby warmly, shade eyes from sun, protect skin from sunburn and insects. Somewhere around six months a child starts to take a positive interest in wildland attractions, dabbling

fingers in sand, picking up pebbles, watching ants.

When does backpacking begin? As far as the baby is concerned, from three or so months on he can be as happy in the backcountry as at home. With one notable exception: up to about twelve months a baby's respiratory system cannot adjust readily to major changes in elevation. If his home is at sea level, during extended stays at camps above 7,000 feet or so, as in the High Sierra or Wind River Range, he may fuss continuously.

Usually, though, the problem is the parents—more specifically, parents with their first child, still fearful of breaking it. Initial trials should be short, so if something goes wrong—a sudden storm or one of those alarming fevers infants develop without warning for no apparent reason (until Mama's finger runs along babe's gums and finds a new tooth)—a quick retreat can be made to car and home. Though an adult party may consider a camp only a mile or two from the road hardly worth the trouble of backpacking, this much distance reduces the population to a fraction of that in car campgrounds, and on such forgiving trips parents learn how much special gear is needed—bottles, dried milk or formula, strained foods, teething biscuits, baby aspirin, changes of clothing, and the like. Reading Goldie Silverman's *Backpacking with Babies* may save some learning time.

Actually, a child is easier to carry at 1–1½ years and younger than later on, weighing and wiggling less and—being always on the back —not presenting the problems a toddler does on muddy or rocky trails. However, with one parent hauling the babe and thus not much else, the other must pack most of the gear, and this limits the length of a hike.

Still, after a few overnights the family may be ready for deeper probes into wilderness—5 or 7 miles—and longer trips—several days or a week, with a basecamp chosen for immediate attractions and the variety of day hikes and close enough to the car for a parent to fetch more food and diapers in mid-trip.

Thus far the discussion has assumed an only child. In a larger family with children widely spaced, backpacking a baby can be much easier, the older siblings helping. But two children only a year or two apart (or in the extreme case, twins) may be entirely too formidable on the trail until both are well past babyhood; parents probably had best give up extended backpacks the first two or three years and (lacking fond grandparents) take turns baby-sitting.

TODDLERS

The awkward age for backpacking is roughly two to four, when a child is usually too much of a load to be carried any great distance, yet can't walk very fast or far. Also, he has developed definite opinions on how the world should be operated, has a loud wail and not the slightest sympathy with adult goals. Frequently his attachment to Mama is so firm that more than momentary separation is simply not tolerated, making it hard for Daddy to be an effective baby-sitter or to share dawdling duty on the trail.

Hiking with a toddler demands the utmost patience. A pace of ½ mile an hour may be too swift, and a trip longer than 4 miles too rigorous. Probably he must be carried part of the time, but aside from the fact that parents may find the weight more than they can bear, the lump typically grows bored and wants to get down and walk—or rather stumble. A warning about piggyback rides: they eliminate the

child-carrier pack and are thought great fun by little darlings but place such pressure on neck muscles and nerves as literally to cause temporary paralysis. If extended hauling is planned, a child-carrier is essential.

Paradoxically, parents may have to plan shorter trips (and certainly slower) with the toddler than with the infant. As compensation, none of the special gear is required and packs thus are lighter. They are, that is, if Mama doesn't lose her head piling up shirts and pants, skirts and shoes, sweaters and mufflers and pajamas. Daddy must sternly inform her: the toddler is no longer a baby and needs as much clothing as an adult but no more—with the sole major exception of one or two complete changes for when he falls into a creek, and moments later into a second. Oversolicitous, overloading mamas are a major cause of back trouble among daddies.

Many toddlers, though potty-trained, continue to be bed-wetters. Parents may try such devices as withholding liquids past suppertime and routing the kid out periodically in the night, but nothing works. The best solution is *not* to have the wetter sleep in Mama's bag but in his own—filled with polyester, *not* down.

For all the difficulties of the toddler age, it is a most exciting family era: fresh young imaginations are stimulated by the richness around them—and their visions can at least be glimpsed by elders. One time a two-and-a-half-year-old boy spent a whole afternoon sitting by himself on a grassy tussock a few feet from the shore of a meadow pond,

dabbling a stick in the water, totally absorbed, and when asked what he was doing, said, "Sailing my boat." To what fantastic seas?

And this is the age when trail country puts to shame the playgrounds built by recreation experts. A fallen log wedged between two trees becomes the most exciting teeter-totter ever; on being torn away to go home, the kids ask, "Can we come back again? When? Next week?" Boulders become forts, snowfields toboggan slides, alpine tarns the most-fun swimming and wading pools. Beautiful stones are gathered by the pound, and hours spent combing bushes for mountain-goat wool.

If parents do not insist on too-long, too-tough trips, do not force incomprehensible adult destinations such as summits and fishing-type lakes but learn to accept and enjoy the goals of kids, chances are another generation will be converted for life to the wildland way.

SELF-PROPELLED PACKS

Seen on the trail: a mother and father suffering under huge burdens, their large, loutish kids running about packfree and happy. Something has gone terribly wrong in this family. The loving daddy doubtless is the same guy who piggybacks his darlings up to the moment they make the high school football team.

Also seen on the trail: a small mountain of gear mysteriously in motion, two legs protruding from the bottom—a self-propelled pack. Tender-hearted adult strangers cry out in horror, packless, drooling louts sneer, but in this family something has gone right.

At a certain age the child must pay the price. He outgrows Mama's sleeping bag and needs his own. Though he doesn't require as many changes of clothing as when he fell in every creek, his body is bigger and clothes heavier. And he eats more, as much as an adult. Unless he starts sharing the burden, the family backpacking becomes too strenuous for parents.

What is that certain age? No absolute rule can be stated; obviously the size and sturdiness of the child are factors as well as parental attitude. It is important, however, not to wait too long, but rather to ease the kid into responsibilities gradually—by being saddled when too young to know what's happening, he grows up with the stone and supposes God put it there.

Actually the average toddler, especially if he has older siblings, feels that to lack a pack is to be denied full membership in the family and demands one long before his folks think he's ready. In this case parents should be utterly permissive. Thus, at three or four the kid starts with a little rucksack containing a sweater and a toy. Inevitably the rucksack is taken over by a parent or sibling before the end of any long walk, but the precedent is established.

At four or five a child can proceed beyond tokenism. One time a girl of this age was given strong motivation by being assigned the family's entire candy supply for a whole week and marched as proudly as if carrying Fort Knox.

At around five or eight the self-propelled pack appears, the child carrying sleeping bag, clothing, and perhaps some food, no longer in a rucksack but a packframe-bag; part or all the load is often transferred to bigger backs before camp.

Year by year carrying capacity increases. But parents must not be misled by the youngster's apparently unlimited energy into overloading his growing, still-soft bones, lest in later years he suffer backpacker's backache.

At around nine or twelve the child carries all his own gear plus a fair share of the food, and parents dream about hiking with steadily lighter packs. However, along about this age independence is declared and Mama and Daddy experience new tribulations.

For one thing, youngsters want to walk faster than the family bunch and discover the country by themselves. The freedom should be encouraged within limits, such as ordering kids to stick strictly to the trail and wait up at forks; stay close to the folks in confusing terrain; give a blast on the emergency whistle if lost or confused; fall only into small rivers and over short cliffs.

For another, children grow bored with parents and seek more exciting tribal relationships. Inviting a pal on a hike adds a new

dimension of fun for toddlers; with moody teens a confidant may save the trip. Ideally, compatible families with compatible children should be sought. But when two or more compatible families march into the wilds with their two to twenty compatible children, they must enforce discipline in order not to render an entire valley uninhabitable. Particular attention must be given to sanitation, since the ordinary human takes a dozen years to learn the manners a cat does while still a kitten.

A few years more, and no matter how closely Mama clutches her baby, he is gone with friends on his own adventures, perhaps to rejoin the old folks on family reunions. The pity is that just as Daddy thought he had it made, a packmule or two thoroughly seasoned, they leave him in the lurch.

Well, there are always the grandchildren.

Harvey P. Manning and Trapper Nelson on the Pacific Crest National Scenic Trail. Photo by Harvey H. Manning.

19:

19:   ON INTO WINTER

Most hikers confine trail trips to summer, and for novices it's just as well, since wildlands are then friendliest and basics of walking and camping can be learned with least discomfort and danger.

Others, who love leaves budding in sudden warmth to green youth and turning in frost to yellow-and-red death, roam in spring and fall, seasons also offering more solitude.

Fewer think of winter as hiking time, yet the dark months can be bright, and when somber, speak perhaps more profoundly than the months of hot sun. Moreover, in winter the wilderness expands enormously beyond summer boundaries, reclaims large portions of its primeval domains.

The following brief discussion does not amount to even the sketchiest manual on winter travel, but this book cannot conclude without suggesting to the beginner the opportunities that await once he broadens horizons from a "hiking season" to the "hiking year."

BELOW SNOWLINE

In parts of America—including the entire South and the Pacific Coast west of the mountains—snow is unknown or infrequent in

386

lowlands and foothills; trails are open most, if not all, of the winter. A few air hours from the mainland are surfs and volcanoes and subtropical forests of Hawaii, magical over Christmas vacation.

Ocean beaches are never more exciting than in winter, and though the word is getting around, the January population on the sands is still a fraction of that in July.

Winter is the height of the season in some Southwest deserts. The semideserts of the Columbia Plateau and Great Basin often offer delightful walks over rolling ridges and up secret canyons dusted by sun-bright snow while windward slopes of coastal ranges are drenched by rain.

Not to be overlooked are low valleys reaching deep into wild mountains and in a normal winter snow-free (and snowmobile-free) all but several weeks. This is the lonesome time; even the roads, deserted by picnickers of summer and hunters of fall, provide quiet walks. Despite the camper-truck and vacation-trailer revolution, most

Winter hiking at sea level.

auto campgrounds are comparatively empty and rarely does a walker feel crowded on trails.

For good reasons. In the latitude of Washington State at the winter solstice the sun is technically up just a bit more than eight hours and is so low in the south that during cloudy weather the entire short day is twilight; on backpacks the camp evenings are almost as much of the trip as actual travel; tent fever may rage. More clothing and other equipment are required to stay warm and dry—safe from hypothermia. From beaches to mountains, the storms are fierce.

The beginner is wisest to sharpen skills in summer, then try spring and fall. But he should not forget winter.

OUT IN THE GRAND WHITE

As winter white expands and contracts, so most hikers retreat and advance. However, more and more of those who value lonesomeness are breaking through the snow frontier, whether on frosted hills near

home or in high mountains where the landscape is totally transformed.

To be sure, North America is suffering a plague of snowmobiles and some time must pass before the patient consents to be cured. Until then, terrain too rough for machines or off-limits through administrative ruling or by law (as in the case of National Wildernesses) remains a land of surpassing white peace.

Again there are reasons. Snow country is blizzard country, avalanche country, hypothermia country. Yet with the right equipment and technique any hiker of average strength and determination can experience the vast quiet (of spirit, that is; winds may be loud, very loud).

BOOTING

The most elementary method of snow travel is booting, identical to trail-walking except for the surface differences, which range from minor to considerable.

A foot of early-winter fluff or slush impedes passage only slightly. A solid midwinter crust permits a good pace—until destroyed by sunshine, warm wind, or rain. On a late-spring snowpack, feet may sink to the ankles in cool morning—to the shins in hot afternoon.

When legs plunge knee-deep, as they jolly often do after a fresh

Into the winter woods at low elevations.

snowfall, the death of a crust, or the creation by sun, wind, or rain of a snow swamp, the hiker progresses by "post-holing," a technique needing no explanation and deserving no recommendation; a strong party alternating leads may find ½ mile an hour a heroic pace.

Much snow-booting is so easy that a hiker wonders, once he's tried it, why he ever shied away. Even in the extremity of midwinter post-holing, though the effort demanded to get ¼ mile from plowed highway perhaps exceeds that of 4 miles on bare trail, the reward may be 16 times greater, may lead straight to faery. In such ranges as the Cascades, fanatic post-holers begin their travels of high valleys and ridges in April, two to three months earlier than conservatives who wait for trails to turn from white to brown. Fanaticism pays.

SNOWSHOEING

When a hiker sinks to the knee, the hip, the waist, the chest, the eyebrows, booting is definitely inferior to webbing. A half-century ago snowshoes rather abruptly gave way to skis in the favor of American recreationists, and for decades were virtually extinct. Then, with the general increase in every variety of winter outdoor activity, reflecting the need of urban people for the solace of nature in all seasons, webs made a comeback, were radically improved, and are now more popular than ever.

Snowshoeing is a go-anywhere sport, at the most advanced becom-

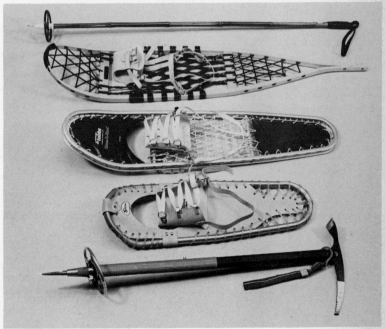

Several popular snowshoe models. The upper one is of an old traditional design, built of wood and rawhide. The lower two are newer, made of aluminum and nylon and plastic. For balance, snowshoers ordinarily use either a ski pole or an ice ax with "basket" attached.

ing winter mountaineering. The main attraction, however, is simplicity. The only significant addition to summer gear is a pair of snowshoes, costing about $100 (rentals available at many backpacking shops), and probably one or two ski poles. Shops with the shoes usually have manuals on equipment and technique.

No extended training is necessary; with experience a hiker learns refinements, but his very first day he can go for miles and after a few trial runs is ready to hoist pack and penetrate deep into the heart of winter.

CROSS-COUNTRY SKIING

Until the late 1960s the original form of skiing, cross-country touring, had been so overwhelmed in America by downhill running as to

Equipment for cross-country skiing: pole, Nordic ski and boot, spare tip, blowtorch (for waxing), waxing kit, scraper (Some skis require no wax.) Ordinary hiking gear completes the outfit.

be little more than a memory. Even the few who kept the spark alive mainly used Alpine equipment which had evolved for tow-hill conditions and was ill suited to mixed terrain. Then, the old Nordic skis returned to America in force and the cross-country revolution (or reaction) began.

Cross-country skiing is a sport quite different from that of the resorts, lacking the day-long succession of high-speed thrills and/or balletlike patterns, and of course the effortless ascents and the mass socializing. In compensation? An easy grace all its own. No lift tickets pushing the family toward bankruptcy. The virgin white, and quiet, and wildness.

The technique, though not so elementary as snowshoeing, is far less complex than downhill running or alpine touring. Under expert tutelage a novice can learn enough on his first outing to cover many miles. In contrast to snowshoers, who do well to make 2 miles an hour and 10 miles a day, cross-country skiers of just ordinary strength and competence often slide along at 4 miles an hour on the flat, much faster on slopes, and in proper terrain consider 20 miles merely an average day.

Texts on equipment and technique are available at shops that sell the gear.

CAMPING

Booters, snowshoers, cross-country skiers all may wish to enlarge their knowledge of winter to include nights. Since pure water is all around, by use of a lightweight backpacker's snow shovel, camp can be made anywhere, excavating a flat bed, digging or molding tables and chairs and windbreaks—and in spring the architecture melts, leaving no evidence of the stay, no damage to underlying plants. With the equipment described in earlier chapters, snow camping can be as comfortable as on bare ground, and in much of America offers the only guaranteed opportunity to get absolutely away from mobs.

AN EARTH FOR ALL SEASONS

Many hikers hibernate in winter, doing their share of the work of the world so they may vacation in summer with a clear conscience. But it's too bad for a person who loves trail country to know it in only one season, to miss the full experience of nature from birth to maturity to wearying unto death—the complete cycle of life.

Some wildlanders don't accept the analogy of winter as death, or the connotations of loss and sadness. They say winter is only gloomy viewed through a window from the stupefying interior of an over-heated house. Fly the coop, get out in it, and blood runs fast and spirits rise. For such folk, often of a classical temper as opposed to flower-loving romantics, winter is the uncluttered season, the months of cleanest wildness, the best time of year.

20:

THE NEW ETHIC

Nature once certified outdoorsmen . . . But now there is such ease of transportation and so much improvement in equipment that anyone can become a wilderness traveler.
J. V. K. Wagar, in *American Forests* (November 1940)

People have scraped the world clean . . . and now they want to run from the dreadful places and find some nice safe country . . . All of them are on the run. They are frightened of the fire.
V. S. Naipaul, in *New York Review of Books* (May 3, 1979)

FROM cities and suburbs, from coast to coast, Americans are on the run. They run as they live—noisily. As long ago as 1920 Clarence Day, in *This Simian World,* said the din of a modern metropolis is precisely what any person familiar with zoos would expect of monkeys once they'd invented the internal-combustion engine. He hadn't heard nothin' yet. Were Day to revisit this planet and witness the Great American Run—passenger cars and four-wheel-drive pickups and jeeps, camper trucks and motor homes and trailers, motorcycles and snowmobiles and dune buggies and swamp buggies, motorboats and jet boats and Hovercraft, airplanes and helicopters—he'd add his voice to the growing prayer that Someone on high rip open the sky, lean through the hole, and bellow in Commandment, "KNOCK IT OFF DOWN THERE!"

Still, damaging as the racket is to ears and nerves, it's merely a by-product, a symptom. The serious and lasting harm is the squandering of fossil fuels, drowning of rivers, slashing of freeways through jungles and tundras, smelting of mountains, paving of farmlands with suburbs, proliferating of radioactive time bombs.

Only the most depraved real estate speculator could imagine the revels of the past half-century continuing another half-century—or quarter-century. The party is ending, and as is usual with any orgy, in the jangles that are the prelude to crying jags, family quarrels, fistfights, and spitting up. Not nice at all. And so Americans are on the run.

Many—one sometimes feels, most—are evidencing saner instincts by running for the backcountry. However, some are so deranged by the fire, the city, they've lost all notion why they're running. Mounted on ORVs and ATVs, they're not escaping the orgy but simply moving the scene, destroying as they come. Seeing them razz into a wildland, a Disney chipmunk might well chitter, "Saints preserve us!"

And praise be, there truly are saints eager to live clean lives and do good works, and not a lonesome few but a splendid many. A paradox for philosophers: Can there be too much goodness? Apparently. For when the saints shoulder packs and come marching into the backcoun-

try by the platoon, the regiment, the division, the army group, Mr. Chippy amends his chitter to "Saints preserve us from the saints!"

As is often said nowadays, "Formerly the problem was how a small band of travelers could survive in an enormous wilderness. Now it's how a small wilderness can survive an enormous number of people."

The number of people a wilderness can accommodate and survive —that is, remain "wild"—is its "carrying capacity." Everywhere, now, land managers are engaged in studies to determine the capacities of individual wildernesses, valleys, campsites. Again, they are required to be philosophers as well as scientists, to define "wilderness" in a modern context—since, obviously, there is no more wilderness anywhere on earth in the old sense, pre-population explosion, pre-airplane.

One thing they know for certain: a wilderness can "carry" vastly more light-foot walkers and no-trace campers than it can woodcrafters, packtrains, and motorcycles. The way to make a wilderness larger is to go slower, quieter.

The U.S. Forest Service blundered in the late 1950s, early 1960s, by complacently accepting on trails the first ridiculous little putt-putt machines. Soon there was nothing to laugh about because the factories in Japan had tooled up and the American backcountry was a-roaring with trailbikers, who by the 1970s were claiming "historic rights." Better call them "wrongs." The mistake must be corrected. Machines must be banned not just from dedicated wildernesses but from all the traditional horse-hiker trails of the nation, from all roadless deserts and prairies and beaches and tundras.

Horses are no noisier than hikers, and in appropriate terrain, in limited numbers, properly handled, little more destructive. Room must be saved for them. Though not for the olden-style thundering herds resembling the U.S. Cavalry headed for the Sand Creek Massacre.

Increasingly the command will be, "Lassie, go home." And Fido, too. Dogs are already excluded from National Park trails and recommended against in popular National Forest wildernesses.

So much for machines and beasts. What about people? When Porky said, "We have met the enemy and he is us," he didn't mean just him and Pogo and Churchy and the rest of the Okefenokee folks. Albert's cigar ain't the only one in the lemonade.

What to do about people? In 1978 the U.S. Forest Service published *Wilderness Management* (a book by John C. Hendee, George H. Stankey, and Robert C. Lucas, with contributions by such other scholars as Roderick Nash and Jerry Franklin), which tells the history of the wilderness concept and discusses the current state of the management art. Not only managers but hikers should study the text so they can participate intelligently in the parliament of wildlanders now planning the future.

Plans currently are sketchy. Time since the population deluge has been too short to inventory lands and determine carrying capacities, perfect management techniques through trial and error—or agree on definitions of the "wilderness experience." Debate is unlikely to cease soon. And the end product probably will be plans that differ, as they do now, for National Parks, for dedicated wildernesses in National

Forests, National Wildlife Refuges, and other jurisdictions, and for places not formally designated "wilderness" but regulated as "backcountry" or "roadless area" or "scenic area" or such.

The crux of any plan is: How should population be controlled? Everyone agrees that if the carrying capacity of a meadow, say, is determined to be X, when Mr. $X+1$ wants to visit he must be denied, lest his boots stomp the flowers to a field of mud only swine could love. But how to handle Mr. $X+1$? First, of course, by educating him away from that particular meadow to others equally pretty, or from weekends to midweeks, summers to springs-falls-winters. What if that doesn't work? Must he then be "rationed" in his use of wildlands by issuance of permits? Probably. But then, should the permits be issued at trailhead, ranger station, or headquarters? By mail, months in advance, as firm reservations, or in person, at time of entry, on a first-come first-served basis? In summary, how can a system be designed and fine-tuned to allow maximum visitation and freedom consistent with minimum impact?

The crux of population control is control of camps, where the average hiker spends 60 percent of his wilderness life and focuses more than that of his damage. Some managers, observing that for generations hikers have camped quite happily on bare dirt, argue for "sacrifice areas" where impact is concentrated to spare the surrounding pristinity. (The howls arise when any particular spot is proposed for sacrifice.) Others favor dispersion/minimal impact, accepting the sacrifice inevitable when sleeping bag touches ground but distributing the wear so widely as not to flagrantly mar the natural appearance of a valley. (The moans arise when tennyrunner friars urge hammocks, sleeping on snow, walking all night.)

Very understandably, in view of the enormity of the task and the shortage of funds and personnel, managers love simple rules, such as no camping in sight of trails, no wood fires above 10,000 feet. The favorite is a ban on camps within a certain distance of water—100, even 200 feet—because waterside camps sometimes foul the water or crush plants, homesteading campers may hog the viewpoints, and such camps are so prominent that their sight and sound over the water is wastefully solitude-consuming.

While granting all this, other managers cite studies made in typical areas that show 90 percent of all campsites—those used by hikers over many generations—have a view of water and 85 percent are within 200 feet of water, nearly half within 50 feet. Can it be that people *like* camping near water, with views of water, and don't really mind bare dirt? Then perhaps it is officious to ruin their fun for the sake of a simple rule. Can it be that in many a valley the geological history has been such that the only campable ground is near water and that a distance of 200 feet would put campers up on cliffs with the goats or out in the swamp with Albert? Then perhaps a manager should walk through his jurisdiction before posting rules at trailheads. Possibly, simplicity can be impractical, shortcuts that don't work can breed contempt for all regulations, however necessary and wise. The alternative is to judge each campsite on its own merits. Close those with unacceptable physical impacts on land and water or social impacts on the quality of the experience. When closing camps, provide enough others. Beware of personal prejudices, of inflexibility. The manager who breeds contempt for his regulations and himself breeds contempt for the wilderness ideal, endangers proposals to preserve more wilderness.

A policeman's lot is not a 'appy one. But policing there must be, even of wilderness, despite the internal contradiction so hard for old libertarians to stomach. However, management cannot be by simple rules. Rules are words. The language of the land is more complex. Managers must learn it. And not in classrooms and convention halls of the frontcountry. On the trails in the backcountry.

Hikers have a double responsibility. They must read and obey the rules, like them or not. But to debate them coherently when they don't, they must study the land. "An ecosystem includes all the organisms of an area, their environment, and a series of linkages or interactions between them." Ecology, the study of ecosystems, should be the hiker's passion, not merely to enrich his trail pleasure but so he can understand the functioning of the systems and how he can fit in unobtrusively.

The hiker should be a bird watcher and animal watcher and bug watcher. He should be curious about rocks and minerals, and note the slow process by which soil is created. And gain a feel for the dynamic balance of a river, of a glacier, and how they carve valleys. And grow intimate with trees and flowers, mosses and lichens, fungi and molds. And learn the meaning of a progression of clouds, a change in winds, and the relationship of the atmosphere to the mantle of living green and underlying rocks. And at night he should look out to the moon and stars and deeply comprehend this is the only earth we ever will have.

Comprehending that, he may well realize that the light foot and no-trace camp are barely a start. More, much more "de facto wilderness" (wildlands man hasn't yet got around to plundering) must be statutorily protected as dedicated wilderness. More, much more "reconstituted wilderness" (lands plundered but now recovering, growing wild again, or with the potential to do so) must be set aside.

But wilderness is only a part of a large planet. Or rather, a very small planet. For man to achieve a balance with the ecosystem of earth, whose carrying capacity of superconsumers already is far exceeded, wildland ideals must be transferred to the city. The hiker must work for zero population growth, minimum energy consumption, complete recycling of resources. To quote the old New England adage,

> Eat it up.
> Wear it out.

Make it do.
Do without.

Let the purified-in-wildness saints come marching in to city halls, county councils, state capitols, halls of Congress, the White House. In a democracy that operates through pressure groups, this means renouncing anarchism and joining up—adding voice and weight and dollars to one or several groups working to save the frogs in the local pond, forests of the skyline wilderness, whales in the ocean, man on the planet.

By such means Thoreau could be proven right in saying, "In Wildness is the preservation of the World." Let it be so assumed. Let the word go out that the wilderness expects every pedestrian to do his/her duty.

Index

Index

Index

Index

HARVEY MANNING, wildland backpacker since the 1930s, edited the first two editions of *Mountaineering: The Freedom of the Hills,* contributed chapters to *Wilderness USA,* and is the author of *The Wild Cascades: Forgotten Parkland, The North Cascades National Park, National Parks of the Northwest,* three trail guides to the Cascades and Olympics, and a dozen other books on hiking, climbing, and conservation. For his four-volume series, *Footsore 1–4: Walks and Hikes Around Puget Sound,* he walked 3,000 miles and wore out three pairs of boots surveying trail routes from the cities to the wilderness.

KEITH GUNNAR, free-lance photographer, has hiked and climbed from Alaska to Peru, New Zealand to the Alps to the Himalaya, and throughout the American West. His work has been published in several books and numerous magazines.

BOB CRAM, free-lance commercial artist, is well known among climbers for his lively cartoons in *Mountaineering: The Freedom of the Hills* and among skiers for his contributions to *Ski* and *Skiing* magazines. He is an avid alpine and cross-country skier but has taken time off from the snows to illustrate a number of books on various subjects and to make frequent appearances on television as spokesman for a supermarket chain.